D0743454

RAGAS OF LONGING:
THE POETRY OF MICHAEL ONDAATJE

In *Ragas of Longing*, Sam Solecki offers the first book-length study of Michael Ondaatje's poetry and its place within his overall body of work. Relating the poetry to various poetic traditions from classical Tamil to postmodern, Solecki presents a chronological critical reading of Ondaatje's six volumes of poems. Among the study's concerns are the relationship between the poet's life and work, his poetic debts and development, his theory of poetry, and his central themes. It also includes close readings of Ondaatje's monographs on Leonard Cohen and Edwin Muir, the Scots poet and critic.

Solecki suggests that Ondaatje's poetry can be seen as constituting a relatively cohesive personal canon that has evolved with each book building on its predecessor while simultaneously preparing the ground for the following volume. He argues that Ondaatje's writing has a narrative unity and trajectory determined by crucial events in his life, especially the early breakup of his family and his subsequent exile from his father and place of birth. The result is a body of poetry whose vision is post-Christian, postmodern, and despite an often humorous tone, fundamentally tragic.

SAM SOLECKI is a professor of English at the University of Toronto.

SAM SOLECKI

Ragas of Longing
The Poetry of Michael Ondaatje

UNIVERSITY OF TORONTO PRESS
Toronto Buffalo London

© University of Toronto Press Incorporated 2003
Toronto Buffalo London
Printed in Canada

ISBN 0-8020-3763-1 (cloth)
ISBN 0-8020-8543-1 (paper)

Printed on acid-free paper

National Library of Canada Cataloguing in Publication

Solecki, Sam, 1946–
  Ragas of longing : the poetry of Michael Ondaatje / Sam Solecki.

  Includes bibliographical references and index.
  ISBN 0 8020-3763-1 (bound)   ISBN 0-8020-8543-1 (pbk.)

  1. Ondaatje, Michael, 1943– – Criticism and interpretation.   I. Title.

  PS8529.N283Z877 2003   C811'.54   C2003-900683-2
  PR9199.3.O5Z877 2003

'One Art,' from *The Complete Poems, 1927–1979* by Elizabeth Bishop,
copyright 1979, 1983 by Alice Helen Methfessel, reprinted by permission
of Farrar, Straus and Giroux, LLC.

University of Toronto Press acknowledges the financial assistance to its
publishing program of the Canada Council for the Arts and the Ontario
Arts Council.

This book has been published with the help of a grant from the Canadian
Federation for the Humanities and Social Sciences, through the Aid to
Scholarly Publications Programme, using funds provided by the Social
Sciences and Humanities Research Council of Canada.

University of Toronto Press acknowledges the financial support for its publishing activities of the Government of Canada through the Book Publishing
Industry Development Program.

It snowed and snowed the whole world over
Snow swept the world from end to end,
A candle burned in the window
A candle burned.

(After Pasternak's 'Winter Night')

This one, 'the last waltz,' is for the keepers of the candle

My sister, Lydia Powers

My dear friends Susan Addario and Audrey McDonagh

And the children Vanessa, André, Tara, Tannis, and Bronwyn

Contents

viii   Contents

Acknowledgments

The chapter on *the man with seven toes* originally appeared as 'Point Blank: *the man with seven toes'* in *Canadian Poetry* 6 (Spring–Summer 1980); parts of the chapter on *Rat Jelly* were published as 'Nets and Chaos: The Poetry of Michael Ondaatje' in *Studies in Canadian Literature* 2 (Winter 1977); the chapter on *Secular Love* appeared in the *University of Toronto Quarterly* 70 (Spring 2001); an earlier version was published as a review in the *Canadian Forum* 745 (January 1985); earlier versions of the chapters on *There's a Trick with a Knife I'm Learning to Do* and *Handwriting* were published as review-articles in *Books in Canada* in September 1979 and November 1998 respectively.

My warm thanks to Dr Maria-Jesus Llarena Ascanio of the University of La Laguna for a continuing dialogue about Michael Ondaatje's work that has lasted nearly a decade.

And especially to A.M. for encouragement during a period of doubt.

Abbreviations

RAGAS OF LONGING:
THE POETRY OF MICHAEL ONDAATJE

Introduction

'the slight silver key'

Only his writing was calm. His writing which had in more ways than one saved his life.

Woody Allen, *Deconstructing Harry*

Teacher: Last question – even simpler. 'Where is the father?'

François Truffaut, *The 400 Blows*

According to the proverb, each book has its history. This one began or, perhaps more accurately, took on momentum because of what might be called two non-events: the relative lack of attention to poetry in the special Ondaatje issue of *Essays on Canadian Writing* (Summer 1994) and, four years later, the relative silence in 1998 in Canada and abroad surrounding the publication of *Handwriting*, to my mind one of the decade's most original books of English poetry. Given the warm critical reception of the early poetry and the international success of *The English Patient* as novel and film, I find it difficult to explain this neglect. Though on my bad days I tend to agree with Randall Jarrell that modern society isn't aware of its poets, I'm still surprised when a significant body of work by a writer of Ondaatje's stature and reputation – the two aren't synonymous – is ignored even by academic critics, the linebackers of poetry's crumbling last line of defence. Part of the problem, of course, is that poetry is more difficult than fiction to treat ideologically, to reduce to the expectations and demands of the critically fashionable identity politics or one of the currently dominant critical 'isms.' It can't be turned as easily as fiction into a discourse that 'proves' some point of gender, class, politics, or social critique. In a word, poetry is more resistant to contemporary critical theory, unless it follows Kenneth Burke in its orientation, than prose. It also requires what Frank Kermode calls 'close literary criticism, nose to the text,'[1] an attitude that smacks of the old New Criticism and is therefore almost automatically suspect. Despite this situation, I still expected that at least readers with an interest in postmodernism or post-colonialism would be as attentive to *Handwriting* as to *The English Patient* and *Anil's Ghost* – and they haven't been. Feminist-oriented critics such as Lorraine York and Christian Bök, who have written about the poetry, have done little beyond stating the obvious about the presence of violent males, passive, uncreative, or commodified females, a male gaze, and traditional gender assumptions. York even seems to suggest that feminists have avoided Ondaatje's work because of the phalanx of intimidating male critics – myself included – standing guard over it.[2] Though both York and Bök are occasionally perceptive, one senses that for the most part the literary texts are primarily occasions for the scoring of points, with the author's total going up or down depending on his perceived attitude to women. In Paul de Man's words, the focus is on 'the external politics of literature,' to the detriment of attention to the text itself.[3] These aren't so much misreadings as swerves away from reading towards a preconceived thematization.

This situation has provoked me to take another look at a body of work that I have admired for nearly four decades and to write a book in which I make as strong a critical case as I can for Ondaatje's poetry. I shall simultaneously provide what Billy the Kid called 'the slight silver key' to Ondaatje's central concerns; examine the relationship between the life and the poetry; offer a chronological overview of his body of poetic work; comment on influence, development, and continuity; and give close readings of those poems that seem to require them. Though the focus will be on the poems, I will refer throughout to *The Collected Works of Billy the Kid, Coming through Slaughter, Running in the Family, In the Skin of a Lion, The English Patient*, and *Anil's Ghost*, as well as Ondaatje's critical writing, whenever they help to illuminate the reading of a poem or whenever I can use them to show continuity and development. Implicit throughout will also be a continuing act of self-criticism as I revisit some of my own early work on Ondaatje.

Some readers may wonder why I have organized *Ragas of Longing* around individual chapters devoted to the volumes of poetry. I was originally tempted to structure the book, like *The Last Canadian Poet: An Essay on Al Purdy*, on the basis of central topics or topoi, but I decided to turn to this format because Ondaatje organizes his collections very carefully and they repay readings that respect them as wholes and see the poems and volumes as related one to another. I think that George Elliott Clarke overstates the point, but he's on the right scent when he comments, 'Ondaatje's works are so alike that each is best read as an adjunct of the others. They form a canon: they must be read in the light and the shadow of each other before their individual illuminations or obscurities can be seen.'[4] I would qualify this perspective slightly by seeing Ondaatje's personal 'canon' as an evolving one in which each book of poems builds on its predecessor while simultaneously preparing the ground for the following, often quite different, volume. Signature words, images, motifs, and topoi recur from book to book, often linking scenes that echo across decades. I agree with Ondaatje's comment that each new book has 'a new vocabulary, a new set of clothes,'[5] but I would add that it also uses much of the old lexis and wardrobe. As a result, his career as a poet has what might be called a deep narrative and a certain narrative trajectory that is best studied, because most obvious, when the books are read in chronological order.

Such an approach also helps to foreground the evolution of Ondaatje's treatment of himself and what one might call his family romance. The presence of the life in the work will be one of the threads holding the book together. Needless to say, poets write about their lives in a variety of ways, with Anne Sexton and Robert Lowell at one end of the autobiographical spectrum and Wallace Stevens and Zbigniew Herbert at the other. The former are confessional; the latter deal obliquely and impersonally with urgent personal needs. As Stevens put it, 'The subjects of one's poems are the symbols of one's self or of one's selves.'[6] In other words, if a poet like Lowell tries to say it all in as unmediated a fashion as possible, a poet like Stevens deals with his life obliquely and symbolically. As I will argue, Ondaatje uses both approaches. In *Secular Love* the style creates the impression of an unmediated narrative; elsewhere the life is less an explicit presence or reference than an intimated autobiographical pressure behind image and scene. The 'plot' of the narrative in Ondaatje's body of work is implicit in my main title – taken from *Handwriting* – whose first word, 'ragas,' points to a song of exile and whose closing phrase, 'of longing,' intimates the desire to return. Some readers may wonder why I have ignored *The Collected Works of Billy the Kid*, which is strongly, if indirectly, marked by Ondaatje's life. For two reasons: first, I don't think of the book as 'poetry' despite the presence in it of a handful of lyrics I admire; and, second, it has drawn a substantial body of perceptive critical commentary, beginning with Stephen Scobie's 'Two Authors in Search of a Character: bp Nichol and Michael Ondaatje.' By contrast, the 'real' poems became critical orphans after *In the Skin of a Lion* (1987), when Ondaatje achieved international popularity.[7]

My own view, and it will be elaborated in this study, is that Ondaatje has produced a substantial body of verse with an original style and a profound vision, as well as a handful of contemporary classics; among these are 'King Kong meets Wallace Stevens,' 'Burning Hills,' '"The gate in his head,"' 'White Dwarfs,' 'Light,' 'Moon Lines, after Jiménez,' 'The Cinnamon Peeler,' 'Rock Bottom,' 'To a Sad Daughter,' 'The Story,' 'Last Ink,' and 'Letters & Other Worlds' (I agree with Stephen Scobie's comment that the last is among 'the greatest of Ondaatje's poems.')[8] From his early poems to his latest, readers would not mistake his voice – cool, laconic, controlled, wryly humorous, and inflected by striking metaphors – for that of another poet. The adjustments in that voice from poem to poem and over time are co-extensive with 'the structural and symbolic aesthetic strategies to which [he] has been driven in coping' with what Helen Vendler has called 'some personal *donnée* which the poet could not avoid treating.'[9] Czeslaw Milosz's suggestion 'It is possible that there is no other memory than the memory of wounds' may be an exaggeration, but in Ondaatje's case it hits close to the mark; 'wounds,' after all, is one of his signature images, and readers as different as Susan Glickman, Ed Jewinski, and Lorraine York have suggested the presence of a primal wound in the poems' figure in the carpet.[10] His vision of human life is post-Christian, postmodern, and fundamentally tragic – 'There are no prizes' (*CTS*, 156). Reading him, I'm reminded of Bertrand Russell's comment about Joseph Conrad's world view: 'I felt, though I do not know whether he would have accepted such an image, that he thought of civilized and morally tolerable human life as a dangerous walk on a thin crust of barely cooled lava which at any moment might break and let the unwary sink into fiery depths.'[11] It is worth recalling that Conrad, another fatherless exile writing in a foreign language, is referred to in *Rat Jelly, Running in the Family,* and *In the Skin of a Lion.* Order in Ondaatje's poems, as in Conrad's novels, is often tenuous and temporary, menaced by violence or chaos.

Something of this sense of threat is apparent in one of the finer lyrics in *The Collected Works of Billy the Kid*:

I have seen pictures of great stars,
drawings which show them straining to the centre
that would explode their white
if temperature and the speed they moved at
shifted one degree.

Or in the East have seen
the dark grey yards where trains are fitted
and the clean speed of machines
that make machines, their
red golden pouring which when cooled
mists out to rust or grey.

The beautiful machines pivoting on themselves
sealing and fusing to others
and men throwing levers like coins at them.
And there is there the same stress as with stars,
the one altered move that will make them maniac.   (41)

Because Billy, the machines, and the stars are on some deep level syn-onymous, the poem suggests that an explosion threatens the self, the world, and the universe. All are fundamentally unstable. Ondaatje's is a tragic world in which errors ('the one altered move') are both inevita-ble – life is like *that* – and irremediable because they can never be cor-rected, except in a way that is paradoxically negligible and vital, in the work of art. His theory of art is predicated on a causal relationship between suffering and creativity; several of his most powerful poems are elegies; and the survivors in his novels resemble minor characters in Shakespearean tragedies in looking back over their shoulders at corpses and what Edgar (a 'character' in *Running in the Family*) calls 'The weight of this sad time' (*King Lear* V. iii. 324). The more fatalistic aspect of his vision can be heard in the epigraph, from Christopher Dewdney, to 'Pure Memory / Chris Dewdney': 'Listen, it was so sav-age and brutal and powerful that even though it happened out of the blue I knew there was nothing arbitrary about it' (*TTK*, 100).

In this context, it seems particularly fitting that when asked to con-tribute a poem and a commentary to the *Globe and Mail*'s 'How Poems Work' column, Ondaatje chose Elizabeth Bishop's hard-edged vil-lanelle 'One Art.'[12]

The art of losing isn't hard to master;
So many things seem filled with the intent
To be lost that their loss is no disaster.

Lose something every day. Accept the fluster
Of lost door keys, the hour badly spent.
The art of losing isn't hard to master.

Then practice losing farther, losing faster:
Places, and names, and where it was you meant
To travel. None of these will bring disaster.

I lost my mother's watch. And look! My last, or
Next-to-last, of three loved houses went.
The art of losing isn't hard to master.

I lost two cities, lovely ones. And, vaster,
Some realms I owned, two rivers, a continent.
I miss them, but it wasn't a disaster.

– Even losing you (the joking voice, a gesture
I love) I shan't have lied. It's evident
The art of losing's not too hard to master
Though it may look like (Write it!) like disaster.

The last sentence of Ondaatje's brief commentary could also serve as an epigraph to his body of work: 'And in the end we are left with this precise wonder, not a word wasted or misused, that has pretty well said everything, quickly, casually, in that cautious self-protective voice that in the end blurts out the great hurt of everything.' It seems appropriate that his selected poems begin and end with elegies. Reading the villanelle in the context of Ondaatje's poems, I can't help thinking that had he written it, the clause 'Then practice losing farther' might be read homophonically as suggesting 'Then practice losing father.' Bishop's great loss, like Louis MacNeice's, was her mother; hence the poignant pun on 'mother's watch.'

'The great hurt of everything' is also at the heart of Ondaatje's vision, though we can often narrow it down to the essential underlying *donnée*, which is the breakup of his parents' marriage, their divorce, and his subsequent childhood exile from Ceylon in 1954, an exile that also included a permanent separation from his father, Philip Mervyn Ondaatje. The writer suggests as much in 1993 in the following uncharacteristically self-revealing, though ultimately ambiguous, comment to Eleanor Wachtel about the moves from Ceylon to England and from England to Canada: 'They were all traumatic moves for me, but I don't think I showed it very much. They were traumatic in retrospect. They weren't *bad* traumatic; it was suddenly, "Okay, now you've got to grow up, now you've got to wear long trousers and a tie." It was a physical change more than a mental one.'[13] This observation isn't entirely convincing. I have the impression that Ondaatje realized at the end of the second sentence that he was showing more of his hand than he wanted to and decided to pull back. He did so, however, with an oxymoronic phrase that doesn't quite make sense since there is no such thing as a *good* trauma, just as there is no good wound. To take two examples, 'Letters & Other Worlds,' the elegy for his father, and *Running in the Family* contradict the suggestion that the trauma was more physical than psychological or emotional. The childhood exile from family, father, culture, and island isn't the only subject he has dealt with in his poetry and fiction, but it recurs often enough in a variety of forms to constitute a significant, perhaps dominant structure of feeling and figure in the carpet. It is not a coincidence that he is formally most experimental and imaginatively most daring when responding to the pressure of unresolved personal issues.

I would argue that the absence of the father is an absent presence somewhere behind the missing parental figures in *The Collected Works of Billy the Kid, Coming through Slaughter, In the Skin of a Lion, The English Patient*, and *Anil's Ghost*. In *Running in the Family* the son returns to Sri Lanka primarily to assemble all the available rumours, gossip, memories, and facts about the dead father. He's also the shadow behind the alcoholic Pat Garrett (*The Collected Works of Billy the Kid*), Dashiell Hammett ('White Dwarfs'), and Buddy Bolden (*Coming through Slaughter*). W.M. Verhoeven makes roughly the same point but without mentioning the father: 'Again and again persons (or their identities) get lost in Ondaatje's stories – lost in legend, lost in the bush, lost in the past, lost in history, lost in memory, lost in myth – and in each case people go after them in order to recover them, to remember them, or to recreate them.'[14] T.S. Eliot, discussing some recurrent imagery in Seneca and Chapman, makes the following comment that illuminates this aspect of Ondaatje's work: 'I suggest that what gives [this imagery] such intensity as it has in each case is its saturation ... with feelings too obscure for the authors even to know quite what they were.'[15] I'm not suggesting, however, that Ondaatje isn't aware of what he is doing, though in poetry there is often an element of the poet knowing more than he thinks he knows. Stevens captures something of this: 'While there is nothing automatic about the poem, nevertheless it has an automatic aspect in the sense that it is what I wanted it to be without knowing before it was written what I wanted it to be, even though I knew before it was written what I wanted to do.'[16] I'm more interested here in the possibility of an emotional or psychological economy in which certain emotions or memories are so strong and important that they saturate or overdetermine aspects of a poem. Eliot, of course, is also probably right in seeing that some feelings may result in recurrent images and scenes of remarkable compression and complexity whose full implications the author doesn't understand. These feelings or memories may also be sufficiently important to the writer to require more than one work for their expression. As George Whalley suggests, the poet's 'transmutation' of his feelings to the words and images with which they have associated in his memory and imagination 'is probably never complete; there is always an untranslatable residue. This no doubt explains how poems and even novels tend to be written in families, as a series of approximations to a recurrent complex of feeling.'[17] It's worth adding that, while this 'complex of feeling' may have its source in the writer's life, it often finds expression in poems that do not seem to refer to the life at all. An extreme case is 'The Waste Land,' which Eliot described to Elizabeth Bishop as less a 'criticism of the contemporary world' than 'a piece of rhythmical grumbling' and which John Berryman guessed in 1948 would eventually 'prove to be personal' and 'also appear then more terrible and more pitiful even than it does now.'[18]

In Ondaatje's body of work, the father is also a metaphor for a lost place and culture. As several readers have suggested, this magical tropical world, completely different from the England and Canada to which he emigrated in 1954 and 1962 respectively, appears in Ondaatje's early work in a variety of displaced forms and images. The early interest in the work of Henri Rousseau, 'le Douanier,' for instance, becomes more nuanced if we think of it in relation to Sri Lanka, as perhaps does the interest in exile, isolation, and Australia in *the man with seven toes* (1969). A similar case can be made for Ondaatje's excited reading of *One Hundred Years of Solitude* in his article 'García Márquez and the Bus to Aracataca,' where Macondo recalls Ceylon and the wayward Buendias seem distant cousins to the manic Ondaatjes and Gratiaens of the two major elegies ('Letters & Other Worlds' and 'Light') and *Running in the Family*. As I shall argue in my discussion of Ondaatje's first book, *The Dainty Monsters*, his work in the 1960s regularly shows the poet swerving away from a direct confrontation with disturbing aspects of his past by finding oblique or symbolic ways of treating them. It's as if he knows that he's not emotionally ready to name the Ceylon of his youth and Philip Mervyn Ondaatje, or perhaps hasn't mastered 'the structural and symbolic strategies' that would allow him to deal with this troubling and, for the moment, intractable material. Yet in a brief prose commentary on 'Peter,' he makes the following revealing comment:

> My only emotion about my own work is curiosity. I see my poems as I would a home-movie. I am still conscious of all the bits and pieces / relatives and friends that were just to the left of the camera and that never got into the picture.
>
> I can't remember what was off-screen when writing 'Peter'; the poem grew by itself and went its own way. It probably contains my most interesting hang-ups and I still remain curious about it. I do remember that my appendix burst a few days after I finished the poem.[19]

The imagery in the first paragraph is revealing: a poem is like 'a home-movie,' and even when it isn't about 'relatives and friends,' they constitute both a frame for it and a felt absent presence. The comment about 'Peter' is equally interesting since it suggests a relationship between 'my most interesting hang-ups' and the mythic story of a feral child who becomes an artist and a killer. A handful of sentences written in 1970 may not be much to go on, but they do suggest that other poems of the first decade also might have an autobiographical subtext. It is worth noting, in contrast, that in *Leonard Cohen*, written at the same time, Ondaatje is reluctant to relate Cohen's work to his life, and he comments that 'nothing is more irritating than to have your work translated by your life' (3). It will be another three years, in 1973 in the dedication to *Rat Jelly* and in 'Letters & Other Worlds,' before the past will be explicitly acknowledged in the names of his parents.

Inseparable from this issue is the problem of how to write about himself. With the exception of a handful of casual domestic poems, Ondaatje's early work is notable for the absence of poems of intimacy or self-revelation. In an era dominated by confessional poetry – Lowell's

Life Studies appeared in 1959, Plath's *Ariel* in 1965 – Ondaatje's poems of the sixties and early seventies, even when they have a first-person speaker, are rarely genuinely subjective or revealing of his personal life; even when subjective, they are almost never intimate, and the 'I' is almost a third-person pronoun. Not coincidentally, his creative energies in this period find full expression primarily in the increasingly experimental sequences 'Peter' (1967), *the man with seven toes* (1969), and *The Collected Works of Billy the Kid* (1970), where one senses that the characters are authorial masks. Most readers will recall Billy's teasing suggestion that we 'Find the beginning, the slight silver key to unlock it, to dig it out. Here then is a maze to begin, be in' (20). There seem to me to be two possibilities here. Either Billy is having some postmodern fun with us since he knows that his reality – in this book and in legend – is nothing but an endless verbal and representational maze and therefore without a key. Or Ondaatje is offering this possibility as a feint, distracting us from the significance of the book's final image, a photograph of Michael the Kid dressed as a cowboy in Ceylon circa 1950. Though the photograph appears at the end, a case can be made that we should also imagine it on the opening blank page, where a photograph of Billy is described but not reproduced. However we respond to this final image, my impression is that we can't avoid seeing that it has autobiographical implications for the text. It may not help us to read the sequence autobiographically, but doing so reminds us implicitly of the presence of subjective concerns that have found indirect dramatic and symbolic expression in the story of a fatherless outlaw whose 'collected works,' like those of Peter and Philip Michael Ondaatje, are expressions of violence and tenderness. After 'Letters & Other Worlds' it will be difficult not to read Pat Garrett, Billy's alcoholic stepfather, as an early avatar of Ondaatje's father as well as of the father as artist. It's worth noting that Billy's parents are never mentioned and that Buddy Bolden is almost autochthonous, though his mother is referred to.

I also want to suggest that we need to read one other of Ondaatje's early works in the light of his life, the master's thesis he wrote on the Scots poet and critic Edwin Muir in the mid-sixties at Queen's University.[20] It is the most important of Ondaatje's four works of criticism, the others being the monograph on Cohen, an essay on Howard O'Hagan, and 'What is in the Pot,' his introduction to *The Long Poem Anthology.* I need to discuss the thesis and to quote from it at some length because it is not widely known. Today this early work reads very much like Ondaatje's argument with an alter ego, an older writer aspects of whose life and writing found echoes in himself. Muir's vision of life as chaotic, meaningless, and marked by violence and suffering antici-pates Ondaatje's. And Muir's melancholy and remorseful voice must have appealed to him, not least because his Scots accent, like Ondaatje's, marked him as an outsider in English poetry. Ondaatje's comments on Muir's writing are still valid enough to constitute a use-ful guide to the Scots poet's neglected books. But to anyone familiar with Ondaatje's writing, the commentary also reads like a palimpsest on his own developing central concerns and obsessions and as an early guide to his evolving poetics. My hunch is that Ondaatje wasn't so much learning from or in any substantive way being influenced by Muir as he was finding confirmation for some of his own inclinations and developing thoughts about life and writing. Reading Muir, he indirectly discovered himself, both what he had lived through as a man and what he might become as a writer. His quotations from Muir's work are almost uncanny in anticipating some of his own later writing.

Similarly, some of his comments on the Scots poet's work are equally applicable to his own: 'With each poem, he approaches Ithaca along a new road and discovers a new wound' (103). On the connection between Muir's life and poetry: 'The mental and physical destruction of his family in Glasgow was so grotesque that Muir was unable to write of it in his poetry' (12). In the following description of Wyre, the island home of Muir's childhood, I find it difficult not to sense the presence of Ceylon and Ondaatje's family behind the primary Scots references. 'Wyre was important for Muir's myth-making because it was an island where "there was no distinction between the ordinary and the fabulous." Muir could blend myths with everyday events and turn characters like "Sutherland" into heroes ... Wyre was therefore a landscape very close to the fabulous – when seen with the innocent eyes of a child, and his childhood made the rest of Muir's life seem bathetic' (5).[21] Substitute one or two nouns and a name, and this passage might be a description of the Ceylon of *Running in the Family* which the young Ondaatje was compelled to leave. In other words, for Muir, as for Ondaatje, the personal story or myth includes an idyllic and for the most part innocent childhood on an island, followed by a fall into modern British society. Muir's lines 'My childhood all a myth / Enacted on a distant isle' could have been written by Ondaatje. His sense of the fallen world as violent and chaotic finds its counterpart in Ondaatje's violent characters and scenes and his intuition that life is fundamentally chaotic. Chaos and chaotic occur, often several times, in each of his books. When Ondaatje quotes Muir as saying, 'At its core everything is chaos, and therefore terrible' (22), one can almost feel the author of 'Peter,' *the man with seven toes, The Collected Works of Billy the Kid*, and 'King Kong meets Wallace Stevens' nodding in agreement. Even Muir's tendency to depict the chaos in animal images finds an echo in Ondaatje's animal poems or his occasional use of animals, as liminal figures marking the boundary between surface and depth, reason and instinct, order and chaos.

Muir's poems also showed Ondaatje that a poet could find forms and an adequate imaginative language for his experience without resorting to a confessional poetic. Myth was the answer. Ondaatje's own early interest in legend and myth gives an edge to his discussion of Muir's fascination with biblical and Greek myths, journeys, heraldic animals, and mythic figures. His critical commentary on how myths function in Muir's poems can also apply to his own. Though he acknowledges that a poet can use myths to discover both aspects of himself and 'the patterns of the societies we live in' (81), I will emphasize the former here because in his poetry Ondaatje's interest in society will be almost non-existent until *Handwriting*. It may be worth noting at this point that in *Leonard Cohen* Ondaatje distinguishes between social evils and personal ones, and insists that the former, because 'outside us,' 'are capable of being controlled,' while the latter 'never can be' because they are 'one's own recurring nightmare' (21). In his poetry, he is always less interested in the social dimension of our lives than in the personal. This is also true of his interest in myths. Discussing Greek myths in the thesis, for instance, he emphasizes, 'The events and personalities of Thebes, Troy, and Ithaca run parallel to our own lives. We discover ourselves in them, and, at the same time, enlarge and give them meaning, (105). Ondaatje's use of 'we' in the final sentence is suggestive, even if readers may not have enough information to determine how the lives of Paris and Helen or Peter or Billy may run 'parallel' to the author's or our own. Also of interest here is his suggestion that 'in his more personal poems ... [Muir] discovered himself behind a mask' (90). It's a point that Ondaatje will make in later interviews about some of his own poetry. He would agree with Anne Carson's suggestion 'All myth is an enriched pattern, / a two-faced proposition, / allowing its operator to say one thing and mean another, to lead a double life.'[22]

Although he doesn't discuss this aspect in the thesis, Ondaatje might have mentioned that myths and legends also save a writer the trouble of having to invent a story by providing him with the materials on which he can work. In none of his longer poems or in his fiction has he ever invented *ex nihilo*. He criticizes Muir, however, for his tendency to spend 'nine-tenths of a poem' setting up a scene and for allowing the inherited story or narrative to dominate. He suggests an alternative based on 'Pound's monologues,' which 'instead of following a strict narrative, consist of a string of lyrics which suggest the narrative' (72–3).[23] Ondaatje's stories, whether in verse ('Light,' *Secular Love*) or prose (*Running in the Family, Anil's Ghost*), will always be closer to Pound than to Muir's slower and more ponderously unfolding poems.

While he finds Muir's approach to narrative restrictive, he's attracted to what D.H. Lawrence would have called his 'metaphysic' (see 'Study of Thomas Hardy') and what today's critics would call his 'ideology.' Discussing this aspect of Muir's work, Ondaatje quotes a passage with a distinctly contemporary sound: 'To be a perfectly honest writer – a writer, that is, true to his impressions – one thing is essential, one must not have a system. A system of thought is a method of exploiting impressions, of weaving them into a pattern, decided beforehand, and of crushing and distorting them for that end. All that one can honestly begin with is a starting-point; but better still if one have several; it makes for independence' (84).[24] In a 1990 interview with Catherine Bush, this theme reappears in his Bakhtinian preference for 'a form that can have a more cubist or mural voice to capture the variousness of things. Rather than one demonic stare.'[25] For Ondaatje, as for Muir, the fact that life, including human life, is in some deep sense chaotic and therefore meaningless must be enacted in the poem. Should the poem's vision reflect a too obvious metaphysical system or aesthetic pattern, it would falsify reality. Ondaatje's lyrics, as well as his fragmented, temporally discontinuous works such as *Secular Love* and *Handwriting*, go further in this direction than Muir's poems, whose symmetric stanzas offer the reassurance of rhyme, metre, and a temporally sequential narrative in the face of life's inchoate and meaningless violence. Muir is enough of a high modernist to want to use myths as fragments from the past to shore 'against my ruins' (*The Waste Land*, 431) in forming at least an aesthetic totality that will offer, among other things, a substitute for lost religious and philosophical certainties.

By contrast, at least in his most radical poems, Ondaatje resists almost successfully the temptations of pattern and totality. Like Muir, he wants to acknowledge chaos, but he also wants to find aesthetic strategies and forms to enact it while creating the illusion that it isn't being contained. The danger for both, as I pointed out earlier, is that any transfiguration of existential, psychological, or moral chaos into aesthetic form might in the end misrepresent that chaos and inevitably create an unintended sense of meaning. One of the failings of aestheticism – always a temptation for a writer as highly figurative as Ondaatje – is that it gives priority to beauty over truth, if only because the former distracts our attention from the latter. George Bowering, reading the lyrics through Charles Olson's spectacles, thinks that Ondaatje should have abandoned this view of form and turned to the open-field poetics of William Carlos Williams and Black Mountain. He describes the early work as 'well cut and shaped, but not risky,' not 'seeking the unrested form he requires.'[26] Offering a view of Ondaatje's vision that is in fundamental agreement with mine, Bowering nevertheless insists that it can receive its full poetic articulation only in a postmodernist poetics of process such as the one implicit in *The Collected Works of Billy the Kid*. It is worth noting, however, that while that work as a whole is postmodernist in its thrust, several short poems – 'I have seen pictures of great stars,' 'You know hunters,' 'White walls neon on the eye' – have the characteristics of traditional short lyrics.

To return to the thesis, the future author of 'Peter,' *the man with seven toes*, and *The Collected Works of Billy the Kid* must also have found gratifying Muir's occasional appeal to what Ondaatje calls amorality or a higher morality. Discussing Muir's poems about visions, he focuses on those moments when 'Muir leaves moralities and reason behind, removes his own personality from the poem, and allows us a clear glimpse of his insight into the fable. Colour, style and image combine at wonderful moments, and then like Muir, we must believe the image – where Art and the Real "play." These images are more magnificent because of their rarity, and because delight in their amorality or higher morality is delightful only to the fallen' (51). I linger over this passage and the concern with morality primarily because 'moral' (with its cognates) is one of the most slippery terms in Ondaatje's private poetic lexicon. In *The Collected Works of Billy the Kid*, for instance, Billy comments that 'if I had a newsman's brain I'd say / well some morals are physical' (11), and in 'White Dwarfs' the speaker, in a searing couplet, refers to individuals 'who shave their moral so raw / they can tear themselves through the eye of a needle' (*RJ*, 70). To be moral in Ondaatje's universe is to be free, authentic, more fully human, and, from the viewpoint of conventional morality, amoral. I'll discuss Ondaatje's uses of the word in some detail in the next chapter; here I simply want to note the attention he pays to it in Muir's work as well as his emphasis on scenes in which the Scots poet's use is co-extensive with his own. For Ondaatje, Muir's poems (and poems in general) fail when they reflect 'the limitations of everyday morality' and become too didactic by allowing questions of social utility, moral purpose, and what we now call identity politics to colour the reader's response. In the following passage, note how quickly he moves from commenting on Muir's poetry to poetry in general:

> The central fault with Muir's war poetry is that it is too didactic. To deal with subjects such as war or violence, a poet should look below the surface of the obvious morality. A poet should discover the subtlety or complexity in an event to such an extent that he will keep the reader or himself unreconciled and uncertain of his attitude towards the event. To do this he must avoid approaching the subject with any preconceived morality. His depiction and judgment must be concerned with the 'right sensation' so that it might even appear inhuman. In Yeats's 'Easter 1916,' we are not conscious of a preconceived morality. The poem is [a] reverie upon the unexpected transformation of violence. In the end there is no resolution, only paradox.   (75)

The fragment 'right sensation' is taken from Wallace Stevens's 'The morality of the poet ... is the morality of the right sensation,' (120)[27] the only morality that at his most radical Ondaatje the poet is willing to acknowledge. The various signposts to the poems and fiction of the 1970s and 1980s are obvious. If the discussion's starting point is Muir's poetry, its unstated goal is Ondaatje's own evolving poetic. In it, the objective will be to present characters and events, like life itself, with as few moral, philosophical, and aesthetic preconceptions or mediations as possible, and to leave the reader 'uncertain of his attitudes towards the event.' I suspect that Ondaatje has never reprinted 'Pictures from Vietnam' (1968), one of his rare political poems, because it is too didactic and its morality too obvious.[28]

Ondaatje doesn't mention Muir in any of his poems, essays, or novels, and anyone not aware of the thesis would be hard pressed to see his importance in the writing of Ondaatje's first decade. A study of poetic influence, however, would mention the images that Ondaatje borrows from him – in 'Dragon' and 'White Dwarfs' – and place him among Rossetti, Kafka, Stevens, Yeats, Auden, García Márquez, and Leonard Cohen as one of the authors to whom the young poet is indebted. Ironically, Cohen's place in Ondaatje's career is more widely known, even though he seems to me to have been less influential than Muir on his development. By 1970, when Ondaatje wrote his monograph *Leonard Cohen*, he had published three books, established his reputation as a very promising and original young writer, and won the Governor General's Award for *The Collected Works of Billy the Kid*. He probably agreed to write the book because he still had academic aspirations, what he calls 'the academic stripe up my back.'[29] As an untenured professor of English literature at the University of Western Ontario, he needed to publish a book, no matter how short, to compensate for the fact that he did not have a doctorate. Whatever the reasons and whatever Ondaatje may have thought of the completed book – the dedication to his dogs, Flirt and Wallace, makes one pause – it still stands up as a comprehensive, occasionally insightful introduction to Cohen's work by someone who very much admires it. His comment on *Beautiful Losers*, a novel that has not aged well, catches him at his most enthusiastic: 'As it is, *Beautiful Losers* is a gorgeous novel, and is the most vivid, fascinating, and brave modern novel I have read' (45).

But like the Muir thesis, the study is more interesting today for what it tells us about Ondaatje than about its ostensible subject. He's interested in Cohen partly because the latter is exploring situations and an emotional climate similar to his own. Even their poetic lexicons overlap: beautiful losers, wounds, scars, madness, shattered windows, loons, bones, myth, chaos, rats. On Ondaatje's account, Cohen transforms his characters, even those based on real people, into heroes and myths in the sense that he endows them with charisma and shows their archetypal characteristics. Referring to 'Alexander Trocchi, Public Junkie, Priez pour nous,' Ondaatje comments that 'like the narrator, Cohen is left at the end holding a myth in his hands' (42). As in his own work, one of the essential preconditions for heroism or mythic status is being wounded or scarred, and therefore unique and authentic: 'Cohen is making heroes out of these people not because they, like Philoctetes, have brilliant bows, but because they have magnificent wounds' (43). It's as if a wound is a badge of authenticity that removes a character from ordinary time and bestows charisma on him and aura on the event. The reference to the mythic archer reminds us how close Ondaatje's critical writing at this point in his career is to his creative work (see 'The Goodnight' [*DM*, 58] and 'Philoctetes on the island' [*RJ*, 34]). He's often drawn to those aspects of Cohen's work that have appeared or will appear in his own. He admires 'Ballad' because 'Cohen sees beauty (gardens, potency, and art) grow out of death and violence' (9); and he praises aspects of Cohen's voice (the wry tone and the ironic understatement) and style (the mixing of modes and styles) that resemble his own; he praises the form of *The Favourite Game* because 'each scene [emerges] as a potent and enigmatic sketch rather than a full blown, detailed narrative. As in a poem, the silences and spaces, what is left unsaid, are essential to the mood of the book' (23). He also pays Cohen the ultimate compliment by borrowing some of his images for his own work. He quotes a passage from *The Favourite Game* that foreshadows a scene in *Coming through Slaughter*: 'He leaped up, ran to the window, smashed his fist through the glass' (34). Another sentence from *Beautiful Losers* – 'I was the tattered billboard for his reality' (50) – may lie behind 'Billboards' (*RJ*, 14). The description of molten brass in *The Favourite Game* (104), not quoted by Ondaatje, may have been on his mind when he wrote, 'I have seen pictures of great stars' and '"The gate in his head."' A line from *The Favourite Game* (17) may have inspired 'Birds for Janet – The Heron' (*DM*, 12): 'A loon went insane in the middle of the lake.' And the fireflies in *Beautiful Losers* (134) reappear in the 'muslin dress / with fireflies' in 'Light.' Other examples are given in the chapters on *The Dainty Monsters* and *Rat Jelly*.

Thinking back to the late 1960s, I can't help wondering whether Cohen represented for Ondaatje a slightly older contemporary writer (he was born in 1934, Ondaatje in 1943) whose work provided a counterweight to the influence of the sometimes more radical, if generally less substantial, writers he met with first at Queen's University and then at Coach House Press. With the publication of *Rat Jelly* in 1973, it must have been obvious to Ondaatje that none of these writers were in his league nor, despite occasional borrowing or quotation, could he learn from any of them. Ralph Gustafson noted in 1970 that Ondaatje owed nothing to Williams or the Black Mountain poets; the comment reminds us that, despite bp Nichol's influence on three poems, he didn't share his fellow Coach House editors' assumptions about poetry.[30] Whatever Cohen's limitations, and Ondaatje is aware of them, he represents a more substantial and original figure. One doesn't have to be Harold Bloom to sense the young poet testing himself against the older one in his judgments on the writing, judgments often made with the vocabulary of Ondaatje's own creative work. Criticism always involves intellectual power, and the criticism of a poet adds creative power as well. The original writer rewrites his predecessor in his own image, even when praising him. Ondaatje was too young and insufficiently established to be as assertive with Muir, a nearly canonical figure if a minor one.

Cohen, however, represented a different case and opportunity. An established and, in the late 1960s, potentially major writer, he could be the brother-father figure against whom Ondaatje could measure himself. I wonder if there isn't something of him, as well as of Mervyn Ondaatje, in *Coming through Slaughter* in the 'fathers' that Buddy Bolden mentions as having 'put their bodies over barbed wire. For me. To slide over into the region of hell. Through their sacrifice they seduced me into the game. They showed me their autographed pictures and they told me about their women and they told me of the even bigger names all over the country. My fathers failing. Dead before they hit the wire' (95). This is obviously less a question of literary influence than of presence, and of one writer's profound awareness of another. In this context one can ask whether the poems about poetry in *Rat Jelly* show Ondaatje thinking through some of his responses to Cohen's work, especially his comments on the relationship between violence or suffering and creativity. And if the answer, however tentative, is yes, then is *Coming through Slaughter* on some level a response to *Beautiful Losers*? A historical footnote: the night that Ondaatje launched his novel in Toronto with a reading at A Space, he was almost late because he had attended a Cohen concert that went into three encores.[31]

The important point here is that the monograph was written at a key period in Ondaatje's development. As with Muir, the study of Cohen's work, especially his poetry, helped sharpen his own sense of his vision of life and of what he could and could not do with lyric. Some of Ondaatje's criticisms of Cohen's poems in *Flowers for Hitler* hint at roads he would not take with his own: 'He presents "Pure lists" – which give the skeletons of an emotion or a scene like trailers from a movie, and there are many stray diary-entries or footnotes to emotions. The most obvious fault in these pieces is that they are not self-sufficient. They belong to Leonard Cohen and need him to bolster meaning' (43). A New Critic couldn't have said it better, nor could a former student of George Whalley. This particular passage reminds us that one of the continuing problems or issues in Ondaatje's poetry will be the representation of the self. With both Muir and Cohen he is attentive to their very different strategies of self-representation. At one extreme is Muir's impersonal, if romantic, mythic poetry; at the other is Cohen's ostensibly confessional approach that nevertheless strives for a mythic dimension. One way of tracing Ondaatje's development as a poet is to note his shift from the first to the second with *Secular Love* and then the retreat into the almost complete impersonality of *Handwriting* (1998), where the self is dissolved and reconstituted in a new and very different mythic poetry. *Secular Love* can be seen as the culmination of the impulse to 'say what happened' and to confront the troubling compulsions of the past and the present.[32] In a manner of speaking, it is implicit in the prose and verse of Ondaatje's first twenty years. Of course, it would not have been written had he not first confronted his father's ghost in *Running in the Family*, a confrontation that had been anticipated during the previous decade by his two elegies for his parents, 'Letters & Other Worlds' (1971) and 'Light' (1975). Having dealt with what happened to his father, he seems to have been able to turn a similarly unsparing eye on himself and his role in the breakup of his own marriage in the late 1970s. Perhaps he could only finally expiate the betrayal and the inevitable guilt involved in telling the father's story by being as ruthless in telling his own in a poetry sequence that is at once a complex act of atonement, an apology, and a love poem.

Since hindsight is always twenty-twenty, it's obvious today that Ondaatje's preface to *The Long Poem Anthology* (1979) was one of the first steps in the writing both of *Secular Love* and *Handwriting*, the two books in which lyrics become part of long, intricate, and relatively open sequences. This brief but important essay marks the turn towards his poetry's last phase. He begins by claiming that 'the most interesting writing being done by poets today can be found within the structure of the long poem' and that our 'best poetry, after we stopped being cocky with narrative, is involved with process and perspective' (11). The emphasis throughout is on poems which 'shift like mercury off the hand' and in which 'stories ... don't matter' because 'what is important' is 'the movement of the mind and language' (12). If we didn't know the author, we might think that he is describing *The Collected Works of Billy the Kid* or the 'Tin Roof' section of *Secular Love*. Even his quotations from the poets included seem like oblique comments on his own subsequent work: 'These poems show a process of knowledge, of discovery during the actual writing of the poem. "You have to go into a serial poem not knowing what the hell you are doing," wrote Jack Spicer. The poets do not fully know what they are trying to hold until they near the end of the poem, and this uncertainty, this lack of professional intent, is what allows them to go deep' (13).

Ondaatje will never be as committed to process poetics as Spicer, John Ashberry, or Frank O'Hara, but there's no doubt that *Secular Love* bears a family resemblance and that *Handwriting* fits Spicer's definition of a serial poem as one that 'deconstruct[s] meanings and compose[s] a wildness of meaning in which the I of the poet is not the centre but a returning and disappearing note' (323). This similarity doesn't make either of these sequences a process poem, but it does seem to indicate that they both owe something, however difficult it might be to define, to Ondaatje's years at Coach House. Considering his strong advocacy of a poetics in which 'stories ... don't matter' because 'the movement of the mind and language is what is important' (12), it may seem at first surprising that his two sequences don't resemble the poems in the anthology more closely in their attitude to language, perception, consciousness, and narration. My hunch is that, however warmly he may respond to process and formlessness in the work of others, Ondaatje is unable to follow them down that poetic road because process, whether epistemological or ontological, is too closely associated in his mind and work with chaos, dissolution, silence, and death. Like Leopardi, he thinks that literary form – the aesthetic structures of the imagination – not only gives life meaning but also makes it bearable. Leopardi puts it this way: 'Works of genius have this in common, that even when they vividly capture the nothingness of things, when they clearly show and make us feel the inevitable unhappiness of life, and when they express the most terrible despair, nonetheless to a great soul – though he find himself in a state of extreme duress, disillusion, nothingness, *noia*, and despair of life, or in the bitterest and *deadliest* misfortunes (caused by deep feelings or whatever) – these works always console and rekindle enthusiasm; and though they treat or represent only death, they give back to him, at least temporarily, that life which he had lost.'[33] For a poet haunted by his past and therefore in need of atonement and consolation, a radical poetics is not enough, though he will learn enough from it to make possible his two formally innovative sequences.

From the viewpoint of style, it's interesting to note that Ondaatje's lexis of key terms, idioms, and images remains relatively stable throughout the shifts in his career. Among the privileged words in his private vocabulary are magnets, acrobats, blood, wounds, scars, knives, cuts, moral, ceremony, choreography, ritual, white, chaos, spiders, flies, ants, dogs, herons, the moon, the room, falling, nets, dreams, bones, madness, and boundaries – all of which can be organized under the two headings 'nets' and 'chaos.' Needless to say, at different times in his career different words are foregrounded and emphasized. This diction makes Ondaatje's style almost instantly recognizable, though it might be more accurate to speak of his various styles, since even poems in the same period can sound quite different. In *Rat Jelly*, for instance, the personal or domestic 'Billboards' and the mythic 'Fabulous shadow' could be by different poets. In general, however, it is possible to speak of the poetry in terms of the early Ondaatje (up to and including *Rat Jelly*), middle Ondaatje (culminating in *Secular Love*), and late Ondaatje (*Handwriting*). Though he never completely abandons the habit of bringing a poem to a point or summary with a powerful or resonant ending, there's no doubt that the poems of the middle and late 1970s – *There's a Trick with a Knife I'm Learning to Do* (1979) – are more open-ended and attentive to process than their predecessors. Their style is more open and relaxed, with the images untroubled by symbolic compulsions; the syntax and punctuation are more casual; the rhetoric is missing the hard angularity, and the images the burnished quality of the major lyrics in *Rat Jelly.* They also show more examples of what David Shaw calls 'unconsummated symbolism,' in which the images have no fixed or assigned connotation.[34] The six poems in *There's a Trick with a Knife I'm Learning to Do* associated with Sri Lanka (I include 'Light') point forward not only to the memoir but also to *Handwriting*. They hint at Ondaatje's turn towards a non-Western poetic that will allow him to immerse and dissolve both his poetry and himself in a past and a culture – an entire way-of-being-in-the-world – that he had left unwillingly nearly half a century earlier. Though the Sri Lankan lyrics in *Handwriting* are still recognizable and discussable *as* lyrics, they are much more fluent than Ondaatje's earlier poems. Their continuity depends less on narrative or the authority of a speaking voice or an underlying symbolic pattern than on what might be called the complex montage between the striking isolated images and stanzas that exist in an almost paratactic relation. As Ondaatje said about Cohen's early poems, 'It is a world where the morals [he means meanings] are imagistic, as they always are in the context of dreams' (14). More than in any of his other books, the poems depend on one another, 'echo and re-echo against one another,'[35] to create a pattern of resonant meaning. Yet however different the most recent book may seem, its more open form and discontinuous structure are foreshadowed in Ondaatje's early criticism and in his first two major sequences, *the man with seven toes* and *The Collected Works of Billy the Kid*. Like them, it leaves the reader uncertain and with 'a sense of paradox.'[36] *Handwriting*, however, differs from Ondaatje's earlier books of poetry in seemingly offering little hint about his possible future development as a poet. The only thing that I'm certain of with respect to *Handwriting* is that the trajectory of the major phase of Ondaatje's career as a poet has come to an end.

A year after writing the previous sentence, I ran into the following comment, made by Ondaatje in a recent interview: 'I don't think I can go back to an earlier style, but at the same time, *Handwriting* did feel like a kind of ending to me. It's like the thin end of the wedge that I'd got to.'[37]

The Dainty Monsters

The Poetry of Myth and Evasion

From the outset Mallarmé's poetry is like a mirage ... in which he recognized himself not by where or how he is but by where he is not and how he is not.

Jean-Paul Sartre[1]

Like its successor, *the man with seven toes*, *The Dainty Monsters* is an impressive apprentice work. Though none of the poems are of the standard of Ondaatje's best later work ('We're at the graveyard,' 'White Dwarfs,' 'Light,' 'The Cinnamon Peeler,' 'To a Sad Daughter'), and while 'the language Ondaatje uses is the language of conventional late-twentieth-century discourse' (J.E. Chamberlin),[2] one can't miss the presence of a technically adroit new voice with a supple range, an often violent verbal expressiveness, and a fully realized imaginative world. Also impressive, especially in a poet with an MA in English, is the relative absence of echoes, allusions, and quotations from the tradition. There are a few exceptions: Yeats's 'The Second Coming' and Joyce's *Ulysses* surface in 'The Inheritors,' and I also hear the former in 'Come to the Desert'; Stevens lends a line to 'Eventually the Poem for Keewaydin'; 'Henri Rousseau and Friends' shows that Ondaatje shares Leonard Cohen's interest in the Douanier (see *The Favourite Game*); there may be two or three echoes of D.G. Jones; and the uncharacteristic interest in Troy owes much to Edwin Muir's many poems on Trojan topics. Similarly, one hears only occasional ghosts of iambic-based metres in the rhythm of his lines (see 'O Troy's Down: Helen's Song'). In other words, the young poet, despite a conventional attitude to lyric, rarely looks back to the old masters, whether American, British, or Canadian. He also seems untouched by the fashions of the 1950s and

1960s: if not quite poetically autochthonous, he nevertheless seems to have avoided the influence of Black Mountain, the Movement, the Beats, and confessional poetry. In contrast to many young poets of the period – George Bowering or Mark Strand – one doesn't have the sense that he has come out from under Olson's or Stevens's overcoat. Read three decades after publication, *The Dainty Monsters* rarely reminds one of its era or where Ondaatje came from poetically; more often, the reader thinks of the later poems and works that it anticipates. If few of the poems have what Dylan Thomas called, in a letter to Vernon Watkins, 'the strong inevitable pulling that makes a poem an event, a happening, an action perhaps, not a still-life or an experience put down, placed, regulated,' still a handful hint at the 'creative destruction, destructive creation,' which he saw as the mark of genuine poetry and which will become part of the grain of Ondaatje's best work.[3]

I

In most of the relatively short poems the focus is on a character, scene, or event – Thomas's 'still-life or an experience put down, placed, regulated.' For the most part, the lyrics reflect the assumption that a poem can recreate unproblematically any aspect of reality or re-enact any experience which the poet chooses. Only in the poems about poetry – 'Four Eyes,' 'The Martinique,' and 'Eventually the Poem for Keewaydin' – is the question raised, though only implicitly, to what extent is such an assumption valid, and if it is valid, what are the epistemological and formal problems involved in transfiguring life into poetry? 'Peter,' the book's last poem, shifts the focus to the relationship between the poet's life and the creation of the poem (I will return to this theme below). Many poems describe life dualistically in terms of a suggestive dialectic between a dark, instinctual or surreal world and one of reason and daylight. The former is shown variously as coexistent with the latter ('The Republic'), vaguely threatening to it ('Gorillas'), or in danger of being overwhelmed by it ('Dragon'). Ondaatje is primarily concerned with showing the relationship between antithetical kinds of reality or modes of being. 'The Republic' (20) is representative:

This house, exact,
coils with efficiency and style.
A different heaven here,
air even is remade in the basement.

The plants fed daily
stand like footmen by the windows,
flush with decent green
and meet the breeze with polish;
no dancing with the wind here.

Too much reason in its element
passions crack the mask in dreams.
While we sleep
the plants in frenzy heave floors apart,
lust with common daisies,
feel rain,
fling their noble bodies, release a fart.
The clock alone, frigid and superior,
swaggers in the hall.

At dawn gardenias revitalize
and meet the morning with decorum.

The scene is reminiscent of those old cartoons in which brooms and buckets come alive when people are absent. The voice is cool and detached, occasionally wry; the idiom is conversational; and there is little interest in literary decorum ('release a fart'). During the day this is the realm of reason and order, but at night the Dionysian world of primal vitality reasserts itself and establishes the republic of the title. But this world, anterior to consciousness and language, is there unperceived all the time. It is a necessary counterbalance to a repressive world of masks and 'too much reason.' The final couplet even suggests that its vitality and chaos 'revitalize' the order and light, and, by extension, poetry itself. It is typical of Ondaatje that the relationship between the two worlds is presented as a complex one and that no simplistic resolution is offered. Thus although 'decorum' is restored at the end of the poem, 'revitalize' serves as a disturbing reminder of nighttime anarchy. The final couplet subtly reiterates the emotional tension created by the central juxtaposition of two opposed realities. This tension, as it relates to the theme, works against the formal closure that arises inevitably with the last word of any poem, and in doing so, it implies a deliberate thematic irresolution that gives the poem the open-endedness or ending without closure characteristic of Ondaatje's best work.

While 'The Republic' is primarily concerned with describing a scene or an event, 'Four Eyes' (46) shifts the emphasis to an examination of the actual process by which a poet transforms a lived, dynamic moment into poetry. This focus anticipates 'Peter,' *The Collected Works of Billy the Kid*, '"The gate in his head,"' 'What is in the Pot,' and the 'Tin Roof' section of *Secular Love*. The speaker, choosing to see only what is within his companion's field of vision, breaks from the moment in order to record it:

Naked I lie here
attempting to separate toes
with no help from hands.
You with scattered nightgown
listen to music, hug a knee.

I pick this moment up
with our common eyes
only choose what you can see

a photograph of you with posing dog
a picture with Chagall's red
a sprawling dress.

This moment I broke to record,
walking round the house
to look for paper.
Returning
I saw you, in your gaze,
still netted the picture, the dog.
The music continuing
you were still being unfurled
shaped by the scene.

I would freeze this moment
and in supreme patience
place pianos
and craggy black horses on a beach
and in immobilised time
attempt to reconstruct.

'Four Eyes' does not deal with the relationship between life and art as perceptively as the later, more ambitious poems, but it nevertheless explores a similar area of creative experience. It is concerned with what happens when a poet tries to 'reconstruct' a lived moment as art. The first consequence of such an attempt is his necessary separation from the experience itself, as if he must choose between the perfection of life and the perfection of art (Yeats). In order to write about it, he must leave it: 'This moment I broke to record.' With its double meaning of separating from and shattering, 'broke' questions the writer's choice of art over life while also suggesting that in some ways he betrays or commits violence against life in order to turn it into art. Instead of being a participant, he becomes a detached observer who prefers searching for a verbal equivalent of a lived moment to life itself. As in so many of Al Purdy's poems, the woman in the original scene is the norm against which we judge the speaker.

While 'record' indicates the possibility of a point-by-point imitation, the final stanza reveals that the reconstruction will be figurative. The writer will use 'pianos / and craggy black horses on a beach,' romantic images not present in the original scene. The poem ends by suggesting that the essential qualities of a scene 'still being unfurled' can only be captured in metaphors that perhaps are intended as an objective correlative for emotions implicit in the scene or felt by the speaker when he was in it. But Ondaatje's final lines simultaneously point to the possibility that even this reconstruction may misrepresent the original moment. The connotations of 'freeze' and 'immobilized time' imply that the poet will ultimately fail to do justice to the dynamic dimensions of life. If my reading makes sense, then 'Four Eyes' offers both a solution to the problem it poses and a critique of that solution. It is not the best poem in Ondaatje's first volume – 'Dragon,' 'Henri Rousseau and Friends,' and 'The Time Around Scars' are better – but, together with 'The Martinique' and 'Eventually the Poem for Keewaydin,' it is the one in which he most profoundly questions the possibilities and limitations of his early poetry and poetics.

Though Ondaatje rarely comments on his work – his early interviews are usually masterpieces of evasiveness – a 1967 review of Margaret Atwood's *The Circle Game* gives some indication of his views on poetry at this time. The review is roughly contemporaneous with the publication of *The Dainty Monsters*, and at several points one has the uncanny impression that Ondaatje is commenting simultaneously on

Atwood's collection and his own. The following paragraph, for instance, is as pertinent to his book as to hers: 'Margaret Atwood brings all the violence of mythology into the present world. Her exceptional imagery and discipline survive each other, and her imagination can lend itself well to humour, as in "This is a photograph of me." The book is also well edited: there are no tangents into themes which do not fit the book, and no bad poems – a relief after the total exposure, good and bad, of poets like Layton and Cohen.'[4] This is a short passage, but almost every comment is equally relevant to Ondaatje's first collection: the attitude to myth and violence; the tense relationship between 'exceptional imagery' and 'discipline'; humour; the concern with the book's unity; and the rejection of 'total exposure.' Similarly, several of the illustrative quotations deal with scenes and have images – oranges, woundings, cuts, chaos – that could have come from his early poems. Atwood's 'An Attempted Solution for Chess Problems' catches Ondaatje's eye and is described as showing people at 'play in this world of archaic machinery' while using 'the legends casually or with banality' (22). Atwood's poem emphasizes the contrast between a room in which a game of chess is being played and the antithetical non-human order or disorder in the landscape outside the window and in 'the cellar / darkness looming.' Structurally and thematically, this antithetical situation occurs, as I pointed out, in several of Ondaatje's poems – 'A House Divided,' 'Henri Rousseau and Friends,' 'The Republic.' In the last he and Atwood echo each other: 'The house *recoils* / from the brightedged vacancy / of leaves' (Atwood); 'This house, exact, / *coils* with efficiency and style' (Ondaatje, 20; my italics). Even her title, 'Against Still Life,' would work as the title either of 'Four Eyes' or '"The gate in his head."' Both poets suggest that beneath or beyond or within this 'ordered, too-clean world' is another 'world of monstrous battles' (Ondaatje on Atwood) co-extensive with it. In Atwood's words (quoted by Ondaatje),

(there are mountains
inside your skull
garden and chaos, ocean
and hurricane; certain
corners of rooms, portraits
of great-grandmothers, curtains
of a particular shade;

your deserts; your private
dinosaurs; the first
woman).   ('Against Still Life')[5]

Ondaatje begins his review by contrasting Gwendolyn MacEwen's use of traditional myths with Atwood's. The latter either relies on 'her own personal mythologies' or, when she does use myth, 'gives it such immediacy and humanity that we scarcely recognize it' (22). Again, he could be writing about himself. Though he tends to treat myth and legend as nearly synonymous and avoids definitions, what he means by these terms is relatively clear from his poetry and from his critical prose. In this review, for instance, 'personal mythologies' seems cognate with the exploration and representation of archetypal or authentic aspects of the self and its world. Lawrence's comment to Edward Garnett on fictional characters may be helpful: 'You musn't look in my novel for the old stable *ego* of the character. There is another *ego*, according to whose action the individual is unrecognisable, and passes through, as it were, allotropic states which it needs a deeper sense than any we've been used to exercise, to discover are states of the same single radically unchanged element.'[6] Atwood probes beyond surfaces and expected myths and symbols, and, as a result, discovers and represents a more comprehensive and profound vision of self and reality. She offers 'a fully realised imaginative world' in which 'garden and chaos, ocean / and hurricane,' are acknowledged as simultaneously present 'inside your skull.' One can understand the appeal of this world to a poet for whom King Kong and Wallace Stevens are parts of a symbolic equation and who, had he studied philosophy, would, like Lawrence and Ted Hughes, have been drawn instinctively to Schopenhauer. Ondaatje's myths, like Atwood's, will take various forms. Like other poets of his generation, he will draw occasionally on traditional myths. More daringly, he will take historically marginal figures and inflect his reinterpration of them with a personal edge. And as often as not, he will take commonplace scenes, often from his own life, and invest them with a suggestive, if indefinite, resonance and 'translate the banal into the mythic' in order to make it memorable.[7] He criticizes the heroes of Cohen's novels for conducting a 'Breavman-like search for an ideal,' thus missing 'the myth and the story that is taking place' (*LC*, 51) around them.

'Eventually the Poem for Keewaydin' (39) shows the poet attentive to what is around him and turning it into a myth:

Taking nature into our routine
we accept more than to write about it,
and the superficial is the poet's paradise.
Poems do not leave you when all this air and leaf
and mass of stars weave in the censoring lake
to become your own myth.

I assume that 'the superficial is the poet's paradise' because, as for Stevens, it gives him the raw matter which he then transforms into poetry, though there is the possibility that it is also his paradise because he must fall from it or break with it in order to write. Speaking of Stevens, it's worth noting that Ondaatje's line has its source in 'The Poems of Our Climate': 'The imperfect is our paradise.' The lake is described as 'censoring' because, unlike the poet's imagination, it distorts and leaves things out of its picture. But the line most pertinent to the present argument is the last, 'to become your own myth.' It echoes Ondaatje's reference to Atwood's 'own personal mythologies' and alerts us to the subjective dimension of his interest in myth. Here myth seems to be nearly synonymous with the poet's 'fully realised imaginative world.' That world is mythic because it constitutes a profound, comprehensive, and original vision of reality that is shared when the reader encounters the poem. More generally, a way of seeing and being in the world is mythic when it encompasses the unconscious, the oneiric, and the chthonic. Although Ondaatje is wary of psychological terms, it might be helpful to characterize this area of his creativity as touching on the archetypal, though his emphasis falls most often on what could be called the personal, rather than the collective, unconscious.

Why we need a new myth or vision is never quite clear even when, as in 'In Another Fashion' (34), Ondaatje ventures a generalization and a near imperative:

We must build new myths
to wind up the world,
provoke new christs
with our beautiful women,
bring

plumed
thin boned birds

to claw carpets
to betray
majesty in a sway

Pale birds
with rings on ugly feet

to drink from clear bowls
to mate with our children

This is playful and whimsical, but it's not clear what it adds up to as a reflection on the need for a post-Christian myth, necessary fiction, or way of being in a postmodern world. It seems to be pointing in the same direction as the well-known last stanza of Stevens's 'Sunday Morning,' which reminds us 'We live in an old chaos of the sun, / Or old dependency of day and night, / Or island solitude, unsponsored, free, / Of that wide water, inescapable.' Ondaatje's 'provoke new christs' seems more of a rhetorical flourish and an unconsummated symbol unsupported by anything within the poem than part of an integrated thematic development.[8] And the force of 'wind up the world' seems to be no more than the idea that the new philosophy or poem will sum up reality. The place of the 'plumed / thin boned birds' in this escapes me.

The birds are part of the book's menagerie of 'dainty monsters.' Like *Rat Jelly*, the title of Ondaatje's first collection is an oxymoronic tease. We understand the adjective 'dainty' and the noun 'monsters' without understanding the reference implied in the phrase. However long we may linger over it, we won't discover a defining content until we read the poems, several of which can themselves be described as 'dainty monsters' about 'dainty monsters.' The collection's eponymous monsters are both animal and human, though more often than not, the former are less monstrous than simply different or radically other. Like most poets in the Western tradition – Lawrence and Marianne Moore are the telling exceptions – Ondaatje uses the animal poem primarily as a means of dealing, however obliquely and symbolically, with his own concerns and obsessions. However individually realized, his gorillas, herons, sows, and dogs are, to paraphrase Freud, a royal road to a private iconography that we only begin to understand fully with the book's successors. The same can be said of the mythic and historical dramatic monologues of the second part of the book – 'Troy Town'

– which ends with 'Peter,' a poem about a nearly feral child who, despite or perhaps because of abandonment, mistreatment, and torture, becomes an artist who

> ... formed violent beauty.
> He carved death on chalices,
> made spoons of yawning golden fishes;
> forks stemmed from the tongues of reptiles,
> candle holders bent like the ribs of men.   (75)

Thirty years later, it is impossible not to read the poem as anticipating the later reworking of the theme of the relationship between chaos ('monsters') and form ('dainty') in the poems of the final section of *Rat Jelly,* in the poetics of *Coming through Slaughter,* and in the title *There's a Trick with a Knife I'm Learning to Do.* The continuity between Ondaatje's first and second collections of lyrics is also established by the presence of 'loathing' in the final stanza of 'Peter' (the book's last poem) and in the last line of 'War Machine' (the first poem in *Rat Jelly*), in which the speaker dreams of becoming mute in order to 'just listen to the loathing' (*RJ*, 11) he feels towards the world.

But if the book's title is initially evasive about its content, the trochaic oxymoron hints at a poetry capable of startling shifts of tone and mood both within and between poems as well as between the two sections, 'Over the Garden Wall' and 'Troy Town.' The hieratic solemnity of the second section is preceded by the first's playfulness, sureality, humour, sentiment, and recurring vague sense of menace. Even the arrangement of the poems in the first part functions to unsettle our expectations, to keep us off balance as we move through the book page by page, shifting from one side of the garden wall to the other, often in the same poem. For instance, the comic and slight 'Song to Alfred Hitchcock and Wilkinson' (17), which may owe something to D.G. Jones's 'For the Birds,'[9] is followed by the oneiric and sombre 'Dragon.' In the former, the poet reminds us that his often heavily metaphoric descriptions of animals say more about him than about them. Like Stevens's 'The Snow Man,' the playful poem reminds us that there are aspects of being prior to or beyond our words and concepts.

> Flif flif flif flif very fast
> is the noise the birds make
> running over us.

A poet would say 'fluttering,'
or
'see-sawing with the sun on their wings.'
But all it is
is flif flif flif flif very fast.

The reader who has read the poems in sequence will recall that the book's first poem, 'Description is a Bird,' is a good example of what 'a poet would say,' while the 'Song' perhaps shows us what he should; even the successful poem acknowledges its failure. Together the poems comment on some of the ways that a poet uses animals in his work and some of the problems he encounters in trying to represent them.

Less circumspect about its concern with poets and poetry is 'Sows, one more time' (31) in which a herd of pigs is described in a series of unexpected metaphors with different connotations and emotional registers.

Sunlight on pigs
a herd of slow pale wounds.

Warm saints milling round the cross,
waiting for weather to break,
speaking gently
appreciating the day.

Wearied intellectuals in the sun.
Shelley and others on the Poet's Coast
taking in the view or lack of grass.
Caustic laughs,
dry about their sensitivity.
Poets
in a poet's world.

The second line's long vowels, culminating in 'wounds,' one of Ondaatje's signature images, suggest a potentially solemn poem that might stand in an ironic relationship to its title. The enigmatic line 'Warm saints milling round the cross' continues the tone and mood, but the next three lines introduce the suggestion of a social outing that defuses and leaves unresolved the religious potential of 'saints' and 'cross.' The third stanza continues the representation by metaphor –

'intellectuals,' 'Shelley and others,' and 'Poets' – and ends with a subtle reminder that the sows are poets only 'in a poet's [that is, Ondaatje's] world.' I suspect that Ondaatje refers to Shelley because the latter died before his time; as, I assume, will the sows, who will be, in a manner of speaking, sacrificed. Hence, perhaps, the image of the cross, not entirely appropriate in the context.

In the end, the poem is less about sows than about poets; if sows are poets, then we can reverse the metaphor and follow Ondaatje's playful suggestion that poets, in some senses, are sows, as well as, by extension, the other metaphors that help define the pigs. Both the most interesting and the most troubling tropes – they seem almost from another poem – are 'wounds' and 'saints milling round the cross.' It's not clear why or how either the sows or the poets are 'saints,' or what 'cross' they casually mill around. As so often in Ondaatje's lyrics, an image or a situation suggests what might be called a pseudo-reference when it is simply a fact of the poem's world. But these images are particularly intriguing not only because they announce in his first book an association between wounds and creativity – the wound and the bow – but also because one senses here an early trying out of the images and situation of the daring climactic stanza of the simultaneously colloquial and hieratic 'White Dwarfs.'

> that silence of the third cross
> 3rd man hung so high and lonely
> we dont hear him say
> say his pain, say his unbrotherhood
> What has he to do with the smell of ladies
> can they eat off his skeleton of pain?   (RJ, 70)

This stanza doesn't include 'saints,' but I wonder whether other readers wouldn't agree that their behaviour in 'Sows, one more time' ('milling ... / waiting ... / speaking ... / appreciating') distances them as decisively from 'the cross' as the 'ladies' are removed from 'that silence of the third cross.' Both poems are about poetic creativity, and each implies that the poet is in some sense a sacrifice or martyr. The earlier is a playfully wry, ironic, and self-reflexive commentary on a generation of poets. The later is Ondaatje's version of Coleridge's 'Dejection: An Ode.' Nearly twenty years later, he will return to this trope and topos when he wonders about a poem in Secular Love, 'Will this be / testamentum porcelli?' (47).

The dreamlike 'Dragon' (18) shows a more symbolic, even allegorical use of an animal. It's possible that it originated in Ondaatje's memory of two passages in Muir, the first from *An Autobiography*, in which the Scots writer discusses his dreams, and the second from the lyric 'The Fall.'

> I had this dream a long time after I left Orkney; I was living in London and being psychoanalysed. I had so many dreams about this time that I could hardly keep count of them. In a great number of them I encountered dragons and mythological monsters, the explanation of the analyst being that I had for many years suppressed the animal in myself, so that it could come up now only in these wild and terrifying shapes. He was right up to a point in assuming this, for I had grown up a Puritan, and though I had liberated my mind, my senses were still bound. But he was right only up to a point, for the strange thing about these monsters was that they did not terrify me; instead I felt in a curious way at home with them.[10]

> Did I see there the dragon brood
>   By streams their emerald scales unfold,
> While from their amber eyeballs fell
>   Soft-rayed the rustling gold?[11]

Ondaatje's dragon, like Muir's, doesn't terrify the dreamer. The narrator's voice is unexcited, even laconic, and the adverb 'again' at the end of the first line alerts us that this is not his first sighting.

> I have been seeing dragons again.
> Last night, hunched, on a beaver dam,
> one held a body like a badly held cocktail;
> his tail, keeping the beat of a waltz,
> sent a morse of ripples to my canoe.

The second stanza offers a vivid description of the dragon as a prelude to its capture in the third and final verse: 'Finally the others saw one today, trapped, / tangled in our badminton net.' The clotted sound of the piled up t's effectively mimics the sense of the entrapment, while the incidental rhyme 'cocktail' / 'tail' anticipates the more regular rhythms of the 'waltz' and the 'morse.' Despite the presence of 'a body' in the opening stanza, there is less a sense of menace here than of pathos. The human nets, including the 'nets' of the poet's tropes and stanzas, have contained the threat of the old dragon, who releases 'pathetic loud whispers as four of us / and the excited spaniel surrounded him.' The liminal 'beaver dam,' like the 'badminton net' and 'the garden wall,' reminds us that in this section of the book the world – of the self or poem – is usually divided into two opposed yet related areas. Dragons and gorillas appear on a lawn or on a beach; tame dogs dream of 'blood' (16); the bodies of young girls are 'jungles of force' (41); and nearly countless individuals are marked by wounds or scars that literally incarnate and freeze the violence of the past. As with 'Dragon,' these poems usually establish an equilibrium between what is in the garden and what is over the wall, even if that equilibrium depends, as it does in 'Gorillas,' on the fact of the poem itself. The desire for order – for, so to speak, a real or metaphoric garden – can be seen in the recurrence of a set of related images that remind us of pace, time, measure, and periodicity. In a dozen poems, Ondaatje refers to the Morse code, metronomes, pendulums, bells, compasses, and watches. Like nets, webs, and locks, these function as tropes for the poems that simultaneously express and contain disorder, randomness, violence, or anarchy.

The volume's first poem, '"Description is a Bird"' (11), offers a subtle and unforced dramatization of this dialectic. Had it been titled 'There's a trick with flight that I'm learning to do,' we would have realized earlier one of the book's primary concerns.

In the afternoon while the sun twists down
they come piggle piggle piggle all around the air.
Under clouds of horses the sand swallows turn

quick and gentle as wind.
All virtuoso performances
that presume a magnificent audience.

The leader flings his neck back,
turns thinner than whims.
Like God the others follow
anticipating each twist,
the betrayals of a feather.

For them no thumping wing beat of a crow,
they bounce on a breath
scattering with the discipline of a watch.

'[P]iggle piggle piggle' anticipates, of course, 'flif flif flif flif' (17). As narrative, this is the story of swallows doing what swallows do best – fly. That the flight takes place 'under clouds of horses' and that these are 'virtuoso performances' with the presumption of 'a magnificent audience' alerts us to the possibility of another context and another dimension of meaning. Like the poet, the swallows are performers who, as they 'bounce on a breath,' avoid the pentameter monotony of crows – 'For them no thumping wing beat of a crow' – while showing 'the discipline of a watch.' The line 'the betrayals of a feather' anticipates, without developing it, a major theme in Ondaatje's work: the idea that the poet inevitably betrays himself and others in his work by using, however obliquely, his and their lives as his subject matter. 'Betray' and its cognates appear six times in *The Dainty Monsters*. In this poem the word seems synonymous with 'indication,' in the sense that the feathers show which way the sparrows will be flying, but its primary meaning unsettles the semantics of the line by introducing the possibility of death.

The question of betrayal usually occurs in those works in which the poet – agreeing with Lowell's comment 'Yet why not say what happened?' – reveals unexpected, often troubled intimacies. Here, Ondaatje's use of the word is interesting because the volume's few poems that deal with his relationships show a poet happy in his life with his wife and children. Few readers in 1967 would have known about his parents' divorce, the son's permanent separation from his father, or the relatively tangled history of his own courtship of his wife, who had been previously married to D.G. Jones, one of his early mentors. Rereading *The Dainty Monsters* three decades later, after the publication of 'Letters & Other Worlds' and *Running in the Family*, one senses an occasional autobiographical presence and pressure both in details and in larger concerns. 'Dragon,' for instance, no longer seems primarily a poem about the unspecified anxieties of its anonymous speaker. Aspects that on first reading seemed to provide local colour and narrative detail now seem to point to a private subtext. Now that we know from the elegy, the memoir, and 'Light' – 'as they hold their drinks' (*TTK*, 107) – that the father was an alcoholic who liked parties and dancing, the lines 'a body like a badly held cocktail' and 'the beat of a waltz' become both clues to the dragon's identity and details in the concealed father's portrait. If, on the one hand, the dragon is potentially threatening, on the other, he sends 'a morse of ripples' to the speaker, a message from the past that is also, like the letters in the elegy, an SOS from halfway around the world; 'a morse of ripples' now also carries with it the withheld 'remorse' that is a tinnitus in so much of Ondaatje's work. In 1967 the 'four of us' were simply anonymous characters on a lawn who had been playing badminton; today they are the four Ondaatje siblings – Christopher, Gillian, Janet, and Michael – who survived the wreck and to whom the author dedicated both *Rat Jelly* and *Running in the Family*. The unidentified 'body' held by the dragon anticipates the woman held by King Kong, who is described as

> ... our lady in his fingers
> like a ring, so delicate
> he must swallow what he loves
> caressing with wounds
> the ones who reach for him.   (*RJ*, 44)

Both the dragon and Kong inhabit what Ondaatje calls 'the zoo of night,' the world of dreams that generates the poems' tessera of images and obsessions. If the dragon and the gorilla are thematically cognate with the father, as I have suggested, then I wonder whether the sex of the body the dragon holds isn't also female. If the poem is at some level a family portrait, then the only missing member is the mother, Doris Gratiaen, about whom Ondaatje will only be able to write a decade later in the elegy 'Light.' I can't resist quoting here Rilke's comment on dragons, which captures something of the poem's quality of feeling: 'Perhaps all the dragons of our lives are princesses who are only waiting to see us once beautiful and brave. Perhaps everything terrible is in its deepest being something helpless that wants help from us.'[12]

Not every poem dealing with the dark side can be read in this way, but I want to suggest that the cause or causes of the fear of disorder, displacement, loss, exile, or chaos in them are usually traceable to events in the writer's life that he won't be able to deal with directly in his writing for nearly another decade. At this stage in his career, Ondaatje would have agreed with Jasper Johns's comment 'Art springs from life experience, but you don't have to be self-expressive.'[13] I don't want to be misunderstood as suggesting that the wounded archer Philoctetes abandoned on an island ('The Goodnight') is simply a symbol of the father, but I have a hunch that Ondaatje's interest in him both here and in *Rat Jelly* ('Philoctetes on the island') is ultimately inseparable from the figure of the father left behind in Ceylon. I doubt that he would have written poems about the archer had he not been separated from his father. Similarly the obsessive, self-contained, and suicidal herons in 'Birds for Janet – The Heron' and 'Heron Rex' (in *Rat Jelly*) probably owe something not only to Mervyn Ondaatje but also, as we will learn from *Coming through Slaughter* and 'Tin Roof,' to his son's anxieties both about his resemblance to his father and about his own life and art.

There is a sense in which the happy-family poems are as much a screen for the past, though of a different kind, as are the various animal poems noting the possibility of disorder and/or violence. Something similar is true of the several historical and mythological narratives, lyrics, and dramatic monologues of 'Troy Town.' These may have been less a wrong or, in the long run, fruitless turn in a young poet's career than a deliberate choice of safe characters and subjects that would let him write what one might call allegories of evasion. Like *the man with seven toes*, the poems, though often concerned with suffering, violence, and death, allow Ondaatje to explore characters and situations ostensibly far removed from his life. As I mentioned earlier, it is only with the photo at the end of *The Collected Works of Billy the Kid* of the young Michael Ondaatje dressed as a cowboy that he offers a hint that these texts have an autobiographical origin and substratum and that the young poet is using some of his characters as masks. As Ondaatje told Catherine Bush, 'in the first longer works, the first serial works like *the man with seven toes*, there was a jump from the self to a mask of some kind. I was writing lyrics at that time, and so the landscape in which I lived was reflected only in the lyric poems. But *Billy* is a personal book, very much about my world then, even though it's set in a different country and it's about an absolute stranger to me. I found I could both reveal and discover myself more through being given a costume. I could be more honest about the things I wanted to talk about or witness.'[14] My own impression, as I suggested earlier, is that some of the poems in *The Dainty Monsters* also show the poet already trying out some costumes and disguises.

II

The poems in 'Troy Town,' two of which are sequences, continue the imaginative engagement with the relationship between disorder and form, unconscious and conscious modes of being, emotion and reason, time and timelessness, violence and creativity. Ondaatje, a fan of Ford

Madox Ford, probably remembered the title from Ford's *It Was the Nightingale*, in which he refers to Dante Gabriel Rossetti's poem 'Troy Town,'[15] though it may also echo Muir's interest in Troy. The first poem, 'Pyramid,' counterpoints the detached and transcendent voice of what I take to be a dead Pharaoh with the frenzied activity of the workers building his tomb. Neither mythical nor specifically historical, the poem introduces a series that show Ondaatje experimenting with the uses of myth and history. The choice of predominantly Greek mythological subjects – Philoctetes ('The Goodnight'), Paris and Helen ('O Troy's Down: Helen's Song') – isn't surprising from an author who wrote these poems while completing a thesis on Edwin Muir. But the more interesting question is why was Ondaatje's imagination drawn to these particular figures and stories? What is it about the fate of the disfigured and abandoned archer Philoctetes that compelled him to devote two poems to him? In *Leonard Cohen*, it is worth recalling, Ondaatje comments, 'Cohen is making heroes out of these people not because they, like Philoctetes, have brilliant bows, but because they have magnificent wounds' (43). As Yeats insisted, '... only an aching heart / Conceives a changeless work of art.' Yeats, one of modernism's mentors about the aching heart, reminds us of the role emotional forces play in determining the selection and the fashioning of the poem's materials. As I suggested earlier, when the Philoctetes poems are read with *Running in the Family* in mind, they are haunted by the figure of Mervyn Ondaatje, another wounded man abandoned on an island who, we learn in 'Light,' also killed birds: 'my drunk Father / tried to explain a complex operation on chickens / and managed to kill them all in the process' (*TTK*, 106). I don't mean, however, that this is all that these richly textured poems are about. Philoctetes may be Mervyn, but he is also himself, as well as a figure or symbol of the artist whose relationship to reality is both ambiguous and ambivalent. These are poems that show the poet of two minds about creativity, since the practice and value of the archer's art or craft is inseparable from his suffering and the deaths of Paris and of the animals on the island. Similarly, one doesn't have to be a psychoanalytic or biographically oriented critic to suspect that the recurring triangular relationships in Ondaatje's work may have some connection not only to the family romance of Michael, Doris, and Mervyn Ondaatje but also, as Susan Glickman suggested, to the later relationship in which a very young poet married the former wife of one of his poetic mentors. (The second story is, of course, completed in *Secular Love* by the narrative of an adulterous passion, a divorce, and the establishing of a new relationship.) There is probably a very complex answer to the questions 'Why write about Philoctetes? Why Paris?' but part of it, I want to suggest, will lie in personal situations and 'emotional forces' that even the writer – especially a young writer just finding his voice and vision – may not be able to explain, except perhaps by referring us back to the complex enactments and emotional cross-currents of his life and his poems. Similarly, he may not be able to explain why he returns to certain images and situations as he does with King Kong, dragons ('The Ceremony: A Dragon, a Hero, and a Lady'), the Crucifixion, dogs, and so on. One explanation, quoted earlier, lies in George Whalley's suggestion that when a poet transmutes certain emotions and feelings into a poem, 'there is always an untranslatable residue. This no doubt explains how poems and even novels tend to be written in families, as a series of approximations to a recurrent complex of feeling.'[16]

Like Philoctetes, Paris is also an archer, and it is his arrow, guided by Aphrodite, that kills Achilles. In turn, he is shot by Philoctetes and eventually dies of the wound. Ondaatje establishes a subtle link between the two by referring in 'The Goodnight' to Philoctetes' 'withering hair' and in the sequence's final poem to 'the mist withering' around Paris as he dies. He tells Paris's story in a seven-part sequence, though as Douglas Barbour has perceptively suggested, it is tempting to treat 'The Goodbye' and 'O Troy's Down: Helen's Song' as prologue and epilogue to the work's main body. 'The Goodbye' deflates any plot-oriented anticipation by asking the reader to imagine, in lines charged with metaphor, Philoctetes killing Paris.[17] Disposing of the myth's climax frees Ondaatje from having to accommodate a plot in his narrative structure. And though he follows the chronological sequence of events, from Paris's stay on Mount Ida with the nymph Oenone to his death, he does so in self-contained lyrics that, like most modernist treatments of mythic subjects, take for granted some acquaintance on the reader's part with the whole story.

Since Barbour has written perceptively at some length about the sequence – though I'm not persuaded by his suggestion that it foreshadows Ondaatje's shift from conventional modernism to postmodernism – I will deal with a handful of what strike me as suggestive details. The first involves Paris and Oenone (spelled Oinone in the poem), both of whom are abandoned or deserted in the original myth. Paris, we know from the Greek sources (though Ondaatje doesn't mention it), was exposed at birth because Hecuba, his mother, had dreamt that she would give birth to a firebrand. A seer interpreted this dream to mean that the child would destroy Troy. Paris was rescued, however, and grew up tending sheep and eventually married Oenone, a nymph of Mount Ida. The first two lyrics celebrate their time together, a time when Paris did not know that he was Priam's son. Both poems have pastoral moments in which the lovers share idyllic experiences in nature and in which the boundary between the natural and the human, as in myth and in stories of metamorphoses, seems momentarily to dissolve.

> She stretches out her palms,
> curves them to circle stars.
> 'I am collecting the sky for you, Alexandros.'   (59)

> Then her gentle body
> frail in the mornings
> and white in the streams
> gleaming among the dark rocks of Ida
> while dawns grew over the hill.
> Those days we sprawled on banks
> or toed dust in silence.

> 'For Alexandros who understands.'
> 'Who understands what?'
> 'Everything.'   (60)

In both poems, however, these moments exist in tension with intimations of Paris's fate. The opening poem closes with the reminder that 'she removes my dreams,' in the sense that she calms him. The second begins with a scene in Troy in which Paris, not yet aware that he is a prince, participates in a chariot race in which 'among my tears of speed, / hunched my body into a gracious bow / and left the chariot in a vast / ignoble, timeless tumble' (60). The 'gracious bow,' in the sense of a bending or stooping, anticipates homonymously the bow that will bring Paris to earth.

In the white between the second and third poems, Paris, once abandoned, abandons the nymph, who had warned him not to go to Greece, where, as we know, he will meet a woman who will abandon her husband for him. The sequence and the story end with the confrontation between two archers, each of whom had once been abandoned and left to die. To stay with this particular set of feelings and emotions, it is worth adding that in the myth itself we have two further abandonments or betrayals. Philoctetes' poisoned arrow only wounds Paris, and when the Trojan prince turns to Oenone, who had once promised that she would heal his war wounds, she rejects him. When she changes her mind later, Paris is already dead. In despair, she hangs herself.

By including the Paris-Oenone relationship in the sequence and ending the Troy poems with Helen's monologue about her life with Menelaus after the war and her memories of Paris, Ondaatje directs our attention to two triangular relationships each of which ends with separation, suffering, and death. Oenone-Paris-Helen ends with two deaths; Paris-Helen-Menelaus ends with one and in a re-established loveless marriage. The frustration and pathos of Helen's situation are intensified by the absence of anyone to whom she can describe her past. The poem's eight stanzas move fluently from her present life in Sparta back through sixteen years to her life with Paris.

> He had nightmares of an egg;
> inside the egg
> two inverted lovers
> strained against the shell
> with their passion.
>
> Oh how we yelled with love!
>
> My frail white daughter
> if I should breathe
> these thoughts to you at night
> I would with all the senses
> left now to me call
> Paris, Paris, Paris, Paris, Paris.   (67)

The 'nightmares of an egg' recall Paris's disturbing dreams in the first poem. But they also bring to mind – thus taking us further back in the myth – Leda, the swan, and the egg that contained Helen and her equally destructive sister, Clytemnestra. But having brought Leda's egg into the poem, Ondaatje then relegates it to a secondary level of meaning by describing this egg as containing 'two inverted lovers / strained against the shell / with their passion.' Leda, Helen, and Cly-

temnestra fade to provide the background for Helen and Paris straining against 'the shell' of their social situations, myth, and fate. The
withheld image here is the original broken egg, which contained
within it the destruction and burning of Troy. Looking ahead to *Rat
Jelly*, the egg will reappear in 'White Dwarfs' as 'This white that can
grow / is fridge, bed, / is an egg – most beautiful / when unbroken'
(71). To return to the above quotation, the past participle 'inverted' is
particularly fine, as is the simple exclamatory 'Oh how we yelled with
love!' which stands between a stanza tensive with metaphor and one
with sinuous enjambment, deliberately awkward syntax, and the ghost
of iambic metre. While Barbour notes two brief echoes of *Antony and
Cleopatra* (II. ii. 235), I wonder whether the poem's simultaneously
despairing and ecstatic line – 'Paris, Paris, Paris, Paris, Paris' – doesn't
owe something to Ondaatje's memory of Lear's 'Never, Never, Never,
Never, Never' (V. iii. 310). Whether he was aware of the allusive echo
or not, I assume that for most readers the emotional force and meaning
of his line are subtly intensified and altered when each iteration of
'Paris' comes accompanied by the equally trochaic 'Never.' To look forward across fifteen years, *King Lear* will return in *Running in the Family*
in one of Ondaatje's finest scenes.[18]

In retrospect, the most unexpected and unusual poems in the collection are the two historical monologues dealing with Queen Elizabeth
the First, 'Elizabeth' and 'Elizabeth – a Slight Ache.'[19] They surprise
because, though the young Ondaatje is interested in legendary and
mythic individuals and events, he is almost never drawn to major historical ones. The latter bring with them too much historical baggage to
allow room for him to invent, project, and elaborate. Still, in image,
theme, and situation the Elizabeth poems are continuous with others
in the volume. In the first poem, as in three shorter ones not collected,
the poet chooses to focus on her youth. With verbal energy and brilliant imagery, the poems convey a sense of undefined menace and
threatened violence. In the brief unreprinted dramatic monologue
'Elizabeth – Anne,' the daughter's version of her mother's meeting
with Henry VIII, her future husband and Elizabeth's father, emphasizes the violence of the encounter.

My mother was a long white viper,
sir, she loped the lilac trees
and fell on Henry's shoulder

slung white down
tore legs apart,
took him with a flying tongue

The several successive words with a labial – long, loped, lilac, fell, shoulder, slung, legs, flying – combine with the flowing enjambment of the poem's single sentence to evoke the impression, as sound and structure echo sense, of Anne's sensual slithering towards Henry. Her violent tearing – 'tore legs apart' – both implies fellatio and ironically anticipates the execution in which she will be torn apart. Her death is dealt with in the also uncollected 'Elizabeth – the House.'

The axe walks seasonal in this house:
the blade like quick birds, sharpened white,
wood as bright as witches' boots.
It flew to take my mother's head
through long hair, bone, then kissed the wood.

With the exception of the curious and distracting simile of 'wood as bright as witches' boots' – there is no answer to the questions 'Which witches, what boots?' – this is an impressive short lyric. The five sibilants in the opening line help evoke the axe both visually and aurally, and the soft 's' sound is then capped with the poignantly ironic and weighty 'kissed' in the second half of the final line. The verb also takes us back to the kiss 'with a flying tongue' at the beginning of the relationship. But the opening's sibilants are immediately counterpointed to the hard plosives of the second line: 'the blade like quick birds, sharpened white.' And this counterpoint, in which meaning exists on the level of sound and rhythm, culminates in the dramatic and rhythmically right placing of 'bone' just before the caesura in the final iambic tetrameter line: 'through long hair, bone, then kissed the wood.' The d's in 'kissed the wood' bring the poem to a close with a thud, echoing the sound of the axe hitting the block.

Though 'Elizabeth' is, as I said, a historical poem, Ondaatje takes as many liberties with the historical facts as he will in *The Collected Works of Billy the Kid*. Less than a page and a half long, the poem covers nearly fifty years of her life, from early childhood to her fifties, when she favoured the much younger Earl of Essex. Each stanza deals with a different period of Elizabeth's life in a style that evokes the voice and sensibility of her age. In the first stanza, we hear the voice of a very young girl: 'Catch, my Uncle Jack said / and oh I caught this huge apple / red as Mrs Kelly's bum.' The closing couplet offers a confident, controlled, and detached account of one aspect of her later life: 'And I find cool entertainment now / with white young Essex, and my nimble rhymes.' These lines are startling because in the poem they follow a long stanza describing the beheading of Thomas Seymour, once lord high admiral, for leading a rebellion against Edward VI. The execution took place in 1549, but Ondaatje places it after Mary's marriage to Philip II of Spain, which took place in 1554. But more important than the freedom with which he treats history is the subtle emphasis on Elizabeth as a poet – 'my nimble rhymes' – something we could have guessed from the monologues' mastery of tone, lineation, and metaphor. ('Nimble' also functions as a displaced epithet in its relationship to 'young Essex,' who, we assume, was nimble where and when it counted.) An apple in her room rots and shrinks 'like a face / growing eyes and teeth ribs.' Her breast, when fondled by Thomas Seymour, moves 'like a snail.' And when Seymour is executed, the blood settles anapaestically 'on his clothes like a blush.' Like the poet of *The Dainty Monsters* and, with important differences, like Peter, Elizabeth is a survivor who has learned how to turn the contingency, menace, and violence of her world into 'nimble rhymes.' When she cuts her hand on broken crystal in 'Elizabeth – a Slight Ache' she confesses, 'I prize pain like this.'

Elizabeth's closing sentence contains both *Rat Jelly* and *Coming through Slaughter*, and it is a succinct summary of a major aspect of Ondaatje's poetics between his first collection and *Secular Love*: pain and prizes, destroying and creativity, King Kong and Wallace Stevens are, so to speak, the signified and the signifier of the work of art. 'Peter,' the seven-part poem that closes *The Dainty Monsters*, offers the first extended treatment of this set of concerns. Though most readers probably suspect that the narrative, like those of the other poems in 'Troy Town,' has a source in some myth, the sequence seems to be a 'translation' or reconfiguration of a variety of sources, echoes, and what Ondaatje has called 'my most interesting hang-ups' into an original 'myth.' As Gillian Harding-Russell has suggested, 'Rather than following any one borrowed mythological structure, "Peter" as a creative myth which is built around the tale of the beauty and the beast echoes *The Tempest*, the Golden Fleece, and Minotaur stories. Here the artist as Caliban and Minotaur figure expresses his sense of persecution and personal frustration at physical handicaps (literally inflicted by society in this story) first through his art, and later by victimizing the young beauty Tara, who has been the one person to treat him with kindness. Accordingly, Tara may be seen as an Ariadne or Miranda figure.'[20] Though Harding-Russell's mythopoeic approach too often leads her into what I.A. Richards calls 'mnemonic irrelevance,' she at least points us in the right direction. That one of the characters is named 'Jason,' however, does not indicate a debt to the story of the Golden Fleece. Similarly, the fact that Jason's daughter is named 'Tara' does not automatically allow the reader to assume that Ondaatje wants him or her to recall 'the Irish home of kings and a Buddhist deity who provides life energy to *everyman*.'[21] I'm tempted to add, Why stop here? why not bring in *Gone with the Wind*? Still, Harding-Russell understands that the poem draws together many of the volume's concerns, and that Peter's troubling story, told in an often surrealistic and tormented lyricism, is in some crucial senses the story of all Ondaatje's artists. This last point is worth emphasizing as a corrective to her curious and slightly trendy claim that 'Ondaatje jolts us into a psychological world where we recognize elements of ourselves through what must be considered a post-modern extension of the artist as *everyman*.'[22] How a wild child who is captured and tortured and who then, in a creative metamorphosis, turns his suffering into a tormented art can be seen as a postmodern everyman figure escapes me. As does the suggestion that tenured English professors and their students will 'recognize elements of ourselves' in Peter. Surely, it makes more sense to see Peter as the figure of a certain kind of artist that fascinates Ondaatje.

Since we know that the poem was the last one in the book to be written, it is not surprising that its images and concerns are both retrospective and prospective. Some, such as scars, wrists, wounds, and splayed, bring earlier poems in the volume into play as we observe the poet's modulations on what we recognize as his signature words and soundscape. When Peter drags his legs 'like a suitcase behind him' (74), the simile drags into the poem the following lines from 'The Goodnight,' Ondaatje's first poem about Philoctetes, another wounded artist obsessed with suffering, violence, and death: 'imagine Philoctetes / the powerful fat thighed man, / the bandaged smelling foot / with rivers of bloodshot veins / scattering like trails into his thighs' (58). Other images we will encounter in *Rat Jelly* or *Coming through Slaughter*. The most interesting of these is the cross or crucifixion already mentioned with reference to 'Sows, one more time' and, I want to suggest, implicitly present in the verbs 'stretched' and 'splayed,' which appear over a dozen times in the volume. That there is an association between splayed and cross/crucifixion in Ondaatje's imagination seems to be indicated in the last section of 'Peter,' where Peter's rape of Tara is described as follows: 'An arm held her, *splayed* / its fingers like a *cross* at her neck / till he could feel fear thrashing at her throat, / while his bent hands tore the sheet of skirt, / lifted her, buttock and neck to the table' (77, my italics). I will return to this scene in a moment, but first I want to recall the previously quoted lines from 'White Dwarfs' in which Ondaatje again, and more explicitly, imagines the silent artist as the crucified, with the crucial difference that in the later poem his ambiguous silence can imply not only distance but also escape from or transcendence of an intolerable situation. (It's noteworthy that Buddy Bolden is twice described as crucified.) For Peter, however, being tortured and 'splayed' eventuates in a grotesque art that mimics his condition and in a 'loathing of fifteen years' that is the immediate cause of his attack on Tara.

It is worth recalling that Peter's captors not only hamstring him – the leg wound links him to Philoctetes, Potter, Billy, and Buddy – but also 'cut out his tongue.' His silence, however, is not the wished for silence of 'White Dwarfs.' This is the silence of Philomela, whose tongue is cut out by Tereus after he rapes her. The self's incapacity to utter human sounds leads to an alternative form of communication: where Philomela weaves a tapestry that tells her story,

... Peter performed violent beauty.
He carved death on chalices,
made spoons of yawning golden fishes;
forks stemmed from the tongues of reptiles,
candle holders bent like the ribs of men.

He made fragments of people: breasts
in the midst of a girl's stride,
a head burrowed in love,
an arm swimming – fingers heaved
to nose barricades of water.

His squat form, the rippled arms
of seaweeded hair,
the fingers black, bent from moulding silver,

poured all his strength
into the bare reflection of eyes.   (75)

The kinetic verbs and the comparison of the inanimate and the human lend an expressive and surreal quality to the verse, though 'fingers heaved / to nose barricades of water' is a good example of Ondaatje's imagination and lyricism slipping out of control. In an anticipation of Billy's shooting and Bolden's cornet playing, Peter transfigures the physical and emotional violence of his life into an equally 'violent beauty.' But as Ondaatje recognizes even in his first book, art isn't and cannot be life; it also cannot compensate for the tragedy of human suffering and what Shakespeare calls death's 'all oblivious enmity' (sonnet LV). Even though Peter 'poured all his strength' and all his rage into a self-expressive compensatory creativity in which art mimicked or reflected life, enough rage, resentment, and frustrated affection remained for him to attack Tara and

... shape her body like a mould,
the stub of a tongue sharp as a cat, cold,
dry as a cat, rasping neck and breasts
till he poured loathing of fifteen years on her,
a vat of lush oil, staining,
the large soft body like a whale.

Then he lay there breathing at her neck
his face wet from her tears
that glued him to her pain.   (77)

In this poem, as in the next three books, violence, suffering, chaos, and evil are simply a given in the book's universe, an implicit psychological or metaphysical ground for the characters and events. The characters, whether animal or human, are suffering loners, almost autochthonic. Peter, Potter, Billy, and Buddy don't have families, a fact that discourages the search for a psychogenetic cause for their behaviour. In a manner of speaking, 'Peter' is the first of the longer works to show Ondaatje running *from* the family by finding ways to deal with his memories and with his feelings of expulsion, abandonment, and betrayal. The most interesting of the animal poems, those organized around dreams, and the 'mythic' poems are all, to varying degrees, forms of autobiographical metamorphosis. One senses in them some suggestion of surplus meaning produced by images hinting at a personally inflected symbolism, overdetermination, or a recurrence of certain topoi that cannot be accounted for within the poem or the book. Looking back at the first four books, for instance, I can't help wondering whether the fact that so many of Ondaatje's heroes have names that begin with a plosive – Paris, Peter, Potter, Billy, Buddy, and Bellocq – is the result of the fact that Philip is his given name as well as his father's. If we take seriously his comment that some of his early characters are authorial masks, then this onomastic pattern links the characters not only one to another but to the author and his father as well. Readers who might think that this suggestion is a bit of a stretch should keep in mind that there are very few details in Ondaatje's work – whether numbers, images, allusions, quotations, or references – that function as furniture or filler.

The concern with the relationship between violence, suffering, and creativity in 'Peter' points us towards the poetics of all Ondaatje's books. It represents a complex ethical and epistemological step forward from 'The Martinique,' 'Eventually the Poem for Keewaydin,' and 'Four Eyes,' the earlier and theoretically more conservative lyrics about representation and creativity. As such, it raises some of the troubling questions about the relationship between the ethical life and art more prominent in the later work. A comment in *Leonard Cohen* provides a short cut to the issue: 'Beauty is all [in *Let Us Compare Mythologies*], and violence is one of the sources of beauty – for knife wounds are seen as caresses. It is a world where the morals are imagistic, as they always are in the context of dreams' (14) (or in the context of certain kinds of poems, I'm tempted to add). This observation is about Cohen, but it could just as easily describe the moral climate of Ondaatje's body of work. 'Beauty is all' brings us troublingly close to aestheticism and Wilde's claim that 'there is no such thing as a moral or an immoral book. Books are well written, or badly written.'[23] If beauty is all and if knife wounds are caresses, then moral discriminations and judgments of the kind that we make daily in our lives have little or no place in poetry; they are set aside for the duration of the reading act as the reader follows Kant and Schopenhauer in assuming that questions of utility, moral purpose, ideology, and identity politics have no place in a poem. In the uncollected 'Pictures from Vietnam,' Ondaatje writes admiringly of 'Beautiful photography / that holds no morality.'[24] In a 1971 interview with *Manna*, he comments that the 'recent fashion of drawing journalistic morals out of literature is I think done by people who don't love literature or who are not capable of allowing its full scope to be seen.'[25] In the final clause, literature's 'full scope' is also life's, a point implicit in Jean Renoir's defence of Truffaut's *Jules et Jim* against charges of immorality: 'The observation of a consequence can't be immoral. Rain wets; fire burns. The resulting wetness and burn have nothing to do with morality.'[26] As readers, we may bring our moral values to the poem, but the poem will counter with what I'm tempted to call an amoral or value-free definition of morality or with an insistence that the reader suspend moral criteria, in an act of negative capability, for the duration of the encounter with its multi-faceted reality. If one does so, then it is easier to accept the moral equanimity of 'Peter,' 'Spider Blues'(*RJ*, 63), or 'Sallie Chisum / Last words on Billy the Kid. 4 a.m.' (*TTK*, 98). In this context, the clause 'the morals are imagistic' can be paraphrased as follows: the morality of a work is co-extensive with and inseparable from the complexity and comprehensiveness of its presentation (what Ondaatje calls imagery) of its characters and events. In this sense, morality is less a matter of specific ethical judgments than of totality of presentation or comprehensive understanding. In Ondaatje's sense, to be moral when writing or reading is to allow oneself to imagine what it is to be a radically different sort of individual by suspending the moral criteria of one's everyday world. Kenneth Burke suggests something of this position when he argues, 'The artist, as artist, will be more concerned with moral imaginings than with moral stability.'[27] Moral stability is the morality of 'journalistic morals' as well as, more recently, identity politics.

It's also tempting to understand Ondaatje's comments as simply another case of the relativistic or pluralistic postmodern view of the moral dimension of art. If we keep in mind the particulars of his youth, however, I wonder whether the desire to avoid moral judgment in the text doesn't also indicate an autobiographical pressure to refrain from judging, as far as possible, oneself and one's father. If 'beauty,' in the widest sense of the word, is the sole criterion or end of art, and if the author has tacitly redefined moral in a way that brackets, suspends, or excludes judgment, then he protects, as he does also by using myths and masks, some of his most emotionally explosive personal material from moral comment by himself and by the reader. Even the characteristic restrained, nearly monotone voice may be one of the signs of a desire to remain objective and uninvolved. One can see this trait even in a comic poem such as 'Application for a Driving License' (35):

Two birds loved
in a flurry of red feathers
like a burst cottonball,
continuing while I drove over them.

I am a good driver, nothing shocks me.

I am tempted to paraphrase the last line as 'I am a good poet, nothing shocks me.' To make this event and his response acceptable to the reader, the poet develops a style that makes emotional and physical, private and public 'violence' bearable by aesthetic mediation and pleasure. But this comment also raises the troubling possibility that this approach implicitly makes acceptable the moral chaos or violence that is one of the sources of beauty – Peter's rape of Tara, Pat Garrett's mounted birds, the father's alcoholism and violence. Perhaps Ondaatje found myth and legend attractive early in his career because it is easier to give equal treatment to seemingly opposed figures – Philoctetes and Paris, Billy and Pat Garrett, King Kong and Wallace Stevens – in mythic, legendary, or surreal narratives than in realistic ones: in *Handwriting*, for instance, than in *Anil's Ghost*. In all cases, however, there is always the possibility, as Adorno reminds us, that when this kind of work gives aesthetic pleasure – beauty in Ondaatje's sense – it is at the expense of the sufferers and suffering depicted.[28] That Ondaatje is aware of these troubling implications is suggested by his recurring concern with betrayal, as an aspect both of relationships and of creativity. That concern will become more prominent after *The Dainty Monsters*.

COVERS

Ondaatje's long association with Coach House Press put him in touch with poets at the cutting edge of contemporary poetics as well as with book designers such as Stan Bevington who made him attentive to every aspect of book production. His sensitivity to the book as an aesthetic artefact is evident in his comment, in an interview in 1984, that 'it's so important to me how a book looks – the quality of the paper, the way the words look on the page, the cover. I really feel that the writer is responsible for this as well as for the writing ... There's pleasure for me in the physical beauty of the book.'[1] With this comment in mind, I want to suggest that we should 'read' the covers of Ondaatje's books almost as attentively as we read his poems.

Take *There's a Trick with a Knife I'm Learning to Do*. The photo on the cover – Harry Frost's 'Minnesota State Fair' – shows a woman, part of a knife-throwing act, standing against a large board with nine knives outlining her figure. She's middle-aged, she wears a long dress with a bow at the waist, and her expression is somewhere between resignation and anxiety. What we don't see until we look at the back cover is that the male knife-thrower is working with his left foot. Why the left foot? Perhaps it's a wink to those who remember that *The Collected Works of Billy the Kid* is subtitled 'Left Handed Poems' and that in *Rat Jelly* the author's note informs us that the poems 'were written before during and after two longer works – *the man with seven toes* and *The Collected Works of Billy the Kid* – when the right hand thought it knew what the left hand was doing' (72). George Bowering's puckish comment that 'the woman ... looks like Dorothy Livesay' points us to Ondaatje's problematic relationship with that part of the traditional Canadian canon represented by Livesay.

Three of the collections – *The Dainty Monsters*, *Secular Love*, and *Handwriting* – come with covers that point east. The first is the most interesting because at first glance the cover seems unconnected to the poems. To anyone attentive to this sort of detail, a design based on a fabric made by 'Ena de Silva Fabrics of Colombo, Ceylon,' must seem an authorial whim or, at best, a riddle, since there are no Ceylonese poems in the first collection and only one in *Rat Jelly*, the elegy for Ondaatje's father. So why the Ceylonese cover of exotic birds in sea blue and dark brown on a green background? Perhaps the images are a hint that the poems, whatever their ostensible setting and subject matter, come from somewhere else and are other than they seem. Even the epigraph from Auden's 'The Witnesses' faces a full-size illustration based on the Ceylonese fabric. It's almost as if Ondaatje wants Auden's lines read within the Ceylonese context suggested by the illustration:

We've been watching you over the garden wall
   For hours:
The sky is darkening like a stain;
Something is going to fall like rain,
   And it won't be flowers.[2]

The cover and the interior illustration suggest a context and a set of semantic and symbolic possibilities that remain undeveloped in the text unless, that is, they seep an almost subliminal Ceylonese aura around poems with tropical settings or images such as 'Henri Rousseau and Friends,' 'You Can Look But You Better Not Touch,' and '"Lovely the Country of Peacocks."' Whether the cover is also a clue to the real meaning of 'Dragon' is a question of another order.

The cover of *Secular Love* shows a photograph of what appears to be a rock, cliff, or wall painting of two women (probably from Sigiriya), visible from just above their breasts. Both wear turbans. Each is expressionless and looks across the painting to the viewer's right. Behind them and again to the viewer's right rises a large hand offering what appears to be a ceremonial greeting or perhaps a gesture of forgiveness. The photograph, by Dominic Sansoni, is so closely cropped that it's not clear whether the women are in water or whether the painter has simply chosen to represent them only in part. But this aspect is less important than the question of the relationship between the cover and the book's contents. Though their expressions are as enigmatic as the book's title – what, after all, is 'secular love'? – the two painted figures anticipate the two women of what Ondaatje has called the book's 'plot' (remember that he has described *Secular Love* as a 'novel').[3] They also anticipate the explicitly Sri Lankan poem 'Women like You' (*SL*, 90), which comes with the note 'the communal poem – Sigiri Graffiti, 5th century.' Anyone familiar with Ondaatje's previous book, *Running in the Family*, will recall that this poem appears there as well. In other words, like the painting, it links *Secular Love* not only to Sri Lanka but also to the Sri Lankan memoir, whose central figure is the father whose alcoholism was one of the causes of the breakup of his family. *Secular Love* begins with the son drunk and in the process of breaking up his marriage as he shifts from one woman to another.

The cover of *Handwriting* has a sepia photograph of a recumbent figure, either a girl or a young woman, with only her head and shoulders visible. She is lying on a rattan mat, her left hand under her head, perhaps asleep, and the focus is on her rich, long, and darkly lustrous hair. The photo, taken by the Sri Lankan photographer Lionel Wendt, is like the title in that it reveals nothing about the book's contents; each refuses to summarize and simplify what is to follow, though the title does link the sequence to a comment in *Running in the Family* about the sudden alteration in Doris Gratiaen's handwriting when her marriage ended. It's a fine example of what Adorno calls 'good titles,' the ones that are so close to the work that they respect its hiddenness.'[4] The photo's significance, however, remains elusive until we reach the climax of the narrative of 'The Story,' in which as the seven warriors – four men and three women – attempt to escape from the palace, 'They take up the knives of the enemy / and cut their long hair and braid it / onto one rope and they descend / hoping it will be long enough / into the darkness of the night' (66). There is also the possibility that if the figure is a sleeping child, then the image anticipates the sleepers in 'The Story' as well as the sleeping child, Michael Ondaatje, implicitly present both in the dedicatory poem and in the second part of 'Wells.'

the man with seven toes

Point Blank

Australia is so far away it hardly exists.

After Jorge-Luis Borges[1]

After the publication of *The Collected Works of Billy the Kid* (1970), *the man with seven toes* (1969) became something of a critical orphan in Ondaatje's corpus. This outcome is unfortunate because this long sequence, though minor, is a problematic apprentice work, interesting in its own right, and a pivotal transitional book in his development. Its continuity with the books that surround it is obvious from some of the poet's signature characteristics, though it reveals less of a felt autobiographical pressure. Ondaatje mentions in an interview that with *the man with seven toes* 'there was a jump from the self to a mask of some kind,' but he doesn't indicate, as he does in discussing *The Collected Works of Billy the Kid*, that the poem is 'a personal book.'[2] The poem's characters are without family and abandoned; the setting is southern or tropical; anxiety is the predominant emotion; the world is chaotic and violent; and the central figure has a fragile sense of self. And as so often in Ondaatje, the events involve the struggle for survival, but the characters, action, and setting are not Canadian. If we turn to form, it is with *the man with seven toes* that we first see him moving towards the longer and more experimental sequential, rather than serial, forms – with the thread of a narrative or a ghost of a plot – that will become characteristic in *The Collected Works of Billy the Kid, Coming through Slaughter,* and *Secular Love,* and that will eventually lead him to concentrate on the novel rather than the lyric. And although *the man with seven toes* does not go as far as they do in the direction of a temporally discontinuous form, aspects of its style and structure nevertheless clearly anticipate the later developments.

The final section of *The Dainty Monsters* showed Ondaatje's interest in the longer poem. 'Paris' and 'Peter' deal with some of his recurring concerns: the borderline between form and formlessness, civilization and nature, the human and the natural, reason and instinct, and the relationship between violence and creativity. But they do so primarily on the level of content by means of contrasted actions, settings, or images. In *the man with seven toes*, on the other hand, it is the style and the form as well as the content that push the reader into the unfamiliar ground of the work, to the point that the reading of the poem's temporally discontinuous and ostensibly unconnected sections mimics what is happening in the story, the heroine's harrowing journey through a wilderness. Beginning with this book, Ondaatje turns to a soft variant of what Roland Barthes terms a *scriptible* text, one that demands the reader's active participation as an interpreter of a reality that is often not only ambiguous but even chaotic.[3]

To achieve this, he attempts to make new both the form and the content of his work so that neither will predispose the reader towards a preconceived approach or what in his thesis he calls 'a preconceived morality' (76). I mention both form and content because at the same time as Ondaatje is creating a new form that will eventually develop into the discontinuous forms of *Coming through Slaughter, Running in the Family, Secular Love*, and *Handwriting*, his choice of subject in *the man with seven toes* foreshadows as well some of the later characters and themes. Where the medium-length narrative poems in *The Dainty Monsters* had dealt with figures drawn from classical mythology ('Paris') or who felt as if they belonged in classical myth ('Peter'), *the man with seven toes* is based on the experiences of a semi-legendary Englishwoman who, like Billy the Kid and Buddy Bolden, exists on the edge of history and about whose experiences there are contradictory accounts.[4] The life stories of these characters provide Ondaatje with a ready-made but incomplete and ambiguous narrative straddling the border between fact and fiction, history and legend. Each of these received narratives frees him from the creative burden of having to invent a story – never his strong suit. But because the received story is incomplete or exists in contradictory versions, it gives him the freedom to develop it in directions that reflect his concerns and obsessions. *The man with seven toes* shows Ondaatje turning towards mythic poems based on materials not usually associated with traditional myths but rather on what we normally refer to as legends. His several near-definitions of myth will seem idiosyncratic to anyone nurtured on *Mythologiques* or *Fables of Identity*, but as was mentioned earlier, there is a consistency in his various references to the subject in his thesis, poems, prose works, critical writings, and films. For him, a myth is any powerful story with an archetypal or universal potential; but in order for the story to become truly mythic, to have what in the article on *Tay John* he calls 'the raw power of myth,' it must be represented in such a way that 'the original myth [story] is given to us point blank.'[5] What he means is that readers must be exposed to as direct and seemingly unmediated a representation or, better, re-enactment of the original event as art will allow; they must feel as if they have become participants in it, experiencing what George Elliott Clarke has called 'the primeval power of story.'[6] To paraphrase Ondaatje's comments about some of the poems in *The Long Poem Anthology*, *the man with seven toes* shows 'a process of knowledge, of discovery during the actual [reading] of the poem.'[7] Though he is concerned in the essay with the poet's act of 'discovery during the actual writing of the poem,' I'm assuming that this act of discovery prefigures a similar one by the reader both in the anthology's poems and in *the man with seven toes*.

In the latter the reader enters the nightmare-like world of an anonymous white woman who spends a period of time living with a group of Aborigines before being rescued by a European and taken back to civilization. A brief note at the end of the book indicates that the source of Ondaatje's story lies in the experiences of a Mrs Fraser, who was shipwrecked in 1836 off the Queensland coast of Australia, captured by Aborigines, and finally rescued by a convict named Bracefell, whom she betrayed once they reached civilization. Ondaatje told me in an interview that this version of the story, as summarized by Colin MacInnes and painted by Sidney Nolan in his Mrs Fraser series (1947–57), was the only account with which he was familiar when he wrote the poem.[8] In his hands the story becomes a mythic exploration, in the form of brief and often imagistic poems, of how an unnamed white woman perceives and experiences a primitive and anarchic world totally alien to her civilized assumptions and mode of being. Like Atwood's Susanna Moodie, she is compelled into a confrontation in which she must acknowledge violent and primitive aspects of life within and outside herself previously either not known or ignored. This basic opposition between, on the one hand, aspects of self and, on the other, self and land, from which many of the poem's other dichotomies develop, is also central to Nolan's version. His first painting shows Mrs Fraser naked and crawling on all fours, with her white body against a setting of green jungle and blue sky; her face is covered by lank black hair, and her limbs are slightly distorted, indistinct, already on the point of becoming subtly animalistic.[9] Both the lack of clothing and the absence of identity remove her from civilization; the effect is rather like the first collage in the first edition of Atwood's *Journals*, where Susanna Moodie seems to be drifting down into the middle of the forest: the human being and the landscape are contiguous, but there is no connection between them.[10]

Both Ondaatje and Nolan – and, later, Patrick White in *A Fringe of Leaves* – use Mrs Fraser as the basis of a myth. In Nolan's series she gradually develops from being alienated from the land to the point where she is one with it and can be represented as an aboriginal rock painting. In contrast to Nolan, Ondaatje universalizes the meaning of her experiences by creating her in the image of an anonymous white woman. He further establishes the potential for her development as an archetypal or mythic figure by moving the story from the Australian historical context in which he found it to an unspecified time and place. The overall effect of these changes is to focus attention on the story's essential content: the effect upon an individual of her confrontation with a totally alien landscape and way of life.

But this true story with a potentially archetypal dimension cannot become mythic, in Ondaatje's sense of the word, unless expressed in a form and style that make its reading as unmediated a confrontation with the events as possible. To achieve this, Ondaatje relies on a form made up of brief, self-contained, often cinematic lyrics, each of which flashes upon the reader with a single startling revelation. To read from one to the next, as the woman moves from experience to experience, is to encounter a series of sensory and emotional shocks, until finally, like the character herself, the reader is numbed into accepting this surreal world as real.[11] Acknowledging a debt to Phyllis Webb's *Naked Poems*, Ondaatje has described the book's form as similar to 'a kind of necklace in which each bead-poem while being related to the others on the string, was, nevertheless, self-sufficient, independent.'[12] The continuity is implied rather than made explicit, and the terse, almost imagistic poems are related by the ghost of a narrative, by various kinds of montage (tonal, intellectual, etc.) or juxtaposition, and through the echoing of images from poem to poem. This kind of 'bonding' (Hopkins's term) of essentially separate lyrics by means of recurring images is important to Ondaatje, particularly as it relates to myth and mythic poems. He has written that 'myth is ... achieved by a very careful use of echoes – of phrases and images. There may be no logical connection when these are placed side by side but the variations are always there setting up parallels.'[13] In *the man with seven toes*, for example, the woman is raped both by the Natives and by the convict Potter (32); she is 'tongued' by the Natives (14), Potter's fingers are 'chipped tongues' (21), and he bends his 'tongue down her throat / drink her throat sweat, like coconut' (35); the Natives tear a fox open with their hands (16), and Potter 'crept up and bit open / the hot vein of a sleeping wolf' (29); the Natives have 'maps on the soles of their feet' (13), and at the book's end the woman lies on a bed 'sensing herself like a map' (41).

Ondaatje does not amplify his point to indicate how such echoes and parallels achieve a sense of the mythic, the turning of the ordinary into the fabulous and archetypal, but one of their effects is to create a common ground or structure – even the possibility of an unsuspected pattern, an order, or, to use one of the poet's recurrent tropes, a web underlying the separate lyrics. As in *Secular Love* and *Handwriting*, contrasts and comparisons are established between individual characters, events, and settings otherwise related only on the basis of a tenuous narrative line. But the structure remains implicit and avoids becoming a constricting grid, just as the repeated images themselves stop short of shifting into a symbolic mode of meaning. It is almost as if Ondaatje is playing with the reader, undercutting his or her conventional notions about structure and symbolism. Most readers, for example, assume that an image, repeated often enough in a variety of contexts, will at some point shift in function and meaning from being simply an image to assume the status of a symbol. But Ondaatje sends a semantic or semiotic signal only to deny the reader the expected consummation: the symbolic potential remains unfulfilled. Sometimes cigars are just cigars. Disoriented, the reader is compelled to re-examine the nature of his or her relationship to the text and to move more tentatively through it. Such is also the case with our relationship to the text as material object. The pages are three inches wider than they are tall, with the result that each lyric seems isolated, surrounded by the white silences of the extensive spaces around it, which seem to mimic the empty landscape and the silences separating each event in the heroine's life. Robin Blaser's description of the reading of a serial poem evokes something of the effect of reading *the man with seven toes*: 'The serial poem is often like a series of rooms where the lights go on and off. It is also a sequence of energies which burn out, and it may, by the path it takes, include the constellated. There is further a special analogy with serial music: the voice or tongue, the tone, of the poem sounds individually, as alone and small as the poet is ... but sounded in series, it enters a field ... A 'necessary world' is composed in the serial poem.'[14]

A closer reading through the text will illustrate more clearly some of the general points I have been making. The book opens with the following lyric:

The train hummed like a low bird
over the rails, through
desert and pale scrub,
air spun in the carriages.

She moved to the doorless steps
where wind could beat her knees.
When they stopped for water she got off
sat by the rails on the wrist thick stones.

The train shuddered, then wheeled away from her.
She was too tired even to call.
Though, come back, she murmured to herself.   (9)

Ondaatje's description of Cohen's *The Favourite Game* also applies here: this is 'a potent and enigmatic sketch rather than a full blown detailed narrative.'[15] The opening lyric has a haunting and disturbing quality because it is so brief and because so much is left unexplained. As in one of Alex Colville's dreamlike paintings, there is no explanation of why the train leaves the woman behind or why she is too tired to call. The situation is disturbing precisely because it occurs without an overall explanatory context to give it some kind of causal perspective. The character and the scene are isolated in time and space – 'desert and pale scrub.' The reader, knowing nothing about the scene's past, can make no valid conjectures about the future. By itself and then in relation to the next lyric, this poem establishes how Ondaatje wants the book to be read. It's worth noting that *The Collected Works of Billy the Kid*, *Coming through Slaughter*, and *Handwriting* have similar opening scenes.

Each poem in the sequence presents a new scene or a new experience, with the effect that the reader follows the woman's path, and often her point of view, as she moves from one startling and inevitably defamil-

iarizing event to another. The events of each new poem are literally
unexpected because Ondaatje's structuring has increased the number of
narrative possibilities that each lyric creates, to the point that the reader
simply does not know what to expect from poem to poem. The very
form of each lyric works deliberately against a predictable narrative
continuity, with the effect that each poem stands out separately as a
complete scene. Ondaatje's comment that myth is 'brief, imagistic'[16] certainly applies to these poems. The revelations come in brief and enigmatic flashes that disappear and are then replaced by new ones; the
effect is rather like that of a film in which the director cuts quickly and
dynamically from scene to scene, allowing the various kinds of montage
to create the meaning. The second poem, for example, begins with a dog
sitting beside her, the third with her entry into a Native clearing. There
is no temporal, spatial, or syntactical continuity, nor are there any hints
about what happens to her between poems.

> Entered the clearing and they turned
> faces scarred with decoration
> feathers, bones, paint from clay
> pasted, skewered to their skin
> Fanatically thin,
> black ropes of muscle.   (11)

A sense of immediacy is created by the elliptical syntax of the opening line. Because the terse poem begins with the verb – 'entered' – the
reader's attention is focused on the action itself. The ellipsis of the
subject – either 'I' or 'she' – achieves an abruptness and shocking
directness that would have otherwise been lacking. The effect is then
reinforced by the brief catalogue of images, one piled upon another,
exotic both to character and to reader. The cumulative effect of the
rhetoric is to indicate the woman's disorientation and to achieve the
reader's. Her reaction to this scene is caught in the violently beautiful
imagery and equally violent rhythms of successive lyrics.

> Goats   black goats, balls bushed in the centre
> cocks rising like birds flying to you   reeling on you
> and smiles smiles as they ruffle you open
> spill you down, jump and spill over you
> white leaping like fountains in your hair
> your head and mouth till it dries

and tightens your face like a scar
Then up to cook a fox or whatever, or goats
goats eating goats heaving the bodies
open like purple cunts under ribs, then tear
like to you a knife down their pit, a hand in the warm
the hot the dark boiling belly and rip
open and blood spraying out like dynamite
caught in the children's mouths on the ground
laughing collecting it in their hands
or off to a pan, holding blood like gold
and the men rip flesh tearing, the muscles
nerves green and red still jumping
stringing them out, like you   (16)

The syntax, imagery, and rhythm – the entire whirling movement of the verse – re-enact her confused response to an experience which, prior to leaving the train, she could not even have imagined. Her confusion is registered disturbingly in her simultaneously negative and positive responses to her rape. There is a visceral lyricism in the natural vitality of the men's 'cocks rising like birds flying to you' and in the syntactically awkward description of their ejaculations as 'white leaping like fountains in your hair.' But the 'fountains' suddenly dry on her 'face like a scar,' and the subsequent similes serve to reinforce the hinted-at connection between her violation and the eviscerating of an animal. The cuts in the animal are 'like purple cunts,' the knife pushed into the animal is also the phallus forced into her, and the bleeding animal body is also hers – 'like you.' This kind of comparison allows her to dramatize her emotions by making them part of a response to an event outside herself – the killing of 'a fox or whatever, or goats.' It is almost as if she cannot articulate directly the personal violation that takes place; only through her empathic response to the animal's suffering can she describe her own experience. And her recourse to similes, here and in other poems written from her point of view, is an indication of an analogous attempt to appropriate in slightly more familiar images a primal landscape and a set of experiences she finds almost indescribable. A later poem, for example, begins as follows:

Evening. Sky was a wrecked black boot
a white world spilling through.
Noise like electricity in the leaves.   (32)

The metaphor ('wrecked black boot') and simile ('like electricity') are imported from civilization in order to render this wilderness slightly more comprehensible, to mediate between its natural language, so to speak, and the character's mode of comprehending and describing the world. But even as these more familiar images struggle to mediate between the two worlds, to make the strange familiar, they simultaneously heighten our awareness of their differences.

The woman's return to the world of boots and electricity begins with her rescue by the convict Potter, whose striped shirt, in Ondaatje as in Nolan (see the paintings *Escaped Convict* and *In the Cave*), indicates his connection, however tenuous, with civilization.[17] His limp, as I mentioned earlier, connects him to Philoctetes, Billy, and Bellocq. He rescues her from the Natives – never referred to as Aborigines – but not from the violent existence she had led with them. The expectations justifiably created by the rescue are immediately thwarted.

Stripe arm caught my dress
the shirt wheeling into me
gouging me, ankles manacles,
cock like an ostrich, mouth
a salamander
thrashing in my throat.
Above us, birds peeing from the branches   (32)

The rescue unexpectedly recapitulates the events of the period of capture. Her rape by the Natives is a prelude to this one, and the imagery indicates that Ondaatje wants the two scenes compared: the Natives had 'cocks like birds,' Potter's 'cock [is] like an ostrich'; the Natives had previously been compared to 'sticklebacks,' while Potter's mouth is 'a salamander.' Potter has replaced the Natives as her keeper, but the nightmare quality of her journey through a physical and psychological chaos has not changed. Her rape, for example, is simultaneously violent, terrifying, and ridiculous. The 'birds peeing from the branches' put it into a grotesque perspective, as if to suggest that the rape is just another event in nature, nothing more or less. Our moral response to the event is suddenly qualified by a new and unanticipated context created by the absurd last line. Yet in this poem, as in so much of Ondaatje's poetry, the unexpected, the absurd, and the surreal gradually become the normal and the familiar: a dog runs away with a knife stuck in its head (27), and birds high on cocaine stagger across the sand (28). As Potter says, 'Sometimes I don't believe what's going on' (27). The woman's attitude to these kinds of experiences is finally one of numbed and passive acceptance; had they occurred earlier, they would have both startled and horrified her.

> So we came from there to there
> the sun over our shoulders and no one watching
> no witness to our pain our broken mouths and bodies.
> Things came at us and hit us.
> Things happened and went out like matches.   (38)

Because of the reference to 'broken mouths,' I assume that the speaker is the woman; it is her mouth that has been pried open by the Natives (14) and by Potter (35). The poem's vagueness – 'from there to there,' 'Things' – is an effective register of her numbed emotional condition. The rhythmic and tonal flatness of 'Things came at us and hit us / Things happened' is a fine preparation for the unexpected closing simile. In poetry as in architecture, less is often more, and the final image – the flash of matches being extinguished – closes with light a poem almost devoid of colour and metaphor.[18] The lyric's texture creates a simultaneous awareness in the reader both of the essentially shocking nature of what is happening and of the paradoxical fact that this no longer surprises the woman now inured to it.

After her return to civilization, this violently beautiful world seems to pursue her even into the safe Royal Hotel.

> She slept in the heart of the Royal Hotel
> Her burnt arms and thighs
> soaking the cold off the sheets.
> She moved fingers onto the rough skin,
> traced the obvious ribs, the running heart,
> sensing herself like a map, then
> lowering her hands into her body.
>
> In the morning she found pieces of a bird
> chopped and scattered by the fan
> blood sprayed onto the mosquito net,
> its body leaving paths on the walls
> like red snails that drifted down in lumps.

She could imagine the feathers
while she had slept
falling around her
like slow rain.   (41)

The narrative closes with this ambiguous and densely allusive poem, whose almost every image echoes some earlier image or situation. Given the poem's position in the sequence, it is inevitable that we look to it to provide some kind of summarizing judgment upon the story. It does so, but only through an ambiguous image or metaphor. The key to interpretation seems to lie in the dead bird and the woman's attitude to it. I assume there is an implicit analogy between the bird's violent death and the woman's brutal experiences in the wilderness. If this is so, then her response to the presence of the slaughtered bird should provide an insight into her attitude to what happened to her. Either her reaction is sentimentally romantic, or it indicates a full acceptance of the violent natural world into which she had been thrust. I tend towards the second reading, first, because this lyric follows a poem in which her attitude towards the convict, now a memory from her past, is completely positive; and secondly, because the opening stanza seems to point to a physical and psychological awareness and acceptance of her new self ('sensing herself like a map, then / lowering her hands into her body'). This new attitude corresponds roughly with Nolan's later paintings of Mrs Fraser and the land as finally indistinguishable from one another.[19] In Ondaatje this merging of self and wilderness is reinterpreted as a rediscovery of the instinctual world within the self. Here, as in D.H. Lawrence's 'The Woman Who Rode Away,' Atwood's *Surfacing*, and White's *A Fringe of Leaves*, the physical journey away from civilization is simultaneously a psychological one as well. M. Travis Lane has described this as a descent into her subconscious.[20] White makes the point explicit by equating the wilderness with 'secret depths with which even she, perhaps, is unacquainted, and which sooner or later must be troubled.'[21] In fact, it is safe to say that here and in his other work Ondaatje is primarily interested in landscape only in so far as it can be used to reveal inner states of being.

The original Mrs Fraser returned to England, married her ship's master, a Captain Greene, and keeping her marriage a secret, was able to exhibit herself at 6 pence a showing in London's Hyde Park. Ondaatje deals with this return to civilization in a ballad – perhaps sung by his central character – which functions as an epilogue offering another ambiguous summary. It is worth noting that *the man with seven toes* anticipates several of Ondaatje's later book-length works in having more than one ending.

> When we came into Glasgow town
> we were a lovely sight to see
> My love was all in red velvet
> and I myself in cramasie[22]
>
> Three dogs came out from still grey streets
> they barked as loud as city noise,
> their tails and ears were like torn flags
> and after them came girls and boys
>
> The people drank the silver wine
> they ate the meals that came in pans
> And after eating watched a lady
> singing with her throat and hands
>
> Green wild rivers in these people
> running under ice that's calm,
> God bring you all some tender stories
> and keep you all from hurt and harm   (42)

The original Scots ballad 'Waly, Waly,' from which Ondaatje borrows his opening stanza, is a song of regret and disillusion in which a woman laments having given herself to her lover:

> But had I wist before I kiss'd
> That love had been sae ill to win,
> I'd lock my heart in a case of gowd
> And pin'd it we'a siller pin.[23]

In 'Waly, Waly' the apparent is not the real: a tree seems 'trusty,' but breaks; a lover seems true, but is not. A similar duality exists in Ondaatje's version: the ostensible order and stability of Glasgow town rest upon people in whom 'Green wild rivers' run under ice that's calm, a motif which, as we have seen, runs through *The Dainty Monsters*. The full force of the contrast between the two images can only be felt, however, if we place them in the context of the entire narrative;

then the ice is seen as relating to consciousness, order, and civilization – everything that was left behind when the woman stepped off the train – and the 'rivers' represent everything that is unconscious, chaotic, and natural – the world she stepped into. The ice does not crack in the ballad, but the reader, keeping in mind the action of the book, realizes how tenuous the order of self and civilization really is, how at any moment the ice could crack and melt, letting through everything implied by the 'Green wild rivers.' If the book has a theme, or what Ondaatje prefers to call a 'moral,' it is summarized metaphorically in the interplay of these two images.[24] As he points out in his thesis, this is also a constitutive concern in Muir's work as well as in the work of Joseph Conrad, a writer both Muir and he admire.

But it is also important to note that, although the ballad summarizes or comprehends the book's dualities and tensions, it does not resolve them. This deliberate irresolution leaves the sequence with a sense of open-endedness reinforced by the grammar of the last sentence, whose verb ('God ... keep you'), in the optative mood, points to the future. Like the present-tense endings of *The Collected Works of Billy the Kid* ('I smell the smoke still in my shirt'), *Coming through Slaughter* ('There are no prizes'), *Secular Love* ('He lies in bed'), and *Handwriting* ('I roam restless'), this gives the book an ending without narrative resolution, struggling against the closure inevitable in every work of art. The reader is left with a sense of the continuity of the story and its implications into present and future time. At the precise moment when the book is being finished and about to be put aside, it forces itself into the reader's real time. One aspect of the book's form – its various discontinuities – compels the reader to enter the narrative as a figure in the story's ground, as a kind of character surrogate; another aspect – lack of closure – reverses the spatial and temporal situation by having the book extend itself into the reader's world. A slight shift in the verb's mood or tense is the final aspect of a narrative form and a poetic rhetoric attempting to achieve a 'point blank' and mythic presentation.

Several of Ondaatje's later works will go further than *the man with seven toes* in bringing the reader into the text or creating a poetic closer to one of process. But the more ambitious and greater achievement of these later books should not prevent us from acknowledging this minor, though by no means negligible, poem, which is as fine an achievement as most of the long poems in *The Long Poem Anthology* and which anticipates the later work in so many respects. There are, however, two particularly important differences between this sequence and

Ondaatje's other work: it doesn't deal self-reflexively with creativity, and it has little autobiographical baggage or residue – one senses that the poet's demons are almost on holiday. The dedication to his next book, *Rat Jelly*, will begin the decade-long journey towards the difficult wrestle with the past.

TITLES

If because of some natural or historical disaster, only Ondaatje's titles survived, the future could follow the curve of his poetic development by reading them in sequence. Their survival would also be enough to hint that he was a magician with titles. Though he hasn't read Gotthold Ephraim Lessing, the titles of his books and poems show him in fundamental agreement with the German writer's comment that 'a title should not be a recipe. The less it reveals about the contents, the better it is.'[1] Adorno paraphrases this as saying that 'the work's substance should on no account, on pain of the work's immediate demise, be put into words, even if the author were capable of doing so. Titles, like names, have to capture it, not say it.'[2] Saying it would entail titling the story of a New Orleans jazz musician *The Rise and Fall of Buddy Bolden*, instead of the non-referential and figuratively elusive *Coming through Slaughter*, a syntactically dynamic title that doesn't reveal the ambiguity of its closing noun until the book's final movement. Similarly, *The Story of Billy the Kid* is very different from *The Collected Works of Billy the Kid*, in which the first three words seem to belong to a phrase like *The Collected Works of Peter Handke* and the last three to a Sam Peckinpah film. In Adorno's words, Ondaatje's titles capture the substance of the work while leaving it room to be heard 'saying' itself during the reading.

This is also true of the titles of the lyrics, which, despite the shift in approach that occurs after *Rat Jelly*, can be divided into three overlapping categories: first, the clearly referential or denotative, such as 'Sows, one more time,' 'We're at the graveyard,' 'Moving Fred's Outhouse / Geriatrics of pine,' 'Translations of my Postcards,' 'To a Sad Daughter,' or 'House on a Red Cliff'; second, the nominative or onomastic, such as 'Song for Alfred Hitchcock and Wilkinson,' 'Philoctetes on the island,' 'Flirt and Wallace,' 'Griffin of the night,' 'King Kong meets Wallace Stevens,' 'Charles Darwin pays a visit, December 1971,' 'Late Movies with Skyler,' and 'To Anuradhapura'; and third, the metaphorical or figurative, such as 'Rat Jelly,' 'Burning Hills,' 'White Dwarfs,' 'Rock Bottom,' 'Light,' and 'Step.'

In the first group, only 'Sows, one more time' points directly to the lyric's content. The other titles in the group simply suggest a setting or do little beyond suggesting a tone ('graveyard'), a smell and mood ('outhouse'), or a colour ('red'). Though the poem amplifies and develops some of the title's intimations, it does so in unexpected ways. Despite the title's deictive quality, the poem remains unsaid or waiting to be spoken.

Poems with names in them – there are nearly thirty – would seem to be not only unavoidably tied to referentiality but committed to saying something about a poem's substance, rather than capturing it. In other words, one might assume that the title would be working against the poem's figurative essence. This is true up to a point of 'Philoctetes on the island,' but that poem is an exception because of its traditional subject matter. In almost every other case, Ondaatje does some trick with a knife in the title to make its meaning equivocal, incomplete, and dependant on the poem to complete it. 'Song to Alfred Hitchcock and Wilkinson,' for instance, contains a comic *hommage* to Hitchcock's *The Birds* and perhaps to Anne Wilkinson, who returns in *In the Skin of a Lion*.[3] 'Proust in the Waters' (*SL*, 122) teases the reader with the image of Proust, perhaps swimming at Balbec, but is then followed by lines in which the poet swims at night at Balsam Lake and reflects, 'We love things which disappear / and are found / creatures who plummet / and become / an arrow.' This is closer to the world of *Coming through Slaughter*, 'White Dwarfs,' and 'To a Sad Daughter' than it is to anything in *À la recherche du temps perdu*. Proust has been named, but he certainly doesn't compromise the poem by 'saying' it in the title. The same is true of 'Charles Darwin pays a visit, December 1971,' in which the date seems to take Darwin out of history and into Ondaatje's world and poetry. The first part of the title creates a set of expectations – perhaps a historical poem or a Richard Howard dramatic monologue – which are then undermined by the date after the comma.

This elusiveness is even more obvious in the figurative titles, which offer only a fragment of the metaphoric equation – in the sense that the title *is* the poem – and let the poem complete it. About a third of Ondaatje's poems begin in this way with the titles enigmatically suggestive, 'so close to the work that they respect its hiddenness.'[4] In 'Light,' for instance, the several possible meanings of the title only become manifest when we have read the poem. The 'light' is the lightning of a summer night, the flicker of the evanescent images on a makeshift screen, candlelight, the light of a match lighting a cigarette, the insubstantiality of memories, and perhaps the unbearable lightness of being. As is so often the case with Ondaatje's titles, it resists our attempts to turn it into a précis of the poem; instead, it depends on the poem to fill it with signification. We can't understand the title unless we read the poem twice. What are 'Burning Hills'? What is 'Uswetakeiyawa'? What is 'Breeze'?

The shift towards a less figurative and more conversational style and open form that takes place in the late 1970s can also be seen in the titles of individual poems. The change may reflect the influence of Ondaatje's prose on his poetry – *Coming through Slaughter* was published in 1976 – or, more likely, he recognized that he had exhausted certain possibilities of style and voice. And 'after such choreography what would [he] wish to speak of anyway' (*RJ*, 71). As so often in his career, he renews his poetry by building on and reconfiguring his earlier strengths. In both *Secular Love* and *Handwriting* the poems carry titles that are less ornate or metaphorically flamboyant than the ones typical of the first two collections. Ondaatje is still capable of surprising us in the play between the title and the body of the poem – see 'When you drive the Queensborough roads at midnight' (*SL*, 121) or 'Last Ink' (*H*, 72) – but the surprises are deliberately muted, subtler. And in *Handwriting*, as we increasingly sense the poems' otherworldly quality, we gradually realize that because the titles are rooted in a cultural tradition not our own, their meaning will become clear only when we have understood the imagined world of the poems. In *Handwriting*, more than in any other volume, the individual titles seem extensions not only of their poems but also of the book as a whole.

Rat Jelly

'right to the end of an experience'

Tolerate chaos.

Richard Diebenkorn[1]

If *The Collected Works of Billy the Kid* (1969) established Ondaatje as a writer to watch, *Rat Jelly* (1973) confirmed the promise he had shown in *The Dainty Monsters* (1967) as a lyric poet. Its finest lyrics demonstrate not only the figurative flair, wit, and surreal imagination of his early work but an ambition in theme as well as a poise and maturity only hinted at a decade earlier. The first two sections of this closely organized collection – 'Families' and 'Live Bait' – develop situations and concerns similar to those in the earlier lyrics, but often display a range in theme and control of voice and tone that show how much Ondaatje developed in the intervening years. This evolution is particularly evident in 'Billboards' (a poem about his wife, Kim) and 'Letters & Other Worlds' (an elegy for his father, Mervyn). But the most surprising and accomplished poems are gathered in the third section, 'White Dwarfs.' Individually, these constitute some of Ondaatje's best work in the genre; as a group, they develop into a poetics some of the hints – and that's all they are – in 'Peter' and in *The Collected Works of Billy the Kid* about the relationship between destroying and making, between wounds and creativity. 'Burning Hills,' 'King Kong meets Wallace Stevens,' '"The gate in his head,"' 'Spider Blues,' and 'White Dwarfs' consolidate and develop in lyrical form the critical hunches and ideas of the thesis on Edwin Muir (1967), the short study of Leonard Cohen (1970), and the lessons that Ondaatje learned during the writing of *The Collected Works of Billy the Kid*.

Though we couldn't have known it in 1973, the book's dedication to his parents, brother, and sisters and the elegy for his father represent the first step towards the writing of *Running in the Family* (1982), in which he finally comes to terms with his Ceylonese/Sri Lankan past. His continuing reluctance to do so is hinted at in the book's three epigraphs. In the first, from Richard Stark's *The Sour Lemon Score*, the female speaker berates the male for his failure to be more communicative:

> She waited and then said, 'Say something, Parker. God to get you to gossip it's like pulling teeth.'
> 'Handy retired.' Parker said.
> 'I *know* he retired! Tell me about it. Tell me why he retired, tell me where he is, how he's doing. Talk to me, Parker, goddammit.'   (8)

The second and third, from Howard O'Hagan's *Tay John* and Herman Melville's *The Confidence Man*, raise roughly similar concerns about silence, lying, and self-revelation. Not unexpectedly, the book's first and last poems – 'War Machine' and 'White Dwarfs' – show a speaker, probably the poet, paradoxically attracted to silence. In the former he brags about the stories and gossip he could tell – '30 jayne mansfield stories' – but concludes with the following ambivalent comment: 'Perhaps / wd like to live mute / all day long / not talk // just listen to the loathing' (11). There's nothing in the poem to explain the 'loathing' or the surprising desire 'to live mute.' And the title metaphor is too strong and too vague for the poem that follows. Whether the title refers to the poet or to poetry, it doesn't quite come off, promising far more than it delivers. If the poem remains in the reader's mind, it does so primarily as a thematic prologue to the more tough-minded and troubling concern with silence in 'Letters & Other Worlds' and 'White Dwarfs,' both of which will be dealt with in some detail below.

Most of the remaining poems in the first section offer various domestic perspectives on the poet's wife, his marriage, and his dogs. Only on finishing the section does one realize that these sometimes playful and affectionate poems are framed, even shadowed, by the more menacing 'War Machine' and 'Letters & Other Worlds.' With the exception of 'White Room,' however, each presents a situation in which there is a division or a sense of separation. 'Notes for the legend of Salad Woman' (18), for example, begins with a playfully exaggerated image of the speaker's wife:

Since my wife was born
she must have eaten
the equivalent of two-thirds
of the original garden of Eden.
Not the dripping lush fruit
or the meat in the ribs of animals
but the green salad gardens of that place.

The 'meat in the ribs of animals' momentarily recalls 'Peter,' but the remainder of the verse combines burlesque and comic book fantasy (Salad Woman, Wonder Woman). The catalogue continues through the second stanza, but while the tone and images remain comic, the reader begins to sense a more sombre note in the references to the destruction 'Salad Woman' leaves in her wake:

She is never in fields
but is sucking the pith out of grass.
I have noticed the very leaves from flower decorations
grow sparse in their week long performance in our house.
The garden is a dust bowl.

The third stanza opens by recalling the 'garden of Eden' mentioned in the first and implies a connection between her compulsive eating and their expulsion from Eden: 'On our last day in Eden as we walked out / she nibbled the leaves at her breasts and crotch.' And though the speaker ends by reassuring us and himself that 'there's none to touch / none to equal / the Chlorophyll Kiss,' the assertion comes in the same stanza as the expulsion from Eden and is inseparable from the earlier images of destruction. If the wife is a life force, she is simultaneously a destructive one; and if life with her is paradisal, the paradisal state is a tenuous one and is dependent on her. She isn't quite La Belle Dame sans Merci, but the poem is tensed about the speaker's ambivalence – admiration and anxiety.

'Billboards' (14–15), a domestic poem about his wife and her children from a previous marriage, shows Ondaatje in a relaxed, reflective mood writing with affection, humour, and some perplexity about his situation. The poem begins by contrasting 'my virgin past' to the domestic complexity, even confusion, of his present, which is filled with 'Reunions for Easter egg hunts / kite flying, Christmases' with his wife's children, who 'descend on my shoulders every holiday.' The poem then shifts into the past, to the time when 'she lay beginning / this anthology of kids' and he

> ... moved – blind but senses
> jutting faux pas, terrible humour,
> shifted with a sea of persons,
> breaking when necessary
> into smaller self sufficient bits of mercury.
> My mind a carefully empty diary
> till I hit the barrier reef
> that was my wife –
> > > > there
> the right bright fish
> among the coral.

The shift to a highly figurative style allows Ondaatje to swerve away from dealing directly with the painful particulars of his past, though 'sea of persons,' 'breaking,' and 'smaller self sufficient bits of mercury' (is there an implication of a thermometer here as well as of a fever?) and the attempt to keep the 'mind a carefully empty diary' hint strongly at potentially troubling events that the speaker wants to avoid making explicit. The suggestive tension is maintained in the third stanza in his comment that before meeting her, he 'was ... trying to live / with a neutrality so great / I'd have nothing to think of.' Whereas 'Nowadays I somehow get the feeling / I'm in a complex situation, / one of several billboard posters / blending in the rain.' The withheld image here is of his wife as a driver looking at various aspects of her past represented by 'several billboard posters.' The image of the billboard probably comes from a passage in *Beautiful Losers* that Ondaatje quotes in *Leonard Cohen*: 'Truth was, I felt that F. was using me like an advertisement for his own body. I was the tattered billboard for his reality' (*LC*, 50). But why 'in the rain,' unless the landscape is an objective correlative for some of his feelings about the situation?

Although the poem begins with a note of domestic comedy and ends with an affectionate evocation of his wife, each of the first three stanzas contains one or more images that suggest anxiety, menace, and unhappiness. In the first the speaker wonders in a parenthesis about when his wife's children will 'produce a gun and shoot me / at Union Station by Gate 4?'[2] In the second, in addition to the already quoted references to 'terrible humour,' 'breaking,' and the 'carefully empty diary,' we also find the speaker describing his first meeting with his wife in terms of a fish hitting 'the barrier reef.' And the third, which ends with 'in the rain,' begins with a reference to 'the locusts of [his wife's] history.' The cumulative effect of these images is to leave one with the impression that the 'complex situation' the speaker refers to is even more complicated and full of emotional cross-currents than one expected from the title and the first stanza. As a portrait of a marriage, the poem reminds us that each partner brings his or her own burdens from the past, whether obvious, like the wife's, or concealed, like the speaker's.

The final stanza, however, also points to the relationship between the poet's life and his writing. As in 'Burning Hills,' we see him writing the poem we have just read: 'I am writing this with a pen my wife has used / to write a letter to her first husband.' But he doesn't stop at this scene, which is charged with ambivalence. He brings his wife more sensuously to the reader's attention by mentioning that on the pen

> ... is the smell of her hair.
> She must have placed it down between sentences
> and thought, and driven her fingers round her skull
> gathered the slightest smell of her head
> and brought it back to the pen.

The run-on lines and the sibilants followed by the assertive closing plosives evoke the scene of writing by means of rhythm and sound. The imagined scene sums up the complexity of the relationship: the current husband writes a poem about his wife writing to her first husband, and he does so with the pen she used. But I wonder whether there isn't also a suggestion that his writing is in some mysterious sense dependent on her, and that his poems are his answer to her 'anthology of kids'? – that this poem, in other words, couldn't exist without her and her complex past. Though the closing stanza doesn't make this explicit, there is a hint of doubling and merging in it: not only does the speaker use the same pen as his wife, but the wife's gestures during the writing of her letter suggest the gestures that he might be making while writing this poem.

'Dates' (21), a poem later in the first section, switches the focus from Canada to Ceylon, from the poet and his wife to himself and his mother. From the perspective of the section as a unit, it can also be seen as preparing the way for the elegy for his father. Read in the context of the volume's concern with poetry and poetics, it shows Ondaatje acknowledging some of his literary debts at a point in his development when he is in the process of leaving his past masters behind. Though the poem alludes to Auden's 'In Memory of W.B. Yeats' and though Stevens is a central figure in it, its style owes nothing to the great moderns. The date in question is that of the poet's birth, 12 September 1943 (though it isn't specified). As he remarks sardonically in the opening stanza,

> My birth was heralded by nothing
> but the anniversary of Winston Churchill's marriage.
> No monuments bled, no instruments
> agreed on a specific weather.
> It was a seasonal insignificance.

The third and fourth lines implicitly draw our attention to the more significant anniversaries and occasions, the deaths of a god and, through an allusion to Auden's great elegy, of Yeats.

The second and third stanzas juxtapose, each in a single, long, flowing sentence, two acts of creation: his mother's pregnancy and Wallace Stevens's writing of 'The Well Dressed Man with a Beard.' If the poet's birth is first mentioned in relationship to 'Winston Churchill's marriage' and under the shadow of two deaths, in the poem's final movement he exists as a foetus whose evolution and birth are counterpointed with the development and completion of a poem celebrating creativity and the imagination.

> Stevens put words together
> that grew to sentences
> and shaved them clean and
> shaped them, the page suddenly
> becoming thought where nothing had been,
> his head making his hand
> move where he wanted
> and he saw his hand was saying
> the mind is never finished, no, never
> and I in my mother's stomach was growing
> as were the flowers outside the Connecticut windows.

Although the syntax, the enjambed lineation, and the idea of organic creation link the poet's mother, Stevens, and the poet, the key verbs suggest a difference between the gestation of a child and the creation of a poem. The words may *grow* into sentences, but they are initially 'put together' and need to be 'shaved' and 'shaped' by the 'head ... making his hand / move where he wanted.' It is worth noting that Ondaatje doesn't italicize or put into quotation marks the words that Stevens's 'hand was saying.' A simple reason may be that the line doesn't quote from Stevens's poem; it paraphrases or creatively misquotes it. The last line of 'The Well Dressed Man with a Beard' is 'It can never be satisfied, the mind, never,' which is not quite 'the mind is never finished, no, never.' I'm tempted to suggest that Ondaatje's rewriting of Stevens, like his casual appropriation of an image from the first stanza of 'In Memory of W.B. Yeats,' is both an example of a strong or original young poet flexing his creative muscles against the major figures in the tradition and an illustration of Stevens's assertion 'It can never be satisfied, the mind, never.' The misquoted line also implies that for the poet *as* poet, the significant dates and filiations are not necessarily the conventional ones. Michael Ondaatje may have been born on 12 September 1943, but an equally important 'birth' occurred when he discovered Yeats, Auden, Stevens, and others who helped make him into a poet.

The 'Families' section ends with two poems, 'Griffin of the night' and 'Letters & Other Worlds,' whose relationship to each other becomes evident only after we have read the second. In fact, it's possible that the full implications of 'Griffin of the night' (23) can be felt only if one has also read *Running in the Family* and the 'Claude Glass' section of *Secular Love*. This isn't to suggest that it is a difficult poem. Its only interpretive crux occurs between the title and the first line, where the reader needs to shift from thinking that 'Griffin' denotes a mythical beast to understanding that the name refers to Ondaatje's son. Since the poem will be about 'nightmares,' which are after all metaphoric monsters, it is a felicitous, ironic confusion. In the end, one understands its complex emotional intensity and the full implications of its last line – 'sweating after nightmares' – only when one sees the relationship between the speaker and his son in the context of the speaker's here unspoken relationship to his father, who is the source of his own nightmares and the subject of the following poem.

I'm holding my son in my arms
sweating after nightmares
small me
fingers in his mouth

his other fist clenched in my hair
small me
sweating after nightmares

The style is spare, almost minimalist: simple diction, an almost monotone or uninflected voice, no punctuation, no affective adverbs or
adjectives, and a palette without colours. By contrast, the subject matter or the story is emotionally charged – a father comforting a son
'sweating after nightmares' – and threatens line by line to overwhelm
the speaker's poise. The tension between the scene and its treatment is
intensified by the chiastic repetition of the second and third lines as the
sixth and seventh. The chiasmus allows a syntactic ambiguity in which
the final 'sweating after nightmares' is allowed to modify both the
father and the son since each is potentially the 'small me' of the sixth
line. The ambiguity intensifies the poem's pathos while simultaneously implicating the speaker and the reader in the temporally withheld earlier scene in which the father was himself a son 'sweating after
nightmares.' Whether someone comforted *him* is the implicit question
with which the poem closes. Three decades after the poem's first publication, it is difficult not to think of it as carrying the subtitle 'Running
in the Family.' The same could be said as well of 'Bearhug' (*TTK*, 104),
a similar poem that introduces 'Light,' the elegy for Ondaatje's mother.

If we remember that Ondaatje has commented on the care with
which he arranges his poems, we won't be surprised that a poem about
himself and his son introduces, in a manner of speaking, his first
attempt to deal directly with his father. 'Letters & Other Worlds' (24–6)
frames the unnamed father's life with two figurative, though stylisti-
cally different, accounts of his death, a structure that Ondaatje also
uses in 'Burning Hills' and 'Light,' two other autobiographical poems
that look back to his family and Ceylon. Though the poem is an elegy
and begins and ends with an appropriately sombre tone, its long middle section of six stanzas shows a startling shift in tone and a deft control in the presentation of the 'terrifying comedy' of his father's life and
his parents' marriage.

As Stephen Scobie pointed out, the epigraph is taken from Alfred
Jarry's 'Descendit ad infernos,' and its description of the hero's ap-
proaching death is also an anticipatory summary of the father's: *'for
there was no more darkness for him and, no doubt like Adam before the fall, he
could see in the dark.'* Worth noting is Ondaatje's omission of Jarry's first
clause, 'But soon he could drink no more.'[3] The letters of the title recur

in the two dirge-like[4] stanzas that open the poem. Written in a style that combines a series of grammatically simple and direct, unpunctuated sentences and a highly figurative language, the lines both amplify the implications of the title and the epigraph and serve as a prologue to the poem.

> My father's body was a globe of fear
> His body was a town we never knew
> He hid that he had been where we were going
> His letters were a room he seldom lived in
> In them the logic of his love could grow
>
> My father's body was a town of fear
> He was the only witness to its fear dance
> He hid where he had been that we might lose him
> His letters were a room his body scared

The several repetitions with the same syntax suggest the effort and resistance involved in the speaker's attempt to address the subject of his father's life and death. The second stanza's near recapitulation of the first suggests that he wants or needs to try again because the first stanza's metaphors and paradoxes don't quite express what he is trying to say. Similarly, the simple diction and style and the succession of short sentences hint at the difficulty and tension involved in dealing with a complex subject towards which the speaker's feelings may be not only ambivalent but conflicted. The figurative progression in the two stanzas from globe to town to room suggests a gradual shrinking of the father's world as he edges towards death. An affective and thematic countermovement is established, however, in the momentarily enigmatic references to his letters – the title has prepared us for their significance – and in the disturbing comment 'He hid that he had been where we were going.' The surrounding lines suggest that he has been in a place of suffering and pain and that his letters, with 'the logic of love,' attempt to shield his family from, in a manner of speaking, 'coming through slaughter.' The last line of the second verse also contains the ambiguous intimation – created by the ambiguous syntax and the lack of punctuation – that he tries to avoid the family in order to shield them from the 'town of fear' in which he has spent much of his adult life and which he himself created.

As I mentioned, the third stanza repeats and amplifies the prologue's concern with the father's death before giving way to the slightly more relaxed stanzas, marked by extensive enjambment, dealing with scenes from his life and his marriage. These anticipate similar, though less unsettling, scenes of eccentric family behaviour in 'Light.' And both poems look forward to Ondaatje's full treatment of the family in *Running in the Family*. Here the humour and 'comedy' are described as 'terrifying,' and are enacted in the shadow of the opening descriptions of the father's death – 'He came to death with his mind drowning.' The events, described almost without emotional inflection, are reports from the abyss, each suggesting others that we are left to imagine.

The last two stanzas return to the father's last years and death with words and images that call to mind Pat Garrett and Dashiell Hammett's alcoholism, the creative but deadly spiders of 'Spider Blues,' the silent imploded figures of 'White Dwarfs,' and Buddy Bolden; more troublingly, they also foreshadow the son's self-portrait in 'Claude Glass,' the first part of the autobiographical *Secular Love*. Here the father is shown as withdrawing to drink 'until he was drunk / and until he was sober.' And in the hard-earned sobriety, he produces 'speeches, head dreams, apologies, / the gentle letters.' The last are written

... in a clear hand of the most complete empathy .
his heart widening and widening and widening
to all manner of change in his children and friends
while he himself edged
into the terrible acute hatred
of his own privacy

The lines grow shorter as the father moves closer to death. Though the overall tone in the last two stanzas is melancholy and rueful, there is also a note of admiration for the desperate and frangible creativity of Mervyn Ondaatje's last phase. Like the work of the spiders in 'Spider Blues' and Bolden's cornet playing, the father's creativity is made possible by pain, guilt, and 'acute hatred.' His writing, like Bolden's music, 'was immediately on top of his own life' (*CTS*, 32). It's as if the clarity, delicacy, and empathy of his vision are only possible because of the suffering; there is even a note of melancholy and menace in the subjects he chooses to write about: 'blue flowers,' 'electricity,' and the sleeping snake disturbed by the speaker's half-sister. The first long sentence of the closing stanza celebrates the flood of grace that occurs during his moments of desperate lucidity; the second continues this motif, but then, as can be seen in the last line of the above quotation, it shifts attention back to the father's collapse and death. The lines become shorter, the clauses more terse, until the last line, whose expansive length and lack of closing punctuation mimic 'the blood searching in his head without metaphor.' I assume that 'his head' is 'without metaphor' because he is dying and, to use the imagery of 'White Dwarfs,' has gone into 'the white,' where he is beyond language. Though we won't know this until we read the collection's final poem, he is one of those 'people who disappear / ... who descend into the code' or 'who implode into silence / after parading in the sky' (71). It is arguable that the answer to that poem's poignant and ambivalent question – 'Why do I love most / among my heroes those / who sail to that perfect edge / where there is no social fuel' – is that the poet loves them because they are surrogates of his father and, as we shall see in 'Claude Glass' and 'Tin Roof,' himself. Had Ondaatje written 'Why do I *admire*' instead of 'Why do I love,' I would be less confident in making this suggestion.[5]

There is very little in Ondaatje's earlier lyrics to prepare one for the complexity, poise, and maturity of 'Letters & Other Worlds.' It is recognizably by the poet who wrote 'Dragon,' 'The Time Around Scars,' and 'Peter.' But in comparison with it, the earlier poems are clearly apprentice work in which the poet was perfecting his style, voice, and masks – his 'tricks with a knife' – in anticipation of a more challenging subject. From the perspective of the later work, it is obvious that this pivotal elegy is simultaneously about his father and about his own tragic view of creativity as often inseparable from suffering. As a poem about poetics, it looks back to poems as different as 'Peter' and 'Dates' while simultaneously anticipating the major lyrics of the final section, in which various aspects of the creative act are a central concern. Together with these, it also points forward to Ondaatje's most profound and extended treatment of his own creativity in *Coming through Slaughter*.

After the tense and tortured autobiographical intensities and the extraordinary sense of personality, even pathology, of 'Letters & Other Worlds,' the thirteen poems of 'Live Bait' seem, for the most part, anticlimactic. They are a disparate, often wryly humorous group in various voices. With the exception of 'Leo,' each one either focuses on an animal or refers to one. And as so often in Ondaatje's early work, the animals intimate or symbolize as 'live bait' the world of instinct, energy, and chaos on which poetry depends for its material and which it transforms, often with violence, into artefacts. I almost have the impression that before confronting the reader with the book's other major poems, Ondaatje felt he needed a section lighter in tone and less intensely focused on poetry. This is not to say that these concerns are completely absent from the second section, they aren't, but they appear in a different form.

The epigraph, as mentioned earlier, alerts readers obliquely to the truth status of the poems they are about to read. Where the first epigraph hinted that the poet's reticence might prevent the poems from offering a sufficiently sincere or honest account of reality, the epigraph from *Tay John* ends with the comment '"See!" she said, "he was a great liar, and the word has choked him!"' Almost as if to contradict the implications of this passage, the section's first poem is 'Rat Jelly' (31), in which, as in the misanthropic 'War Machine,' a sardonic and jaundiced speaker seems to tell us the worst about himself using an image already associated with Billy the Kid (Billy's head, for example, is 'smaller than a rat' [109]).

> See the rat in the jelly
> steaming dirty hair
> frozen, bring it out on a glass tray
> split the pie four ways and eat
> I took great care cooking this treat for you
> and tho it looks good to yuh
> and tho it smells of the Westinghouse still
> and tastes of exotic fish or
> maybe the expensive arse of a cow
> I want you to know it's rat
> steamy dirty hair and still alive
>
> (Caught him last Sunday
> thinking of the fridge, thinking of you.

Though the slightly cryptic references to the Westinghouse and the fridge seem to indicate that the speaker has a particular 'you' in mind, I have the impression that he is also addressing the reader. The fact that this is the title poem of the collection and that some of its concerns are more explicit in 'A bad taste' (42) leads me to assume that 'rat jelly' is a metaphor for poems and poetry. Like the pies in the stained glass window reproduced on the cover of the first edition, the poem ('rat jelly') 'looks good' and seems to taste of 'exotic fish' or 'the expensive arse of a cow,' but in origin and essence it remains 'rat / steamy dirty hair and still alive.' In Yeats's slightly, though only slightly, more decorous tropes, the poem begins in 'The fury and the mire of human veins' ('Byzantium') or 'the foul rag-and-bone-shop of the heart' ('The Circus Animals' Desertion'). Though I can't quite articulate what I think is being intimated by the references to the Westinghouse and the fridge, I have a hunch that it's connected to the fridge in 'White Dwarfs.' There it is mentioned twice, first in the opening lines: 'This is for people who disappear / for those who descend into the code / and make their room a fridge for Superman' (71); it then reappears in the final stanza: 'This white that can grow / is fridge, bed, / is an egg – most beautiful / when unbroken, where / what we cannot see is growing / in all the colours we cannot see.' Though the speaker admires the white and the silence, he simultaneously realizes that his fate *as a poet* lies with language and what Robert Penn Warren calls 'the world's tangled and hieroglyphic beauty' ('The Mission') or John Crowe Ransom 'the rich contingent materiality of things.'[6] The poem's existence confirms that as a poet he has no choice but to deal with what is in the fridge, inside its whiteness.

Like colour, energy, and speech, the 'rat' cannot be kept in the 'fridge,' nor can it be completely baked or cooked if the poem is to be alive. 'A bad taste' (42–3) seems to confirm this reading. It ends with an admiring description of one of the great modernists as a 'rat.'

> But it was the rat in Ezra who wrote best,
> that dirt thought we want as guest
> travelling mad within the poem
> eating up pronunciation, who farts
> heat into the line. You see
> them shaved in the anthology.
> You will be frozen and glib when
> they aim for the sponge under the rib.
>
> God being made fat
> by eating the rat in us.

In the penultimate couplet, it's not obvious to me who is being referred to by the 'you' and why he or she is 'glib' and has a 'sponge under the rib.' The sponge and the rib call to mind the crucifixion, an association that becomes less irrelevant than it first seems when the line is followed by the couplet 'God being made fat / by eating the rat in us.' Though the image is repulsive, it seems to say no more than that by dying on the cross, God redeems humanity by taking its sins upon himself. What that has to do with the poem's central theme is beyond me, unless there is also a suggestion that the poet is Christlike in writing about 'the rat in us' and thus anagrammatically turning rats and farts into art.

It's worth noting at this point that the crucifixion is alluded to twice more in the book, in 'White Dwarfs,' as was already mentioned, and in 'King Kong.' In the latter, Kong is described surrealistically as 'Last seen in Chicago with helicopters / cutting into his head like thorns' (44). The Christological hint is prepared for by an earlier suggestive reference to 'our lady in his fingers.' But if he is a Christ figure, he is a parodic and apocalyptic one who 'perishes magnanimous / tearing the world apart.' Instead of loving humanity, 'he must swallow what he loves / caressing with wounds / the ones who reach for him.' And though we know that he will die, still, as the poem's final couplet tells us, 'we renew him / capable in the zoo of night.' As in 'King Kong meets Wallace Stevens,' discussed below, Kong represents a problematically constitutive aspect of ourselves that links us through the unconscious or through our dreams with non-human life. Both poems also suggest, the second more explicitly than the first, that what Kong represents is an essential component of poetic creativity. Seen this way, he is indeed a savage redeemer if we believe that poetry has redemptive value. The poet – and this theme is made explicit in 'King Kong meets Wallace Stevens' – is the 'connoisseur of chaos' whose creativity is inseparable from his dark side. Ondaatje's artists, from Billy the Kid and Buddy Bolden to the poet-novelist in *Secular Love*, occasionally resemble Kong, who 'must swallow what he loves / caressing with wounds / the ones who reach for him.'

The fascination with wounds, scars, and violence – the three are cognate and related to creativity – is pervasive in this section, and I want to turn now to three very different poems, each of which deals with some aspect of them: 'Loop,' 'The Ceremony: A Dragon, a Hero, and a Lady, by Uccello,' and 'Philoctetes on the island.' At the centre of each is a wounded figure who is in some sense a social outcast. 'Loop' is one of those animal poems in which we understand Stevens's comment 'The bare image and the image as symbol are the contrast: the image without meaning and the image as meaning. When the image is used to suggest something else, it is secondary.'[7] In the pull between Loop as dog and Loop as symbol, we sense that the second is stronger. The issue will be clearer if we compare the poem to the earlier 'Flirt and Wallace' (36), Ondaatje's poem about the two hounds to whom he dedicated *Leonard Cohen*.

> The dog almost
> *tore* my son's left eye out
> *with love*, left a *welt* of passion
> across his cheek
>
> The other dog licks
> the armpits of my shirt
> for the salt
> the smell and taste
> that identifies me from others
>
> With teeth which carry broken birds
> with wet fur jaws that eat snow
> suck the juice from branches
> swallowing them all down
> leaving their mouths tasteless, extroverted,
> they *graze* our bodies with their love   (my emphases)

The focus here is on the dogs as animals, as something other than human, even though their names make an anthropomorphic gesture: one is named after a playful and self-conscious human attitude, the other after Wallace Stevens. The poem may begin and end 'with love,' but each stanza reminds us that this love is as unpredictable as it is unconditional. In the first stanza, the perfect placing of 'tore' and 'with love' startles us into this awareness, and the third ends with a deft verbal ambiguity: 'they graze our bodies with their love.' Throughout the poem we feel the claims of word and image on the poet's domestic reality.

'Loop' (46), however, offers a contrast between the speaker's dogs and

> ... the one
> who appears again on roads
> one eye torn out and chasing.

He is only a space filled
and blurred with passing,
transient as shit – will fade
to reappear somewhere else.

The metaphor and simile of the second stanza develop what has been suggested by 'roads' and 'chasing,' while simultaneously nudging the dog from realism to romance or what Ondaatje calls myth. He becomes less a particular dog than the embodiment and personification of a way of being in the world. The paratactic syntax and sentences give a compressed but comprehensive summary of his life. The effect is to leave the reader with the impression of a life force that transcends not only social categories – 'I leave behind all social animals' – but perhaps even language itself. While the poem says nothing about language or poetry, it is difficult not to read it with '"The gate in his head"' in mind. In the famous closing lines of that poem, the speaker suggests 'that is all this writing should be then. / The beautiful formed things caught at the wrong moment / so they are shapeless, awkward / moving to the clear' (62). The animal 'caught at the wrong moment' in that poem is a 'stunning white bird / an unclear stir.' The dog Loop seems to me an early trying out, without the metaphysical baggage and the burden of poetics, of that poem's final movement. Instead of developing the epistemological implications of Loop's existence, Ondaatje offers a self-sufficient portrait that culminates in a surreal resolution. While Loop tears into the garbage at a drive-in, the bird carrying the 'one eye torn out' 'lopes into the rectangle nest of images // and parts of him move on.' The poem ends with two suggestively ambiguous lines: 'the rectangle nest of images' is both the film on the screen into which the bird 'lopes' and that other 'rectangle nest of images,' the poem. And the plural 'parts' looks back to the eye in the bird's mouth and to the remaining 'parts' of the dog disappearing or dissolving in the metrically regular last line.

In 'Philoctetes on the island' (34–5) Ondaatje returns to the Greek archer who in 'The Goodnight' is shown shooting Paris after his rescue from the island. The poem's presence in this collection is surprising simply because of Ondaatje's lack of interest, after *The Dainty Monsters*, in the classical myths that were so important in his early work and in his thesis on Muir. That Philoctetes was on his mind during this period – the poem was published in 1969[8] – is also indicated by his comment, quoted earlier, that Cohen makes heroes out of certain characters, 'not because they, like Philoctetes, have brilliant bows, but because they have magnificent wounds' (43). The Greek archer of course has both. In the present poem Philoctetes describes his lonely existence on the island in a style compressed and figurative: 'Sun moves broken in the trees / drops like a paw / turns sea to red leopard' (34). The omission of articles, conjunctions, and punctuation continues through the poem. There is the possibility that the images here owe something to Ondaatje's interest in Henri Rousseau. In the 1908 painting *Exotic Landscape*, for instance, the orange-red sun is broken up by the dense green foliage through which we see it. And the 'paw' and the 'leopard' may recall several of the jungle paintings in which a lion or jaguar is shown attacking its prey (see *Surprise* [1891], *The Hungry Lion* [1905], *Combat of a Tiger and a Buffalo* [1908], *Forest Landscape with Setting Sun* [1910]).

The poem is filled with images of violence, including the emotional violence of what 'Letters & Other Worlds' calls 'the terrible acute hatred / of his own privacy.' In words and images that occasionally recall *The Collected Works of Billy the Kid* and anticipate 'White Dwarfs' and *Coming through Slaughter*, the archer articulates his divided impulses – to survive or to die? – and the longing for oblivion that simultaneously produces an acute awareness of self. Though reduced to an animal-like existence, he is nevertheless aware of his radical separation from the animals that he must kill in order to continue to survive.

> To slow an animal
> you break its foot with a stone
> so two run wounded
> reel in the bush, flap
> bodies at each other
> till free of forest
> it gallops broken in the sand,
> then use a bow
> and pin the tongue back down its throat.

The unexpected iambic beat of the last three lines lends a ritual quality to the closing, horrifically violent image that is unsettling. We have already seen it in 'Peter' ('After the first year they cut out his tongue'), and there is a variant of it in 'White Dwarfs' ('The Gurkhas in Malaya / cut the tongues of mules'). Though extreme, the image is emotionally right, reflecting as it does Philoctetes' rage at his abandonment and isolation. It is worth recalling that in Sophocles' play he pleads with Neoptolemus to talk to him:

Take pity on me; speak to me; speak,
speak if you come as friends.
                                No – answer me.
If this is all
that we can have from one another, speech,
this, at least, we should have.[9]

In the poem he aims his arrow at the tongue that is mute to human
ears. But it's also tempting to speculate that Ondaatje's fascination
with the image and with silence has its origins in his continuing fascination with the figure of the silent poet tempted or compelled to
renounce his art. It is also difficult once again not to sense behind the
figure of Philoctetes abandoned on an island the withheld presence of
the silent father, left behind in Ceylon and writing alone in a room.
Philoctetes' isolation is reiterated in the closing couplet, whose lack of
terminal punctuation reminds us that his solitude and pain will continue: 'then they smell me, / the beautiful animals[.]'

Perhaps the most surprising poem in *Rat Jelly* is 'The Ceremony: A
Dragon, a Hero, and a Lady, by Uccello' (39), a traditional three-stanza
iambic tetrameter lyric, with four lines in each stanza, the second and
fourth rhyming. Paolo Uccello painted two versions of *St. George and
the Dragon*, the first in 1439–40 (the Musée Jacquemart-André in Paris),
the second between 1455 and 1460 (the National Gallery, London).
Ondaatje describes the second.[10]

The clouds burn blue, hang like sweat.
The green fields bounce the horse's paws.
A boy-knight shafts the dragon's eye
– the animal with a spine of claws.

In the foreground linked to dragon
with a leash of golden chain
dressed in silk there leans a lady
calmly holding to his pain.

From the mood I think it's Sunday
the monster's eye and throat blood strangled.
The horse's legs are bent like lightning.
The boy is perfect in his angle.

On first reading, it is tempting to treat this simply as an ekphrastic poem which transposes a visual image into a verbal one. But Ondaatje isn't Ralph Gustafson, and this is the only poem of this kind in his early work. Interesting to note is the fact that several of the details in his account of the painting are not quite right. In Uccello the clouds do not 'burn blue,' the fields aren't quite 'green,' the dragon doesn't have 'a spine of claws,' the 'lady' holds what looks like a green rope not a 'golden chain,' and she stands straight without leaning. If these differencs suggest that Ondaatje isn't paying close attention to the tones, textures, details and composition of the painting, then it is worth pausing to speculate on what drew his attention to it. The earlier poem 'Dragon' provides the most obvious and relevant clue. If I'm right in reading it as a symbolic and displaced account of a confrontation between the poet and his father, it's possible that 'The Ceremony' recapitulates the same scene and complex set of feelings in a different form. Read symbolically or allegorically, Uccello's painting offered the young poet another version of the one story and one story only – the family romance – that mattered to him at the time and that, ironically, he couldn't deal with directly. It is also the one story that he will do variations of throughout his career. He could say with Yeats, 'I have spent my life saying the same things in many different ways.'[11]

Here the story becomes an Oedipal one of the 'boy-knight' rescuing the 'lady' by slaying the dragon-father. But in fact, as in Uccello's painting, the dragon doesn't seem to pose a threat either to the town or to the woman, who seems to be holding him with a slack leash. 'The boy' may be 'perfect in his angle,' but as much as in *Running in the Family*, he is excluded from the drama's central couple, who are paradoxically joined by the masculine figure's 'pain.' When St George 'shafts the dragon's eye,' the lady leans solicitously, 'calmly holding to his pain.' As several readers have remarked, 'the boy' seems similarly excluded even in *Running in the Family*. To recall Eliot's words, the poem's dramatic situation and imagery seem saturated with feelings perhaps 'too obscure' even 'for the author to know' what they are. Ondaatje's next stop in exploring this aspect of his autobiographical '*donnee*' will be 'White Dwarfs.' As Jorie Graham reminds us, 'contained damage makes for beauty' ('Mother of Vinegar').

The best poems of the third section of *Rat Jelly* – and they are among the finest in Ondaatje's body of work – are magnificent lyrical footnotes to many of the existential and poetic issues implicit in 'Letters &

Other Worlds': fathers and sons, wounds and creativity, chaos and form, and the temptation of silence in the face of suffering. Read as a group, the poems leave me with the impression of a complex emotional and aesthetic pattern painfully and slowly shaped out of difficult and disparate materials. Though quite different, they seem nevertheless to have a common source, to flow one into another and to overlap in imagery and theme. Particularly fascinating is the felt, often tacit interaction between autobiographical pressures and creative ones. These are most evident in the seven poems about creativity that, as a group, constitute an early poetics: 'We're at the graveyard,' 'Taking,' 'Burning Hills,' 'King Kong meets Wallace Stevens,' '"The gate in his head,"' 'Spider Blues,' and 'White Dwarfs.' These have roughly the same relationship to Ondaatje's body of work of his first decade as Stevens's 'Notes toward a Supreme Fiction' does to his oeuvre. They are a theoretical stock-taking that is a confluence of the various lessons he learned writing the thesis on Muir, *The Collected Works of Billy the Kid*, and his monograph on Cohen. But if they are a summary, they are simultaneously a preparation for the writing of *Coming through Slaughter*, in which, as I argue in 'Making and Destroying: *Coming through Slaughter* and Extremist Art,' Ondaatje pushes the theory to the limit.[12] In the novel he explores the same situations and issues in the story of an artist-hero whose cornet playing enacts the aesthetic assumptions of *Rat Jelly*.

Of the final section's thirteen poems, all but three touch on death (accident, murder, suicide). Even the gentle and finely nuanced first lyric, 'We're at the graveyard' (51), juxtaposes death to the pregnancy of Sally, one of Ondaatje's friends. Its form depends on an antithesis between the stars' clarity, order, imperceptible movement, and seeming permanence and earthly transience, disorder, and mortality.

Up there the clear charts,
the systems' intricate branches
which change with hours and solstices,
the bone geometry of moving from there, to there.

And down here – friends
whose minds and bodies
shift like acrobats to each other.
When we leave, they move
to an altitude of silence.

The complex dependance of our relationships is finely caught in the always ambiguous simile of the mutually dependent acrobats (it will return in *Running in the Family, Secular Love,* and *Handwriting*), which also carries the unavoidable suggestion of falling and danger. And the idea that we live out our lives in the shadow of death, that in a sense we are always 'at the graveyard,' is gently reiterated in the poem's two closing images:

> Sally is like grey snow in the grass.
> Sally of the beautiful bones
> pregnant below stars.

The quietly foregrounded 'g' in 'pregnant' reminds us of 'graveyard,' which is the eventual resting place of all bones. Unlike the 'bone geometry' of the white stars, ours is short-lived. A small compensation is offered, however, in the third stanza's paradoxical first sentence:

> So our minds shape
> and lock the transient,
> parallel these bats
> who organize the air
> with thick blinks of travel.

Our lives may be marked by the various griefs of living, but the mind – which 'can never be satisfied' – attempts to compensate by shaping or making something permanent of our transient existence. I assume that we 'parallel these bats' in being unable to see what is to come and not fully understanding our situation. Though the general sense of the last two lines is clear, I'm as pleasingly puzzled by 'thick blinks of travel' as I was in 1973 when I bought the volume, though I console myself by recalling Cleanth Brooks's comment that 'privacy and obscurity, to some degree, are inevitable in all poetry.'[13]

Though 'We're at the graveyard' is a fine achievement in itself, it is also an effective introduction to the section as a whole and an anticipation, though in an emotionally antithetical mode, to its closing poem, 'White Dwarfs.' The latter will develop in another direction its concern with 'sliding stars,' 'an altitude of silence,' and the implied image of Sally's white, convex stomach concealing and containing a colourful growth. More generally, the poem also introduces the question of the sources of poetry and of the poet's creative relationship with reality.

'Taking' (55), for instance, presents the poet as someone willing to appropriate whatever he thinks he can turn into a poem.

It is the formal need
to suck blossoms out of the flesh
in those we admire
planting them private in the brain
and cause fruit in lonely gardens.

The anonymous voice and the third-person copula, together with the closing image of 'fruit in lonely gardens,' lend these lines an unearned momentary general force. It takes a moment to realize that the speaker – his pronominal mask slips in the second stanza – is describing the relationship between a parasite and its admired host. The relationship may produce something as positive as a blossom or a poem, but it is nevertheless based on exploitation. The second stanza offers a comic variant on this idea before undermining the tone and complicating the theme.

I have stroked the mood and tone
of hundred year dead men and women
Emily Dickinson's large dog, Conrad's beard
and, for myself,
removed them from historical traffic.
Having tasted their brain. Or heard
the wet sound of a death cough.

In other words, everything from a 'large dog' such as Emily Dickinson's Carlo to 'the wet sound of a death cough' is of potential use to the artist, whose justification for his attitude is that he can transform – 'the formal need' – transient, labile, and perishable life into the 'immaculate moment' of the work of art. The various organic images scavenged by the jackal poet are 'rumours' that 'pass on / are planted / till they become a spine.' Like the gossip and the stories in 'War Machine,' they are turned into a poem. Ondaatje's tone may be more bizarre and light-hearted than Horace's, but this is a playful version of the Latin poet's 'Exegi monumentum' (*Odes* III. 30). It is worth noting in passing that the opening lines of the second stanza ('To learn to pour the exact arc / of steel'), slightly out of place in 'Taking,' not only look back to 'I have seen pictures of great stars' (*CWBK*, 41) but reappear as the thematically clinching image in '"The gate in his head."'[14] Also worth noting is the presence of Joseph Conrad, another exile and stranger in a strange land who turned exile into a strength. He will appear twice more in Ondaatje's work.

The troubling question of the poet's relationship to his material is brought closer to home in the next poem, 'Burning Hills' (56–8). The narrative situation here is sketched in the first few lines.

> So he came to write again
> in the burnt hill region
> north of Kingston. A cabin
> with mildew spreading down walls.
> Bullfrogs on either side of him.

> Hanging his lantern of Shell Vapona Strip
> on a hook in the centre of the room
> he waited a long time. Opened
> the Hilroy writing pad, yellow Bic pen.
> Every summer he believed would be his last.

The burnt hills, the mildew, and the Vapona Strip suggest death and decay, while the last line transfers this suggestion to his anxieties about his creativity (as well as, perhaps, his own life). The bullfrogs, as in Lampman (to make the rare CanLit connection), remind us of a simpler, less ambivalent or conflicted music. Like several other poems, this one frames images from the past with opening and closing sections set in the poem's present. It is about its own writing and the poet's realization of the price he pays for being a writer. The three works mentioned implicitly comment on this theme: 'A copy of *StrangeLove*, / of *The Intervals*, a postcard of Rousseau's *The Dream*.' The first prepares us for the poet's 'strange love' for those he simultaneously loves and uses in his work; Ondaatje's comment that Cohen's Breavman treats his friends like 'raw material' and 'uses and translates them constantly into art' (*LC*, 28) also applies here to himself. The second reinforces this motif by describing Stuart Mackinnon's long poem, and by implication Ondaatje's, with violent images in which the poem is 'strict as lightning / unclothing the bark of a tree, a shaved hook.' As I have implied, Ondaatje's poem is about the intervals of time that separate us from our younger selves. The third work of art, Rousseau's *The Dream*, reminds us that the artist's imagined reality will often be different from ours: 'The postcard was a test pattern by the window / through which he saw growing scenery.'

Among the memories that constitute the poem's long central section, the most telling is a remembered photograph:

> There is one picture that fuses the 5 summers.
> Eight of them are leaning against a wall
> arms around each other
> looking into the camera and the sun
> trying to smile at the unseen adult photographer
> trying against the glare to look 21 and confident.
> The summer and friendship will last forever.
> Except one who was eating an apple. That was him
> oblivious to the significance of the moment.
> Now he hungers to have that arm around the next shoulder.
> The wretched apple is fresh and white.

The 'wretched apple,' like most apples in the Western canon, needs no commentary. In the context of the poem as a whole, it is one of several intimations of separation and alienation, such as the third-person narrative voice and the past tense.

The poem might have ended here, but Ondaatje shifts it back to the present and changes the original reference of the title from the 'burnt hill region / north of Kingston' to the act of writing as a scorched earth policy – 'Since he began burning hills.' The suggestion that writing and destruction are in some deep sense co-extensive is immediately reinforced with the mention that 'the Shell strip has taken effect. / A wasp is crawling on the floor / tumbling over, its motor fanatic.' And the slowly paced closing four lines look back to 'StrangeLove,' 'The Intervals,' and 'The Dream.'

> He has written slowly and carefully
> with great love and great coldness.
> When he finishes he will go back
> hunting for the lies that are obvious.

To love with 'great love and great coldness' is to offer the 'strange love' of the artist, who is never completely involved with life because as an artist he inevitably also stands apart and observes. Equally interesting is the teasing closing confession that the revised poem will have only lies that are *not* obvious. Ondaatje has said in an interview, 'There's a great deal of lying in poetry, by necessity. It's not a case of being tactful or misrepresenting something but of making art; art is, to a certain extent, deceit ... I suppose in writing you have to get all the truth down – the qualifications, the lies, the uncertainties.'[15] He is indicating that, despite his attempts at objectivity, his poem may be a creative misrepresentation or lie.[16] And if the lies to be sought out are the 'obvious' ones, there is the disturbing implication that the not-obvious ones remain and are an essential aspect of the art. In either case, the reader has been warned about the poem and the poet's attitude towards getting 'all the truth down.' Like 'The Dream,' whatever its debt to the real, the poem will enact its own version of reality. For Ondaatje, as for Sri Lankans, at least according to his endnote to *Running in the Family,* 'a well-told lie is worth a thousand facts' (176).

The poet's relationship to his subject matter is dramatized again in 'Spider Blues' (63–5), where in the central symbolic fable, the poet is seen as an admirable, because ruthlessly dextrous, spider. Though Ondaatje may know Emily Dickinson's 'The Spider as an Artist,' his is simultaneously more anthropomorphic, comic, calculating, and sinister.[17]

> I admire the spider, his control classic,
> his eight legs finicky,
> making lines out of the juice in his abdomen.
> A kind of writer I suppose.
> He thinks a path and travels
> the emptiness that was there
> leaves his bridge behind
> looking back saying Jeez
> did I do that?
> and uses his ending
> to swivel to new regions
> where the raw of feelings exist.

The spider as creative artist is a cartographer of the unknown, and as the image in the last line reveals – a favourite of Ondaatje's – he brings back a message about some essential or primal reality. But, like the speaker in 'Four Eyes' and in 'Burning Hills,' he can only do so by separating himself from that reality. The spider may be more talented than the fly; yet in terms of the poem's allegory, the fly, because it is closer to life, is the necessary subject matter of art:

And spider comes to fly, says
Love me I can kill you, love me
my intelligence has run rings about you
love me, I kill you for that clarity that
comes when roads I make are being made
love me, antisocial, lovely

.....
And the spider in his loathing
crucifies his victims in his spit
making them the art he cannot be.

Mind distinguishes Wallace Stevens from King Kong, and 'intelligence' the spider from the fly; but the cost of the distinction is registered by the title of the poem, 'Spider Blues': it is sung by Ray Charles, not Céline Dion. The poem is also a blues song because, in the relationship between the spider and the fly, the former creates beauty by 'crucifying' the latter. Though the poem doesn't indicate what other kinds of creativity are possible, the suggestion is nevertheless felt that this is not an ideal relationship between art and life.

But the fable of the self-loathing spider and the crucified fly is also about the spiders and the poet's wife, as we learn from the surreal opening stanza and as we are reminded by the equally oneiric last one. In the first the spiders' attraction to the wife is described by the poet, who also admits to having his 'own devious nightmares' in which, I assume, he identifies with the spiders. In the closing movement, however, he refers to a

Nightmare for my wife and me:

It was a large white room
and the spiders had thrown
their scaffolds off the floor
onto four walls and the ceiling.
.....
they carried her up – her whole body
into the dreaming air so gently
she did not wake or scream.
What a scene. So many trails
the room was a shattered pane of glass.
Everybody clapped, all the flies.

They came and gasped, all
everybody cried at the beauty
ALL
except the working black architects
and the lady locked in their dream   their theme

The metaphor and the homophonic pun (pane/pain) of the 'shattered pane of glass' look back to the cobwebs earlier in the poem and forward to one of the most memorable images in *Coming through Slaughter*, a novel whose hero-spider is unable to escape his friend, the policeman named Webb.[18] Ironically, the creative act gives no pleasure to either of its participants. Only the attendant flies, themselves potential victims, applaud.

It is clear why this is a 'nightmare' for the poet's wife. But to understand why it is also one for him, we need to recall that spiders and poets were compared in the brief third stanza:

Spiders like poets are obsessed with power.
They write their murderous art which sleeps
like stars in the corner of rooms,
a mouth to catch audiences
weak   broken   sick

While there is a slight syntactical ambiguity in the last line (is it the audience or the spider/poet who is 'weak broken sick' or is it both?), the context implies that the adjectives refer to the artist. The poem suggests that whatever we may think of the work of art, its origins, as well as the satisfactions it provides for the artist and the audience, are as troubling and suspect as they are in Plath's 'Lady Lazarus.' Ondaatje's poet isn't quite Stevens's 'The Weeping Burgher,' but he would have to agree with the latter that 'It is with a strange malice / That I distort the world.'[19]

In 'King Kong meets Wallace Stevens' (61) Ondaatje presents this troubling situation in the form of a psychodrama. Both Kong and Stevens have made previous appearances in the poetry: the former in 'King Kong,' where he is evoked as an aspect of ourselves, a Dionysian force that 'we renew ... / capable in the zoo of night'; the latter in 'Dates,' where together with Auden and Yeats, he functions as a tutelary figure – one of three wise men – attending the birth of the poet.[20] The two figures of the title seem to represent two aspects or faculties of the speaker. The poem, the situation suggests, is the product of their tense interaction.

Take two photographs –
Wallace Stevens and King Kong
(Is it significant that I eat bananas as I write this?)

Stevens is portly, benign, a white brush cut
striped tie. Businessman but
for the dark thick hands, the naked brain
the thought in him.

Kong is staggering
lost in New York streets again
a spawn of annoyed cars at his toes.

The mind is nowhere.
Fingers are plastic, electric under the skin.
He's at the call of Metro-Goldwyn-Mayer.

Meanwhile W.S. in his suit
is thinking chaos is thinking fences.
In his head the seeds of fresh pain
his exorcising,
the bellow of locked blood.

The hands drain from his jacket,
pose in the murderer's shadow.[21]

The poem is ostensibly structured upon a series of now familiar antitheses; the primary contrast is between Stevens, the businessman whose 'thought is in him,' and Kong, whose 'mind is nowhere.' But as so often in Ondaatje's poetry, the opposed terms are ultimately related. Kong, after all, is more than just a suggestive photographer's image of directable energy; he is also, as the poem's structure and imagery suggest, both something created by MGM and an aspect of Stevens himself, and the meeting between them occurs not only in the juxtaposing of their photographs but also within Stevens's mind. This association is established by the presentation of analogous situations in the third and fourth stanzas: MGM directs Kong; Stevens fences the chaos and blood within himself. No comma or conjunction appears between the two clauses of 'is thinking chaos is thinking fences' because the poem is suggesting the problematic simultaneity of both the 'chaos' and the 'fences' in Stevens's 'thinking.' If, as I have suggested, Kong and chaos/blood are nearly synonymous – though here Kong is less a figure of the id than in 'King Kong' (44) – then the entire fourth stanza points to Kong's simultaneous presence within Stevens himself: both the containing form and the contained energy are within the mind of the businessman-poet, who, to quote Ondaatje on Cohen, 'sees beauty (gardens, potency and art) grow out of death and violence' (*LC*, 9). This connection between the two is also present in the image of Stevens's 'dark thick hands,' which at the poem's end 'drain from his jacket, / pose in the murderer's shadow.' The poem closes on the alarming association between Stevens and 'the murderer's shadow,' which can only be his own. He is a murderer because he has subdued his chaos or blood, his unconscious self. He hears 'the bellow of locked blood' because he exorcised in a 'locked' poem 'the seeds of fresh pain.'

But the poem also suggests playfully that Stevens is not the only poet with a shadow self. After all, the writer-speaker asks humorously in the opening stanza, 'Is it significant that I eat bananas as I write this?' In view of the almost symbiotic relationship between Stevens and Kong, there can be only one answer. Despite the parenthetical nature of the question, the 'bananas' allude comically to the speaker's Kong-like aspect. Thus the poem indicates that the speaker is in creative contact with everything that the ostensibly antithetical Kong represents; like Stevens, he is able to transform, control, and shape this 'chaos' within the self into an aesthetic construct, into 'King Kong meets Wallace Stevens.' There is also a lingering suggestion, however, that some of the 'chaos' will resist and even escape the poet's act of transformation. Both 'the *bellow* of locked blood' and 'hands *drain* from his jacket' (my italics) raise this possibility. Ondaatje and Stevens are also linked by the younger poet's use of the older's imagery. The 'dark thick hands' hinting at violence may owe something to 'My hands such sharp imagined things' ('The Weeping Burgher'), though there is also the possibility that Ondaatje is recalling Atwood's 'The Green Man' ('They did not look / in his green pockets, where he kept / his hands changing their shape') from *The Animals in That Country*, a book he reviewed. Similarly, the telltale 'bananas' may owe as much to Stevens's 'Floral Decorations for Bananas' as to King Kong's diet.[22] A final point: if King Kong belongs to the same family of images as the dragons in 'Dragon' and 'The Ceremony,' then it is possible that, like them, he is associated with the father, and the poems about him are in some deep sense also about the poet's attempt to come to terms with and perhaps control his intractable past. Poetry, after all, is one of the ways in which humanity tries to control and understand the world, including the world of the self. On one level, then, the tension between Kong and Stevens, chaos and order, enacts Ondaatje's own sense of the tenuous stability of his life.

'"The gate in his head"' (62) suggests what might be the ideal relationship between poetry's nets and life's chaos. I want to approach its engagement with the question of how poetry should represent what the poem calls life's 'sense of shift' by way of Helen Vendler's comment on an aspect of Jorie Graham's poetry: 'To allow the primacy of the material over the spiritual, to admit into art the unexpected detour, the chance event, whimsy even, is to be forced to abandon the neat stanzas of a 'classical' poem ... It is to allow an equal role to the sensual, to make form mirror the unstoppable avalanche of sensations and the equal avalanche of units of verbal consciousness responding to those sensations.'[23] The dilemma Ondaatje faces in such a situation is that in transfiguring 'chaos' or 'the unstoppable avalanche of sensations' into aesthetic form, he might misrepresent both it and his response to it. In this respect, *The Collected Works of Billy the Kid*, *Running in the Family*, and *Secular Love* may be closer to the poetic ideal of *Rat Jelly* than its poems on poetry. As we have seen, the key term or image for Ondaatje, whether his concern is with the self or with external reality, is chaos, a concept also important to Muir and Stevens. Though there are anticipations of this issue in other poems, '"The gate in his head"' is his most explicit articulation of how he thinks a poem should mirror or enact or express reality:

My mind is pouring chaos
in nets onto the page.
A blind lover, dont know
what I love till I write it out.
And then from Gibson's your letter
with a blurred photograph of a gull.
Caught vision. The stunning white bird
an unclear stir.

And that is all this writing should be then.
The beautiful formed things caught at the wrong moment

so they are shapeless, awkward
moving to the clear.

The ideal here is the romantic poem that is less an artefact than a process of discovery. As I wrote, there is an anticipation of this in 'Taking,'
where the ideal is 'To learn to pour the exact arc / of steel still soft and
crazy / before it hits the page' (55). In '"The gate in his head"' 'chaos'
is synonymous with whatever reality the poet has chosen to describe.
It is the basic life stuff or substance – human and non-human – out of
which he shapes a poem. The poem's central tension is between this
'chaos' and the 'mental nets' of imagination, language, and poetic
form. The 'nets,' as well as the 'gate' in the title, recall the 'fences' in
'King Kong meets Wallace Stevens' and the 'webs' in 'Spider Blues'
and *The Collected Works of Billy the Kid*; they are the medium – film or
words – in which the vision is enacted or caught. Although 'caught' is
Ondaatje's word, it does not really do justice either to his essentially
heuristic assumptions about poetic creativity – 'A blind lover, dont
know / what I love till I write it out' – or his concern with registering
as sensitively as possible the kinetic quality of a personality, object, or
event. His concern is that the poem describe or enact 'the unclear stir'
made by 'a beautiful formed thing' perceived 'at the wrong moment.'
This last detail is particularly important if the poetic perception is also
to yield a new, unexpected awareness of reality. Yet as I pointed out
earlier, the poem must deal with motion, flux, and formlessness within
the confines of poetic form. Ondaatje's poem achieves this goal by
hinting at forms – the page, the photograph – and then subtly recreat-
ing through oxymoron and an interweaving of sounds – n's and r's –
the 'caught' reality. The ideal sought is 'not clarity but the sense of
shift.' One of the dangers, of course, is that any attempt to represent
chaos in aesthetic form might in the end create an unintended impression of order and meaning. Despite his several years as an editor at
Coach House Press and his association with postmodernist poets such
as Frank Davey and Christopher Dewdney, and despite his admiration
for Williams, Ondaatje is rarely tempted by the open field or form
poetics of Pound, Williams, or the Black Mountain school. Most of his
lyrics resemble '"The gate in his head"' in displaying several of the
qualities of the modernist lyric: form, concentration, unity, ambiguity,
and an argument or what Kenneth Burke calls 'progressive form' or
'syllogistic progression.'[24] It's only in his longer works that Ondaatje
realizes the full implications of the poetics in *Rat Jelly*.

Ironically, '"The gate in his head"' is an *hommage* to Victor Coleman, whose poems are in many respects closer to what 'all this writing should be' than Ondaatje's lyric. The photograph that is the metaphor for Ondaatje's ideal poem is by Coleman, a difficult, experimental poet whose work reveals '... the faint scars / coloured strata of the brain, / not clarity but the sense of shift. The 'faint scars' are metaphors for Coleman's poems (*One-Eye Love, Stranger*), which, in a mode much more radical than Ondaatje's, attempt to give the reader a sense of life as pure process, 'shift,' or 'chaos.' But the 'scars' are also literally scars. Here, as elsewhere in Ondaatje's work, a physical scar represents caught motion, just as a mental or emotional scar is caught memory. In other words, the scar literally incorporates and records an emotion, an act, or an experience. In terms of the imagery of 'The Time Around Scars,' a scar is a 'medallion' or 'watch' that records a violent and revealing event. One could even say that a scar is finally analogous to an ideal, because non-verbal, poem in which the distinction between word and thing or event has disappeared, and all that is left is a symbolic trace.

Ondaatje's most radical and troubled gesture in the direction of suggesting that there are times when 'all the truth' cannot and sometimes *should not* be stated is the collection's ambitious and powerfully ambivalent final poem, 'White Dwarfs.' The last of the poems about poetry, it builds on the others' images, insights, and questions but re-examines these through lenses coloured by 'Letters & Other Worlds.' As a result, it interweaves two concerns: poetry's struggle to deal with certain kinds of experience and the poet's paradoxical attraction to silence.

In 'White Dwarfs' (70–1) the poet confronts not just the unconscious or chaos but events that in their full human – that is, moral – significance seem to demand a response of awed silence. It's as if the poet simply throws his pen down in despair when he realizes that he may not want or perhaps will not be able to deal with certain aspects of life. There is also a hint that to attempt to describe these might entail betrayal. To recall Adorno, if the work gives aesthetic pleasure when dealing with suffering, it may do so at the expense of the sufferers. Ondaatje focuses on individuals, animal and human, who are the 'white dwarfs' of the title, stars of small volume but high density that have imploded into darkness and silence. The poem is a tribute to those who, for whatever reason, have gone beyond 'social fuel' and language to achieve what might be called a negative sublime or transcendence downwards that Ondaatje evokes by means of the interplay of images traditionally associated with the sublime – silence, height, depth, and whiteness.

> This is for people who disappear
> for those who descend into the code
> and make their room a fridge for Superman
> – who exhaust costume and bones that could perform flight,
> who shave their moral so raw
> they can tear themselves through the eye of a needle
> this is for those people
> that hover and hover
> and die in the ether peripheries

The key word here is 'moral,' which, although slightly ambiguous, seems to be synonymous with one's essential humanity or way of being in the world. Those who 'shave their moral ... raw' live in a condition in which their self exists without a social persona, 'where there is no social fuel'; consequently, they come in touch with the very ground of their being, subtly associated here with heaven or an ultimate state of being ('through the eye of a needle').[25] Like Ondaatje's outlaws (Billy), alienated loners (Pat Garrett and Charlie Wilson), and sufferers (Philoctetes, his father), they are the ones who can provide a disturbing but necessary glimpse of what the elegy for his father calls the 'other worlds' lying beyond or beneath consciousness or social forms. The problem for the poet is that what they come to represent is so radically other that it negates the way of life which makes his poetry possible. Furthermore, their ascesis (or even human kenosis) is an end in itself and not, as in Rilke, a preparation for a more comprehensive and enriching vision. In 'White Dwarfs' the speaker 'loves,' without explaining why, those whose achievement or experience is beyond him as man and poet.

> Why do I love most
> among my heroes those
> who sail to that perfect edge
> where there is no social fuel
> Release of sandbags[26]
> to understand their altitude –
>
> > that silence of the third cross
> > 3rd man hung so high and lonely
> > we dont hear him say

> say his pain, say his unbrotherhood
> What has he to do with the smell of ladies
> can they eat off his skeleton of pain?

Himself afraid of 'no words   of / falling without words,' he loves (as I wrote earlier, not 'admires') those whose language is an expressive and deafening silence; for them, their experience and their expression of it are one. Silence is here, as later in *Coming through Slaughter*, where Buddy Bolden is described as 'crucified and drunk' (*CTS*, 76), a final poetry of authentic being that cannot be improved by the poet's facility with words.[27] It is the white of the page, which, like the white eggshell, makes writing and sound possible; it is a writing degree zero – to adapt Barthes's phrase – which is the ground and perhaps ultimate cause of other less authentic forms of representation and expression. The white also hints at what is beyond language and form, at what poetry and the imagination cannot encompass. Frank Lewis's comment on Buddy Bolden's music is relevant here: 'We thought he was formless, but I think now he was tormented by order, what was outside it' (*CTS*, 33). Don McKay puts it slightly differently when discussing the cognitive status of poetry, but he could be speaking of 'White Dwarfs': 'Poets are supremely interested in what language can't do; in order to gesture outside, they use language in a way that flirts with its destruction.'[28] In other words, the poem's emotional indecision has its source not only in its autobiographical subtext but in the heart of poetry itself.

Incidentally, the image of the implicitly crucified figure probably owes less to the New Testament than to Kafka's 'In the Penal Colony' and 'The Hunger Artist,' stories that Ondaatje doubtless read in Edwin and Willa Muir's translation when working on his thesis. Each presents an execution that resembles a Crucifixion without a cross, though other images suggest that Kafka has the Crucifixion in mind. In the first, the self literally becomes the site of writing on the death machine. At one point, the officer supervising the execution says to the condemned man, '"Here are your handkerchiefs," ... and threw them to [him]. And to the explorer he said in explanation: "a gift from the ladies."'[29] The second describes the forty-day fast of a 'hunger artist.' It ends as follows.

Experience had proved that for about forty days the interest of the public could be stimulated by a steadily increasing pressure of advertisement, but after that the town began to lose interest, ... So on the fortieth day the flower-bedecked cage was opened, enthusiastic spectators filled the hall, a military band played, two doctors entered the cage to measure the results of the fast, which were announced through a megaphone, and finally two young ladies appeared, blissful at having been selected for the honour, to help the hunger artist down the few steps leading to a small table on which was spread a carefully chosen invalid repast. And at this very moment the artist always turned stubborn ... And he looked up into the eyes of the ladies who were apparently so friendly and in reality so cruel, and shook his head, which felt too heavy on its strengthless neck.[30]

In both stories the 'artist' is silent and is himself his greatest creation. Both Kafka and Ondaatje hint at a supreme fiction in which the dualities of language and reality, nets and chaos, Stevens and Kong, Michael and Mervyn, and art and life have finally been dissolved, but only at a price that the writer as writer cannot afford to pay. Even as Ondaatje suggests that poetry in such a situation might be superfluous and perhaps blasphemous – whatever that word means in his secular world – he is nevertheless writing a poem. Like other poets who interrogate the validity of language – Paul Celan, Tadeusz Różewicz, and Ingeborg Bachmann, for instance – Ondaatje uses language. This dialectic of language and silence leads finally, not to despair about poetry, but to an affirmation that in the poem's terms is simultaneously a betrayal of the very things admired and an affirmation of human aspiration. The fundamental and unresolvable contradiction at the heart of the poem's theme is enacted on the level of the imagery by the tension between the images that evoke height and those that point to a transcendence downwards into the self or Being. I almost expect to find Cummings's phrase 'depths of height' ('my father moved through dooms of love') somewhere in the poem. In the end, the confrontation with a reality that at first seemed resistant to the 'nets' of verbal representation doesn't silence the poet; rather, it provokes him into an even more ambitious poetry, an ode in a high style, in which language gives voice to its antithetical and negating other.

The poem's final movement attempts to evoke silence and the unknown.

The Gurkhas in Malaya
cut the tongues of mules
as they were silent beasts of burden

in enemy territories
after such cruelty what could they speak of anyway
And Dashiell Hammett in success
suffered conversation and moved
to the perfect white between words

This white that can grow
is fridge, bed,
is an egg – most beautiful
when unbroken, where
what we cannot see is growing
in all the colours we cannot see

there are those burned out stars
who implode into silence
after parading in the sky
after such choreography what would they wish to speak of   anyway

The poem ends by pointing hauntingly to a beauty ('an egg') and a human profundity (the personified 'star') beyond more explicit description and discussion. The tentative metaphoric gestures are all that can be expected of poetry in such a situation. The mules' cut tongues figure a paradoxical silence that screams for voice and justice and finds them in a poem about the temptations of silence. After certain kinds of horror, silence may be the only possible poetry; to paraphrase Adorno, 'No poetry after ...' – fill in your own favoured place (Rwanda) or experience (torture) or person (Hitler). Ondaatje's willingness to risk these inevitably anticlimactic lines ('after such choreography') to try to evoke the 'the perfect white between the words' and 'the colours we cannot see' is a paradoxical attestation of his belief in poetry. It seems appropriate that the image of the egg, while contributing to the section's unity, is borrowed from Stevens's 'Things of August':

We make, although inside an egg,
Variations on the words spread sail.

The morning-glories grow in the egg.
It is full of the myrrh and camphor of summer

And Adirondack glittering. The cat hawks it
And the hawk cats it and we say spread sail,

Spread sail, we say spread white, spread way.
The shell is a shore. The egg of the sea

And the egg of the sky are in shells, in walls, in skins
And the egg of the earth lies deep within an egg.[31]

Stevens's 'The Poems of Our Climate,' another poem about the insufficiency of white and harmony, may also have been in Ondaatje's mind here since he commented on it and quoted from it in the Muir thesis (118).

But more important than the possible sources of some of Ondaatje's images is the fact that the poem doesn't answer the one question it poses explicitly: 'Why do I love most / among my heroes those / who sail to that perfect edge / where there is no social fuel.' The poem doesn't answer this question, but as I suggested earlier, it offers clues in the verb 'love' and in the fact that Dashiell Hammett was an alcoholic. I doubt that Ondaatje loves Hammett, but on the evidence of the poems and of *Running in the Family*, there's little doubt about his feelings towards the man for whom Hammett is a screen and whose elegy is a distant prologue to the book's closing poem.

Three decades after publication, *Rat Jelly* can be seen as both a summing-up and a re-examination of some of the constitutive personal and aesthetic issues raised implicitly in *The Dainty Monsters* and *The Collected Works of Billy the Kid*, while simultaneously preparing the ground for *Coming through Slaughter* and *Running in the Family*. In the novel Ondaatje imagines the worst-case scenario for the kind of lacerating self-expressive creativity – 'his music was immediately on top of his own life' (*CTS*, 37) – that punctuates his early work and that will reappear in the confessional *Secular Love*. In both, as in some of the poems in *Rat Jelly*, he will write as if responding to Rilke's comment:

Art is always the outcome of one's having been in danger, of having gone right to the end of an experience to where no human being can go further. And the further one goes the more peculiarly personal and unique does an experience become, and the art-object is but the necessary, irrepressible and most conclusive utterance of this uniqueness. Therein consists the immense succour which the art-object gives to the life of him who must create it: it is his integrity, his integration; the knot in the rosary by which his life murmurs a prayer; the ever-recurrent proof of his singleness and veracity, revealed only to him, applicable only to him, affecting the outside world anonymously, indefinably, as necessity only, as reality, as existence.[32]

The new poems in Ondaatje's next book, *There's a Trick with a Knife I'm Learning to Do: Poems 1963–1978*, will show him attempting to shift away from what, after Rilke, might be called an aesthetics of danger.

EPIGRAPHS

With the exception of *the man with seven toes,* all Ondaatje's books of poetry have epigraphs introducing the volume, the individual sections, or the poems. And while he rarely revises his lyrics – 'Billboards' and 'Spider Blues' are important exceptions – he has changed book and section epigraphs when reprinting selections from *The Dainty Monsters* and *Rat Jelly* in *There's a Trick with a Knife I'm Learning to Do* and *The Cinnamon Peeler.* Because epigraphs are so common in Ondaatje – even his master's thesis has two – we tend to forget while reading him that, once we get past Eliot and Pound, modern and contemporary poets who use them regularly tend to be the exception. A quick and random sampling of my bookshelves produced the following figures. There are no epigraphs in the collected Frost, Muir, and Olson, four in Stevens, and none in Auden before 1940. Among the Canadian modernists, Layton's *Collected* has none, and Purdy's has four, while Avison has none before 1989. Among Ondaatje's contemporaries and near contemporaries the numbers are similar: none in Ashberry's *Selected Poems* and two in Creeley's; none in Hughes's *The Hawk in Rain*; two in Plath's *Collected*; none in Newlove's *Black Night Window* and *Lies*; none in Bowering's *Touch: Selected Poems 1960–1970*; three in Lee's *Civil Elegies, The Gods,* and *Night*; two in MacEwen's *Collected*; none in Atwood's *The Circle Game* and *The Animals in That Country.* By contrast, in *The Dainty Monsters* two sections and three poems have epigraphs, while three other poems have epigraph-like titles based on quotations; in *Rat Jelly* each of the three sections has an epigraph, as do three of the poems; *There's a Trick with a Knife I'm Learning to Do* has three section and three poem epigraphs; *Elimination Dance* has two; *Secular Love,* in the first edition, has one introducing the collection, five preceding the four sections, and three in the poems; and *Handwriting* has a dedicatory epigraph.

Epigraphs generally mediate, almost like brief prefaces or fore-words, between the title of a poem or novel and the body of the text. In the majority of cases they introduce the text metaphorically, metonym-ically, or by way of analogy by hinting, however obliquely, at what the text is about. We expect a poem to exemplify an epigraph. More rarely, as Gérard Genette points out, the epigraph elucidates and clarifies 'not the text but the title,' as is the case in Proust's *Sodome et Gomorrhe* or Ondaatje's *In the Skin of a Lion*. In the case of the latter, the epigraph from *The Epic of Gilgamesh* simultaneously indicates the provenance of the title while preparing the reader for one of the novel's key scenes. Without the epigraph, I suspect that most readers would have remained at least partly mystified about the title's meaning and per-haps even its connection to the novel. Some, more accustomed to bibli-cal allusions, might even have thought that Ondaatje was looking over his shoulder at I Peter 5: 'Be sober, be vigilant; because your adversary the devil, as a roaring lion, walketh about, seeking whom he may devour.'

Referring to novels, Genette describes 'an epigraph [as] always a mute gesture whose interpretation is left up to the reader.'[1] I suspect, however, that epigraphs to poems have more force and demand more interpretation than those that occur as chapter headings in Stendhal or George Eliot. The latter are not quite disposable, but I doubt that even critical readers and specialists remember more than one or two from a favourite novel. I also doubt whether more than a handful of readers return to take a second look at an epigraph after having finished a chapter in a novel. By contrast, to read a poem attentively means treat-ing the epigraph as an integral part of the composition, wondering at every point whether it is important by itself or whether it brings its source with it in the way that many allusions do. The former is almost always the case in Ondaatje, whose epigraphs are self-sufficient rather than fragments of an implied whole. 'The Diverse Causes,' for instance, has the following untagged epigraph from Malory's 'The Knight of the Cart': 'for than all erbys and treys renewyth a man and woman, and in lyke wyse lovers callyth to their mynde olde jantylnes and olde servyse, and many kynde dedes that was forgotyn by necly-gence' (*DM*, 22).[2] The quotation establishes a mood and an implicit comparison between two situations involving lovers in spring, those in the epigraph and those in the following lines. The epigraph's original

Arthurian context is irrelevant, and that's why Ondaatje doesn't include the author's name. That the connection between an epigraph and a book's section is less organic than with a poem can be guessed from the fact that while Ondaatje has never dropped or revised the epigraph to a poem, he has done so several times with sections. In the revised version of *Secular Love* that appears in *The Cinnamon Peeler*, for instance, he replaced the first of the two following quotations with the second in introducing 'Skin Boat,' the fourth section:

> On one occasion on the Alaska Peninsula, I heard thin squeaky voices in the tall grass. I watched quietly and had glimpses of tiny forms flashing by the little openings in the dense cover. I could only guess what might be the intimate affairs of those diminutive mammals.
> Olaus J. Murie, *A Field Guide to Animal Tracks*

> *'a sheet of water near your breasts*
> *where I can sink*
> *like a stone'*
> Paul Éluard

Each of these fulfills one of Genette's four functions of epigraph by 'commenting on the text, whose meaning it indirectly specifies or emphasizes.'[3] In this case, moreover, the epigraph both looks backwards to the narrative of the preceding three sections and, in a manner of speaking, awaits that of the fourth. While there is nothing mystifying about either, the fragment from Éluard is closer in mood, imagery, and theme to the love story as it has been represented in the sequence's first three parts. The more equivocating and wry quotation from Murie, by contrast, has the merit of distancing us from the events, giving us some breathing room from the nearly claustrophobic intensities of the second and third sections. It anticipates the fourth part's more relaxed, even occasionally playful mood, the celebration of the middle range of the emotions, and several poems in which landscape is prominent.

Many of Ondaatje's section epigraphs have similar thematic functions in alerting us to some aspects of the poems they introduce. The passage from Italo Calvino's *Invisible Cities* that precedes the 'Pig Glass' section of *There's a Trick with a Knife I'm Learning to Do* seems to anticipate the Sri Lankan poems written after Ondaatje's return in 1978 to his native country, though the reader won't suspect that link until 'The Hour of Cowdust,' the section's tenth poem.

'Newly arrived and totally ignorant of the Levantine languages, Marco
Polo could express himself only with gestures, leaps, cries of wonder and
of horror, animal barkings or hootings, or with objects he took from his
knapsacks – ostrich plumes, pea-shooters, quartzes – which he arranged
in front of him ...'   (71)

As I suggested earlier, the first epigraph in Ondaatje's body of work,
from Auden, doesn't so much comment on *The Dainty Monsters* as
introduce a mood. It's close to Stendhal's view that 'the epigraph must
heighten the reader's feeling, his emotion, if emotion there be, and not
present a more or less philosophical opinion about the situation.'[4] But
taken with the epigraph from *The Brothers Karamazov* to the second section, 'Troy Town' (the title is from Rossetti), it functions to establish
what Genette calls 'the epigraph-effect,' by which a young author
gives himself 'the consecration of a(nother) prestigious filiation' in
which 'he chooses his peers and thus his place in the pantheon.'[5] In
other words, the poet's choice of epigraph, like his allusions and echoes, indicates, among several things, the tradition within which he
wants his work to be read. If we have enough of them, we can also
treat them as a trace revealing what the writer has read, which writers
he admires, and who has influenced him. It's worth noting that only
once after *The Dainty Monsters* does Ondaatje quote from or allude to a
major poet in the Western tradition – Rilke in *Secular Love*. It's as if,
having established himself, he doesn't need what Genette calls 'the
indirect backing' of a major name to enter the tradition. After *The
Dainty Monsters*, the epigraphs will come as often from unexpected
sources such as conversations, the magazine description of a wine, or
popular mystery novels as they will from canonical or nearly canonical
authors. The later epigraphs have a more serendipitous quality.
Encountering them, we feel a bit like Olaus J. Murie surprised by 'thin
squeaky voices' or an unexpected set of animal tracks.

There's a Trick with a Knife I'm Learning to Do

Transition

A change of style is a change of subject.

Wallace Stevens[1]

There's a Trick with a Knife I'm Learning to Do: Poems 1963–1978[2] contains both old work and new; it summarizes where Ondaatje has been – the title alone is an effective trope for the old – and in its Sri Lankan poems announces the shift in his poetics that will make possible the poems in *Running in the Family* and *Handwriting*. There are few surprises among the selections from *The Dainty Monsters* and *Rat Jelly*; of the ones included, I have never been impressed with 'Breaking Green' or 'Sullivan and the iguana,' neither of which strikes me as fine as the omitted 'King Kong' or 'The Ceremony: A Dragon, a Hero, and a Lady,' one of Ondaatje's few ventures into what might be called conservative verse. Also worth noting are the new epigraphs chosen to introduce each selection; where most poets revise poems, Ondaatje revises or rethinks epigraphs. *The Dainty Monsters* is now introduced by lines from 'Ksemaraja,' a Sanskrit love poem: 'The tongue's name is / Morning Star / The name for the end of the nose / is North Star ... // Whosoever does not see this in the sky / will surely die.'[3] The fragment is a riddle, but I doubt that many of Ondaatje's readers will be able to understand it without some sort of commentary and without a translation of the title. Twenty years after first reading these lines I'm still puzzled by them and, to be completely frank, have no idea of their significance for the poems of the 1960s. The selection from *Rat Jelly* is now introduced by a playful description of a wine: 'Deep colour and big, shaggy nose. Rather a jumbly, untidy sort of wine, with fruitiness shooting off one way, firmness another, and body pushing about underneath. It will be as comfortable and comforting as the 1961 Nuits St Georges when it has pulled its ends in and settled down' (33). I assume that this is an indirect general description of the poems that follow, which 'shoot off' in various directions: love, domesticity and family, elegies, art. Its tone, however, is too playful, even frivolous, for some of the more sombre poems, and I can't help wondering whether Ondaatje isn't dropping some of his earlier allusions as a way hiding some of his literary and cultural sources.

The poems written after the appearance of *Rat Jelly* in 1973 are collected in the final section, titled 'Pig Glass' after one of them. As I suggested above, the epigraph from Calvino's *Invisible Cities* seems to have particular relevance to the handful of poems based on Ondaatje's return to Sri Lanka in 1978. I assume that the comic scene is an indirect commentary on his situation and feelings when he returned to his homeland unable to speak either Sinhalese or Tamil. Five poems deal with the return: 'The Hour of Cowdust,' 'The Palace,' 'Uswetakei-yawa,' 'The Wars,' and 'Sweet like a Crow.' In retrospect, it is clear that they represent Ondaatje's first steps towards what might be called the 'nostos' or Sri Lankan phase of his career – the writing of *Running in the Family* (1982), *Handwriting* (1999), and *Anil's Ghost* (2000). I will reserve discussion of them to the end of the chapter.

The most accessible and, in some respects, most conventional of the poems in the 'Pig Glass' section are the ones that grow out of Ondaatje's life in the country north of Belleville. With the exception of 'Walking to Bellrock,' these resemble free verse conversational poems or journal entries based on events in the poet's daily life. Our interest in 'Buying the dog,' 'Moving Fred's Outhouse / Geriatrics of pine,' or 'Buck Lake Store Auction' is primarily in the content or the story, not in the poetic discourse. In some cases, as with 'Country Night' and 'Buying the dog,' I have the sense that the poet is going over very familiar poetic ground ('The Republic' for the former and 'Loop' for the latter). There is an occasional arresting image or idiom in most of them, but they don't repay rereading or extended attention. Within the design of the book as a whole, they seem resting stops between more difficult and more powerful lyrics.

A more interesting, because unexpected, return to earlier subject matter occurs in 'Sallie Chisum / Last words on Billy the Kid. 4 a.m.' (98–9). The style is different from what we recall in *The Collected Works*, but the voice is convincingly Sallie's '37 years since I knew him.' The deliberately fragmented poem is also, of course, another ending to be added to the several 'last words' with which that book ended without closure. The overall structure of this piece, shards of memory framed by scenes in the present, echoes that of 'Light.' The speaker ends where she began – aware of the association between the moon and Billy's image – and in between drifts through fragments of her past. By the end we have had 'last words' not only about Billy but also about Sallie. He remains young in her memory, removing a splinter from her foot with his teeth, firing bullets into 'the dummy / on which I built dresses,' or observed 'having a serious dream.' Sallie, by contrast, is time-bound and, as she realizes, has aged. Billy has escaped time by dying and becoming memory and legend. His timeless quality is also suggested when she identifies him with the moon in both of the framing fragments.

Her address to him in the third lyric – 'Where have you been I ask' – makes this into a dramatic monologue as well as an elegy in which the portrait of the speaker is as important as the ostensible subject matter. Billy remains beyond reach, but the longer Sallie speaks, the more complex does her attitude to him become. The first three brief verses are coloured by loss, affection, and remorse. The fourth, however, shocks with a new, startling note announced without preparation: 'Billy was a fool / he was like those reversible mirrors / you can pivot round and see yourself again / but there is something showing on the other side always.' The laughter produced in the fifth section by the shooting of the 'dummy' leads to a description of Billy 'having a serious dream. / Concentrating. / Angry. As if wallpaper / had been ripped off a wall.' (Notice the near-chiastic sound play in the last sentence.) The remaining four parts, in a form that mimics the failure of memory, reiterate earlier images, closing with Sallie butting out her cigarette 'against the window / where the moon is. / In his stupid eyes.' Instead of the two holes in the dressmaker's dummy, Ondaatje brings back Billy's eyes and the cigarette of the first section, where she said, 'That is a sin he taught me. / Showed me how to hold it and how to want it.' Her use of 'sin' to describe smoking seems surprising until we realize that it also prepares us for the next lines revealing ambiguity: 'Showed me how to hold it and how to want it.' The full force of this comment is felt, however, only the second time around, after we have encountered Sallie's reticence in the remainder of the poem as well as her equivocations and hints of remorse and anger. In one crucial aspect, however, the poem represents an important departure from *The Collected Works*: the emphasis on the intricacies of memory brings it closer to some of the new poems and to *Running in the Family* than to any of the earlier writing. The poem's halting style, with its sudden shifts, emotional cross-currents, and unconscious repetitions, enacts an individual's ambivalent response to her past and her memory's struggle with forgetting. Though only a handful of the new poems make this concern explicit – it is central in 'Pig Glass' and 'Light' – even the ones dealing with the mundane topics leave me with the impression that they were written in part to ensure that the event and its attendant feelings survive.

In 'Pig Glass' (84–5), a deceptively subtle and even mischievous poem, the object and its discovery are directly implicated in issues of creativity, destruction, and survival through time. The piece of glass is introduced casually in Canada's other official language – 'Bonjour' – and offered to the reader for inspection: 'This is pig glass / a piece of cloudy sea // nosed out of the earth by swine / and smoothed into pebble / run it across your cheek / it will not cut you' (84). The green glass is 'slow faded history / waiting to be grunted up / There is no past until you breathe / on such green glass.' In this instance, the survival of the past depends on chance and on the speaker's and the reader's active interest in the object. However trivial the thing may seem, it is 'The morning's green present' (a particularly fine ambiguity) and 'Portland Township jewellery.' But as the next stanza suggests, it is part of a rich trove of random objects – found poems? – that have survived from the past, awaiting rediscovery in the present by readers, poets, or swine. Part of the process of recovery inevitably involves the poetic imagination's ability to enter into the past and to reconstitute it from the surviving fragments. The penultimate stanza's use of the present tense hints at the complexity of the temporal relations involved in a poem in which the past has become the present.

> A bottle thrown
> by loggers out of a wagon
> past midnight
> explodes against rock.
> This green fragment has behind it
> the *booomm* when glass
> tears free of its smoothness

The original event, if indeed it happened this way, is reimagined in a deliberately simple vernacular. What happens afterwards is described in increasingly figurative language as if to indicate the work of the poet's imagination on the bare shards and facts of real life.

> now once more smooth as knuckle
> a tooth on my tongue.
> Comfort that bites through skin
> hides in the dark afternoon of my pocket.
> Snake shade.
> Determined histories of glass.

Evocative as I find this final stanza – 'Snake shade' hisses and is tersely dazzling – I'm not clear on how the smoothed piece of glass is 'Comfort that bites through skin.' On the other hand, 'the dark afternoon of my pocket' compresses at least two notions into a single trope. Not surprisingly, since this is an Ondaatje poem, creation and recreation are inseparable from violence and the memory of violence. As for the pigs? They're just pigs on Ondaatje's farm unless we want to think of them as any individual who stumbles over objects like the glass or 'the band from the ankle of a pigeon' and doesn't see the intricate nexus of relations behind them. It is worth recalling, however, that in 'Sows, one more time' (*DM*, 31) Ondaatje described pigs as 'Poets / in a poet's world.' Both poems are playful enough to engage the question of whether poets are therefore pigs in a pigs' world?

In this section only 'Light' is as concerned with 'determined histories' and memory, but I want to reserve its discussion until the end of this chapter so that I can approach it by way of the Sri Lankan poems, with which it naturally belongs and with which it prefigures *Running in the Family* and that book's handful of similar poems. Before looking at them, however, I want to comment on 'Walking to Bellrock' and 'Late Movies with Skyler,' two poems that introduce an unsettling tone which is a mix of unease, anxiety, remorse, and despondence into the section without quite making clear its precise source. The even more sombre 'Pure Memory / Chris Dewdney' belongs with these more personal poems, but much as I admire it, I must admit that I have little of interest to say about it. Perhaps it's just one of those complex and profound works not in need of commentary? Much of the poetry of Hardy, Lawrence, and Purdy seems to me to be like this. In the other poems, the manifest content – a walk down a shallow river, the watching of the late show – hints at unsettling events and circumstances that are never named. These two poems recall David Schubert's definition of poetry as 'Speaking of what cannot be said / To the person I want to say it.'[4] The unresolved emotional and thematic tension in each prevents closure. In each case I have the impression of having read a section of a novel without knowing what came before and what happens after. The episode is all that seems to matter; the rest is irrelevant or at best to be hinted at, a shadowing or chiaroscuro effect occluding the causes. As Ondaatje wrote about *Tay John*, 'to tell a story is to leave most of it untold.'[5]

In 'Walking to Bellrock' (81–3) the speaker is recognizable as the individual who recounts 'Buying the dog,' 'Buck Lake Store Auction,' and 'Moving Fred's Outhouse / Geriatrics of pine.' He is the poet's persona, and he tells a meandering, descriptive, and reflective narrative about how he and a friend named Stan – probably the writer and editor Stan Dragland – are walking 'the river into Bellrock' in eastern Ontario. The narrative is relatively straightforward: 'The plot of the afternoon is to get to Bellrock / through rapids, falls, stink water / and reach the island where beer and a towel wait for us.' The speaker pauses over various details of the walk, mentions history and neighbours, and, in a curious turn, ends by wondering about what didn't happen, specifically what he and his friend didn't say: 'And all the next day trying to think / what we didn't talk about. / Where was the criminal conversation / broken sentences lost in the splash in wind.' That something troubling but unspoken was in the air is obvious in retrospect from some of the potentially violent images ('the splashed blood of cardinal flower on the bank'; 'our heads decapitated'), from the reference to what is hidden in the 'landscapes underwater,' and in the emphasis on difficulty and potential danger. The ending only seems slightly histrionic if we overlook these details:

Stan, my crazy summer friend,
why are we both going crazy?
Going down to Bellrock
recognizing home by the colour of barns
which tell us north, south, west,
and otherwise lost in miles and miles of rain
in the middle of this century
following the easy fucking stupid plot to town.

Maps in Ondaatje almost always hint at an order that is desired but not actual. The paradox that the two men are lost even though they are

'following the easy fucking stupid plot to town' alerts us to other intimations in 'lost' and 'plot' without providing the information needed
for a fuller understanding of their situation. Dragland's comment
about Ondaatje's work is particularly apt here: '*The* fact about Michael
Ondaatje's writing is its inexplicable residue of meaning.'[6] It's worth
recalling that whenever Ondaatje writes that 'there is no ... metaphor
with us,' he usually deals with a writing degree zero in which some
critical confrontation about ultimate issues is involved. Scenes set at
night function in almost the same way.

A similar sense of tension and crisis is present in 'Late Movies with
Skyler' (96–7). Skyler, Kim Ondaatje's 'restless' son from her first marriage, has come home from Vancouver Island and has spent much of
his time repairing a car, playing blues on his guitar, and watching late
movies with the speaker. Without explicitly judging Skyler's situation,
the speaker nevertheless manages to convey that he is worried about
him. Again, nothing specific is said about his age or his situation, but
the speaker's comments about the Stewart Granger film *The Prisoner of
Zenda* hint at his concern:

> I lie in bed fully awake. The darkness
> breathes to the pace of a dog's snoring.
> The film is replayed to sounds
> of an intricate blues guitar.
> Skyler is Rupert then the hero.
> He will leave in a couple of days
> for Montreal or the Maritimes.
> In the movies of my childhood the heroes
> after skilled swordplay and moral victories
> leave with absolutely nothing
> to do for the rest of their lives.

One gradually senses that the narrator is 'fully awake' because he's
worried about Skyler. Is there a suggestion of immaturity in the fact
that the young man can be both the villain and the hero, or that having
come from one side of the continent, he is now setting off in the opposite direction but without having decided between Montreal or the
Maritimes? As well, there is the earlier contrast between the 'perfect
world' of the adventure film and the implicitly imperfect world of broken cars and adult life decisions. Again, nothing is spelled out, but a
melancholy mood is created and sustained in the poem's final stanza.

If there's a judgment to be made, it's left to the reader to attempt the difficult summing up. As always, Ondaatje's use of 'moral' and 'morals' is slippery and unconventional, synonymous sometimes with conventional morality but more often suggesting an authentic and therefore difficult way of life. Our view of the situation described becomes even more sombre, however, if we notice that several of the poem's images ('star,' 'alone,' and 'moral') and the syntax of the last sentence ('after skilled swordplay') recall 'White Dwarfs,' Ondaatje's troubling tribute to 'people who disappear' by sailing 'to that perfect edge / where there is no social fuel.' Even the subject's name, shortened to 'Sky' in the fourth stanza, recalls 'the ether peripheries' to which the earlier poem's heroes ascend, as well as, more closely, its penultimate line: 'there are those burned out stars / who implode into silence / after parading in the sky / after such choreography what would they wish to speak of   anyway.'

The most obvious difference in the new Sri Lankan material is the change in the speaker or persona. The speaking self becomes indeterminate, sometimes gender-free, no longer connected to the settings or relationships of Ondaatje's earlier work. It's as if having left North America behind, he is able to leave behind as well a particular kind of poetry and to attempt a dissolution of the voice and self in language and a more open poetic that seems unrelated to any of the traditions within which he originally found his voice. It's worth recalling his comment, made in an interview in 1984, that 'one tries to start each new book with a new vocabulary, a new set of clothes. Consciously or subconsciously we burn the previous devices which have got us here but which now are only rhetoric.'[7] These poems don't seem interested in narrative, totality, or the endings that somehow bring a poem to a point. Their images are loosely related to each other but without any obvious striving for a larger aesthetic or narrative pattern connected to or expressive of a symbolic meaning. The poetic unit seems to be the image or the verse paragraph, and these seem more important than the whole, to which they stand in a loose relationship. In Kenneth Burke's terms, the poem's form depends less on a syllogistic than on a qualitative progression. I also have the impression that the poem's form expressively mimics for the reader Ondaatje's own acts of perception and discovery of the landscape and the culture he once knew. It may not be coincidental that several of the poems – 'The Hour of Cowdust,' 'Uswetakeiyawa,' 'The Wars' – take place at night and/or mention the moon, usually a symbol for the imagination in his work. It's worth recalling that 'Country Night' (73) ends with the claim 'All night the truth happens.'

Though 'Moon Lines, after Jiménez' (74–5) isn't one of the Sri Lankan poems, it anticipates their new, freer manner in which words and images seem to find their place in the poem through some sort of free association, perhaps based on the order in which they occurred to the mind. Time and place remain unspecified, as do the poem's two figures. If not for the reference to and quotation from Juan Ramón Jiménez, the poem would be completely non-referential, self-contained. The point of departure is a fragment from the Spanish poet's 'At First She Came to Me Pure.'[8]

Are you going around naked
in the house?

      speaking to moon

from the precise
place of darkness
speaking to
the unnamed woman

The moon has no shoes
undresses itself of cloud
river reflection

In dark bound rooms
the lost men imagine
paths of biography
on their palms

The greatest shipwrecks
are silent
semaphore their bones
through tide
they grow coloured history
wait
for the clock of moon

The abandoned woman
dives through darkness
and then
balances
with the magic fluid of her ear

It is here
it is now
when my thumb
swallows the candlelight

This is one of those poems that, while elusive and obscure, still seems to me profound in what it suggests about a complex situation and therefore about the human condition; though to be honest, I know that my reading of it is a tissue of guesses. I assume that the speaker is a man because of the contrastive reference to 'the lost men' in the twelfth line. He addresses the moon because 'the unnamed woman' is not present, not available. The poem pivots on the two middle stanzas, in which the lost men, living in 'bound rooms' that contrast with his open one from which he can see the moon, imagine what their lives might have been like, had they made different choices in their 'paths of biography.' The stanza about 'The greatest shipwrecks' seems a reality check, a reminder that some choices lead to disaster and silence (the sibilants remind the ear of the silence). Their 'wait / for the clock of moon' may hint at waiting for someone to tell their story, since the moon seems to function as a non-human presence in the poem, perhaps as well as a figure for the imagination. Behind the whole stanza I sense both 'White Dwarfs' and 'Full fathom five thy father lies' (*The Tempest* I. ii. 394–5). Like so much else, the identity of the 'abandoned woman' is ambiguous, as is the meaning of her dive 'through darkness.' Perhaps she dives through darkness *because* she has been abandoned for 'the unnamed woman'? Though there is also the stronger possibility that the two women are the same. The timelessness of the scene is reiterated in the closing 'It is here / it is now' (what does 'it' refer to?), but whether the thumb's swallowing of the candlelight is a positive or a negative development escapes me, though I suspect that it suggests the self's surrender to the moonlight and lines written under the influence of the moon. Perhaps a clue lies in the title – 'Moon Lines' – with its hint of a scene both witnessed by the moon and written under its influence.

    There may also be a clue in Ondaatje's reading of Cohen's 'Before the Story.' In his monograph he quotes the poem's closing stanza:

... the wilderness moon
lives above the whole world,
and in her light
holds us, holds us,
cold and splendid,
in her vast and cloudless night.

His commentary on these lines would make sense as a reading of 'Moon Lines, after Jiménez': 'Cohen often ends with this moon – the final judge, the perfect poet with its precision and constancy – this moon which sees everyone in the total order; so that here, Bathsheba is watched as she bathes and the moon watches the watchers. The ideal state of the poet, for Cohen, is to reach this sort of objectivity, and there are numerous images which deal with the metamorphosis into moon or stars' (*LC*, 15–16). This passage suggests that Cohen's poem may be as important a presence in 'Moon Lines, after Jiménez' as Jiménez's. Since I have confessed to not being sure what this poem means, it may strike some readers as paradoxical when I also admit that I admire it very much and consider it to be among Ondaatje's finest. To modify Genette slightly, even the possible absence of meaning creates the impression or possibility of meaning: 'often the most stimulating or most rewarding: to think without knowing what you are thinking – is that not one of the purest pleasures of the mind?'[9]

If this poem was written before the Sri Lankan ones, then it seems to me to indicate a significant shift in Ondaatje's poetry towards looser paratactical forms, fragmentation, and a freeing of the image from referentiality and a precise context. In the specifically Sri Lankan poems he's more of an impressionist interested in evoking the mood or climate of a scene on the basis of a handful of evocative images. The analogy with painting is substantiated by the renewed interest in light. As I mentioned earlier, the subject or speaker here is less substantial than in the earlier poems. It's as if 'coming home' allows Ondaatje to escape the anxious adult self of the earlier work, to dissolve the self in landscape, cultural traditions, and personal and historical pasts.

The title of 'The Hour of Cowdust' (86–7) could just as easily refer to a genre painting. It's a poem marking a transitional moment on the trip to Sri Lanka, though we infer this only from the poems that follow. Its reference to 'Indian miniatures,' like the use of Indian myth in 'The Wars,' alerts us to the poet's turning away from the cultural tradition that had nurtured his writing until now. He begins with a scene on the Nile dissolved in light and then follows it with further local details, as well as with images from 'Indian miniatures' and books about Asian writing: 'It is the hour we move small / in the last possibilities of light // now the sky opens its blue vault // ... // Everything is reducing itself to shape.' The subsequent images do not seem to follow any obvious pattern or thematic logic, and the transition from the scene on the Nile to memories of Indian miniatures seems to function liminally, more to indicate transition and the journey's destination than to amplify the emotional or thematic implications of the poem's first half. It's as if Ondaatje is stretching the poem's form to the point where it doesn't seem to have one, before returning to the opening concern with perception and disappearance. But, in fact, the long central stanza – beginning with 'In Indian miniatures / I cannot quite remember' – presents a series of images each of which touches in some way on love and separation, a motif planted in the fourth line's mention of the speaker's children – 'I thought this hour belonged to my children.' The barely recalled 'Indian miniatures' and the 'commentaries' offer indirect consolation for his situation by reminding him that others have endured a similar condition.

> Women confided to pet parrots
> solitary men dreamed into the conch.
> So many
> graciously humiliated
> by the distance of rivers

I assume that they were 'graciously humiliated' because of the grace or gracefulness of the art – 'miniatures' – in which their stories have been commemorated. They have been 'humiliated' in two senses: they have been humbled by life, and they have been made small in the art of the miniatures. The adverb 'graciously' may also be present because of its appeal to the poet's auditory imagination; it carries the unspoken 'gracefully' in its wake, and its sibilants fit perfectly into the stanza's sound patterns. The poem then returns to the boat in the river with its 'sails / ready for the moon.'

> there is no longer
> depth of perception
> it is now possible
> for the outline of two boats
> to collide silently

The poem dissolves itself in a sketch or outline of a remarkably subtle tonal harmony in which the plosives surrounding 'boats' struggle almost successfully against the liquids of 'outline ... collide ... silently.' In retrospect, another title suggests itself: 'Nocturne: The Hour of Cowdust.'

The next poem, 'The Palace' (88), also registers the mood of a moment – '7 a.m. The hour of red daylight' – in a series of random images of Rajasthan as it is seen by the speaker. Like the other poems in the series, it reminds the reader of how different this world is from the world of the Canadian poems. Ondaatje makes this point more explicitly in the epigraph – taken from Aldous Huxley's well-known essay – to 'Wordsworth in the Tropics,' a poem he has not republished: 'The essential failure of Wordsworth,' one critic notes, 'is that he never ventured into the tropics.'[10] Like the earlier epigraph from Calvino, this is one of several casual reminders, to himself and to readers, about difference and otherness, a deft gesture showing his awareness of the dangers of Orientalism. This will be an important concern in *Running in the Family, Handwriting*, and *Anil's Ghost*, where Anil, like Ondaatje, understands that a lengthy absence has made her a stranger in her changed homeland. Ondaatje's words in the memoir also apply to her: 'I am the foreigner. I am the prodigal who hates the foreigner' (*RF*, 79). Often the sense of strangeness and estrangement will be announced and intensified by moonlit scenes.

Stan Dragland, focusing on Ondaatje's status as a native foreigner, comments perceptively on 'Uswetakeiyawa' (89–91; the title means 'the night mile'): 'a native could not have found the distance to write "Uswetakeiyawa" and a real foreigner could never have gotten so close. The poem threads a strange nightscape. Everything happens along an edge of suggestion. There is no definition. The eye of the poem is teased with glimpses of regular and unusual life forms apparently metamorphosing in the night, but sight can't get a purchase on what's happening out there. Smell is just as important to reading the night mile, with its thick, thrilling, slightly sinister otherness that seems vast because so little of it is intelligible, to the writer and so to the reader.'[11] The difference between here and there is announced immediately and unmistakably by the fact that the title is in a foreign language. It is then developed in the catalogue of scenes and images glimpsed from a jeep riding through the countryside near Colombo. As Dragland suggests, the riot of smells and sights confuses the speaker, for whom this is 'the dream journey / we travel most nights /

returning from Colombo. / A landscape nightmare / unphotographed country.' What the poet means, of course, is that to someone from North America it seems like a dream or a nightmare, and that its alphabets and codes are incomprehensible only to someone like him who is unfamiliar with Sri Lanka and doesn't speak Sinhalese or Tamil. The new land is a new language and demands a new poetic: the 'bright coloured boats' seem 'like masks in the night / their alphabets lost in the dark.' The poet has to rely on his imagination to make sense of the fragmented images and confusing sensations:

> No sight but the imagination's
> story behind each smell
> or now and then a white sarong
> pumping its legs on a bicycle
> like a moth in headlights
>
>   and the dogs
> who lean out of night
> strolling the road
> with eyes of sapphire
> and hideous body
>   so mongrelled
> they seem to have woken
> to find themselves tricked
> into outrageous transformations,

Though the poem tries to impose imaginative order on these scenes, it ends with a stanza reiterating this sense of confusion:

> Once in the night we saw
> something slip into the canal.
> There was then the odour we did not recognize.
> The smell of a dog losing its shape.

Dogs in Ondaatje's poetry are usually associated with the senses, spontaneity, instinct, irrationality, and madness. Their function is generally liminal and transgressive. He catches something of this aspect when he refers in the penultimate stanza to 'the aura of dogs / in trickster skin.' At their most extreme, as in *The Collected Works of Billy the Kid* and *Running in the Family,* dogs appear as parts of a scene of violence and terror.

Livingstone's 'mongrelled' and inbred dogs attack and eat him in *The Collected Works of Billy the Kid* (61–2); and one of the final images we have of Mervyn Ondaatje shows him coming out of the jungle

> huge and naked. In one hand he holds five ropes, and dangling on the end of each of them is a black dog. None of the five are touching the ground. He is holding his arm outstretched, holding them with one arm as if he has supernatural strength. Terrible noises are coming from him and from the dogs as if there is a conversation between them that is subterranean, volcanic. All their tongues hanging out.
>
> They were probably stray dogs which my father had stumbled on in jungle villages, he had perhaps picked them up as he walked along. He was a man who loved dogs. But this scene had no humour or gentleness in it. The dogs were too powerful to be in danger of being strangled. The danger was to the naked man who held them at arm's length, towards whom they swung like large dark magnets.   (*RF*, 153)

Looking back from *Running in the Family*, it's tempting to see the scene in 'Uswetakeiyawa' as the first hint of the key scene in the memoir. In both works, the speaker talks almost successfully of what cannot be said. After all, the poem's closing lines seem to contradict each other as what might be called the negative synaesthesia of the second undoes the 'not' of the first.

The poem in the volume that most clearly anticipates the return to Sri Lanka and the memoir is 'Light,' the elegy for the poet's mother, Doris Gratiaen. Though placed last, it was published three years earlier than any of the other Sri Lankan poems. It appeared in 1975 in the *Canadian Forum*, while the others were first published in 1979. Like so much of Ondaatje's poetry and fiction, it recalls earlier work and anticipates later. Its most significant link with the past is to 'Letters & Other Worlds,' the elegy for Mervyn Ondaatje published in 1971. As I mentioned earlier, each elegy is prefaced by a brief poem about Ondaatje's son: 'Griffin of the night' introduces the first, the justly admired 'Bearhug' the second. In both a scene involving the reciprocal love of parent and child colours and intensifies the sense of irretrievable loss inevitable in an elegy for a parent. Never careless about the arrangement of his lyrics, Ondaatje has been particularly attentive here.

'Bearhug' (104) is about a child's call for a kiss and hug before going to sleep. It's a poem about need and longing and love, as well as about the withholding or absence of the last. In the first of three stanzas

> Griffin calls to come and kiss him goodnight
> I yell ok. Finish something I'm doing,
> then something else, walk slowly round
> the corner to my son's room.
> He is standing arms outstretched
> waiting for a bearhug. Grinning.

The delay between the father's 'ok' and his arrival in his son's room is rhythmically enacted in the stanza's lineation as time and place stretch across the second, third, and fourth lines, and then is reiterated in the deft enjambment of the fifth and sixth ('outstretched / waiting'). The child's grin makes it clear that for him this is not a Proustian scene of anguish, a fact that ironically makes us more attentive to the father's concerned reaction in what follows. Instead of simply hugging his son, he responds to his grin with a question: 'Why do I give my emotion an animal's name, / give it that dark squeeze of death?' Our response to the first line might be that our hugs are visceral or physical or, as D.H. Lawrence would have put it, 'along the blood.' But the surprising mention of 'death' at the end of the second line makes this answer problematic. Something more is coursing through these lines: perhaps the awareness of the centrality of the parent-child relationship as well as the brevity of its duration; perhaps the troubling pressure from some half-remembered scene in the speaker's own life. We may be joined to our parents or our children by 'a magnet of blood' (line 13), but as the poet's family history shows, the connection may be suddenly broken either by divorce or by death. As much of the pathos of the father's closing question comes from our realization of this reality as from the son's 'arms outstretched / waiting for a bearhug.' And if we've read Ondaatje's body of work, we'll probably also recall that in 'Letters & Other Worlds' and *Running in the Family,* magnets are associated with Mervyn Ondaatje. As we know, they both attract and repel, as do the characteristics that run in a family.

The reflective, remorseful tone of 'Light' (105–7) reminds us that an elegy is often also a meditation on the speaker's own mortality. Though the poem is 'for Doris Gratiaen' and therefore nominally at least an elegy for her, it anticipates *Running in the Family* in its evocation of the now dead individuals of her generation. The Ceylonese or Sri Lankan past is framed by two stanzas in the Canadian present in which the speaker calls to mind 'my favourite slides / re-shot from old minute photographs.' He sits on a porch during a midnight storm watching 'Trees walking off across the fields in fury / naked in the spark of lightning' and 'The past, friends and family, drift into the rain shower.' The long, often enjambed, easily and slowly flowing sentences evoke a dreamlike mood, as if the mind is on automatic pilot and memory and feeling are allowed to flow with minimal conscious intervention. The second stanza describes images or scenes that are sentimental, funny, and innocently outrageous. These seem to come from the speaker's memory in no particular order ending with

> My Aunt Christie. She knew Harold MacMillan was a spy
> communicating with her through pictures in the newspapers.
> Every picture she believed asked her to forgive him,
> his hound eyes pleading.
> Her husband Uncle Fitzroy a doctor in Ceylon had a memory
> sharp as scalpels into his 80's
> though I never bothered to ask him about anything
> – interested then more in the latest recording of Bobby Darin.

(Keep in mind Bobby Darin and especially 'Mack the Knife.') The third and middle stanza focuses on 'my Mother with her brother Noel.' The tone is mellower, closer to sentimental, partly because it shows them as children and partly because she is allowed to describe her brother's death scene. Because this happens *after* we have been told about 'My Uncle dying at 68, and my Mother a year later dying at 68,' it creates the momentary illusion that she is still alive. The illusion is extended by the omission of the verb in the final sentence dealing with her: 'Her voice joyous in telling me this, her face light and clear.' It's as if the speaker recalls the telling as if it had happened recently. Of the three stanzas devoted to the family, this is the most peaceful.[12]

The next deals with the more problematic figure of the father. Ondaatje manages the transition by reminding us of 'the dogs, restless on the porch' and then commenting, 'They were all laughing, crazy, and vivid in their prime.' None of these descriptive terms quite prepares us for the bizarre and violent scene that follows. The other relations have been 'crazy' in the sense of 'eccentric'; the father, when 'drunk,' is crazy in the more troubling sense of the word.

> At a party my drunk Father
> tried to explain a complex operation on chickens
> and managed to kill them all in the process, the guests

having dinner an hour later while my Father slept
and the kids watched the servants clean up the litter
of beaks and feathers on the lawn.

From Mack the Knife to Mervyn the Knife on one page, though we
have also been prepared for the violence by the mention in the second
stanza of 'Pam de Voss who fell on a pen-knife and lost her eye' and in
the third of Uncle Fitzroy's 'scalpels.' The narrator doesn't comment
on the party scene, but his inclusion of the detail of the 'kids' watching
speaks for itself and implies that they are also thinking about what is
happening. Together with three other references to children, this scene
hints at a concern with things 'running in the family.'
    The fifth and final stanza returns the poem to the present with the
acknowledgment that

These are their fragments, all I remember,
wanting more knowledge of them. In the mirror and in my kids
I see them in my flesh. Wherever we are
they parade in my brain and the expanding stories
connect to the grey grainy pictures on the wall

I said that the speaker doesn't comment in a judgmental way on any of
these scenes except to say that the photo he 'loves most' is 'a hand-
coloured photograph' of his mother and uncle when they are '7 and 8
years old.' But there are two details in the setting that function almost
like a self-revealing pathetic fallacy or an objective correlative. The violence of the storm itself and the illusion he has of the trees 'walking off
across the fields in fury / naked in the spark of lightning' and later
'frozen in the jagged light as if snapped in their run / the branch arms
waving' – both of these details seem to be expressive of the turmoil of
his own feelings. And the curious reference to the trees as 'lonely in
their own knife scars' implies the unspoken presence of 'my own scars'
as well as 'scars' in general. He recalls and envisions the past in the
lightning, and it is lightning that also knocks over a tree and knocks
out the lights, forcing 'the kids [to] play dominoes by candlelight.' And
we all know that dominoes, in some children's games, fall over.
    At the end of the poem, as at its opening, the speaker sits alone,
mediating between the past and the present, separated from both. *Running in the Family* and *Anil's Ghost* will also try in very different ways to
establish an implicit dialogue between past and present, between here

and there. In a more radical gesture, *Handwriting* will simply abandon the 'here' in an attempt to immerse Ondaatje's poetry in Sri Lankan history and culture as completely as is possible for a Canadian poet writing in English.

CANON I

I predicted in an over-exuberant essay written nearly twenty years ago, 'Two generations from now all postmodernist fiction/writing will be read as autobiography.'[1] What I think I meant was that Ondaatje's work seemed to me to be shaping itself into a coherent, often self-reflecting narrative which, among other things, could be read as a sometimes oblique, sometimes direct commentary on his life in a way that the work of, say, Margaret Atwood couldn't. From the perspective of the millennium, this reading seems to me even truer than it did then. As I have argued, Ondaatje's vision of life, though it becomes more richly nuanced and complex from book to book, is nevertheless consistent from *The Dainty Monsters* to *Handwriting*. Life in his world is tentative, anxious, and always menaced by the possibility of disaster. Even moments of stability, order, and happiness are presented with reminders of their opposites and are therefore marked by ambiguity and ambivalence. A particularly fine early example is 'I have seen pictures of great stars,' quoted in the introduction, in which 'one altered move' will make the stars explode and the finely calibrated machines 'maniac' (*CWBK*, 41). In 'White Dwarfs' the 'stars' are individuals like Dashiell Hammett, whose response to 'the one altered move' is a shift into alcoholism and silence. If we're not distracted by his wit and humour – these are more obvious in the films – we can see that Ondaatje's vision is as dark as Joseph Conrad's or Peter Handke's. Almost all his books end with a death, and the survivors drift back into life like minor characters in a tragedy. In several of them, the loneliest figure is the surviving writer, alone in a small room trying to make sense of the events by writing about them. And a work of art, whatever claims we make for it, is never an adequate compensation for life.

Our altering love, our moonless faith.

Last ink in the pen.

My body on this hard bed.

The moment in the heart
where I roam restless, searching

for the thin border of the fence
to break through or leap.

Leaping and bowing.   (*H*, 75–6)

The 'thin border of the fence' is cognate with the 'nets' and 'fences' in
the early poems; the implied room takes us back to *Secular Love* and the
endings of *Running in the Family, Coming through Slaughter*, and *The Collected Works of Billy the Kid*; 'Last ink' recalls *From Ink Lake*, Ondaatje's
anthology of Canadian short fiction; and *Handwriting* links the lines to
Running in the Family and Doris Gratiaen. To quote William H. Gass on
Rilke, 'The poet never forgets a metaphor.'[2]

A complete list of echoes and repetitions – some discussed earlier –
would fill several pages. What it couldn't indicate, however, is the
effect of encountering a familiar image in a new setting. Think of the
expected semantic charge of 'magnet' in this sentence. Now compare it
to Ondaatje's figurative use of it in the following couplet in 'Bearhug':
'The thin tough body under the pyjamas / locks to me like a magnet of
blood.' And now, keeping both in mind, recall two scenes in *Running in
the Family*. In the first, Ondaatje turns the post-divorce movements of
the various children into a semi-comic Keystone Kops routine:

Gillian stayed in Ceylon with me, Christopher and Janet went to England.
I went to England, Christopher went to Canada, Gillian came to England,
Janet went to America, Gillian returned to Ceylon, Janet returned to
England, I went to Canada. Magnetic fields would go crazy in the pres-
ence of more than three Ondaatjes. And my father. Always separate until
he died, away from us. The north pole.   (172)

The fragment 'And my father' pulls the tone back to the force field of
the family tragedy, and the drop in temperature is confirmed by the

final 'The north pole,' which is, of course, a *magnetic* pole. In the second scene, quoted earlier, the father walks out of the jungle holding five ropes from each of which dangles a dog: 'The danger was to the naked man who held them at arm's length, towards whom they swung like dark magnets' (153). What I'm getting at is that when we encounter magnets in *Running in the Family*, the word has entered deeply into Ondaatje's private lexicon and has broadened its semantic and symbolic field. Its use here also has the effect of enriching our response to instances earlier in his body of work. Gradually the word becomes one of the many recurring words, scenes, and tricks of the stylistic knife (his habit of beginning with the copula 'there is,' 'there are') that define what we might call the grammar or geography of his body of imaginative work.[3] Having said this, I should point out that Ondaatje doesn't think of these works as related in quite these terms. He told me in an interview, 'When I wrote down the word magnet in the scene about my father [in *Running in the Family*] the last thing on my mind was to write it or have it read as a mirror to "Bearhug."'[4]

And if we think of his books as chapters in a work called *Ragas of Longing*, then it's particularly appropriate that the narrative begins with a book of exile whose cover features a pattern from a Ceylonese fabric and that it ends, for the time being, with one of return whose cover has a Sri Lankan photo and whose half-title page has a rune-like image which 'is an example of rock art, possibly a variation of a letter of the alphabet, found at Rajagalkanda in Sri Lanka' (*H*, 78). Everything connects, and like the acrobats in *Running in the Family* and *Handwriting*, each poem and each book depends on the others. The traditional consolations of totality or of a master narrative may no longer be available in life – or so the postmodernists tell us – but they are still possible in art. At least to a strong writer: the weak float along with the period's tide.

Secular Love

It Runs in the Family

J'aime avoir des personnages pourqui la vie est absolue ...

François Truffaut[1]

Few readers would claim that the poetry Ondaatje published before *Secular Love* (1984) has much in common with confessional writing. If anything, most of his earlier work stands opposed to that school's constitutive assumptions, and even when his lyrics are personal, they are rarely intimate. The speaker in most of them seems to be Ondaatje, but he's rarely interested in dealing directly with his most personal and most problematic emotions and situations: the voice is too laconic, the tone too detached, and the attitude to the self is ironic, on occasion even self-mocking. Yet we often sense that the artifice and control not only shape and present the material at hand but simultaneously hint at repressed or displaced experiences and aspects of the self with which the writer is unwilling or unable to deal. Ondaatje's suicidal herons and artists, his fascination with the jungle, the various hints at autobiography in *The Collected Works of Billy the Kid* (1969), 'Letters & Other Worlds,' and *Coming through Slaughter* (1976) – three studies in pathological creativity – all point obliquely or symbolically to the pressure of personal events on the work. Without resorting to a confessional aesthetic, *Coming through Slaughter*, his novel about a jazz cornetist whose obsessive art leads to silence and madness, and the crucial lyrics 'Letters & Other Worlds,' 'Burning Hills,' and 'White Dwarfs' reveal a compulsive fascination with an intensely subjective and violently self-expressive art. But in these works a confessional approach is not part of what Helen Vendler calls 'the structural and symbolic aesthetic strategies' to which the poet has been 'driven in coping ... [with] some personal *donnée* which the poet could not avoid treating.'[2] By contrast, the local *donnée* in *Secular Love* is a love affair and the breakup of a marriage. And its 'aesthetic strategies' show Ondaatje moving in a new direction in adapting a version of confessional that results in a four-part lyric sequence that is subjective, personal, and even intimate, but on the poet's terms. His answer to Lowell's question is that saying it all in this kind of situation always involves betraying others, and the art, the trick with a knife, consists in writing in such a way that you betray only yourself: 'This last year I was sure / I was going to die' (23).[3]

Ondaatje's basic problem in the book is how to transform an intensely subjective set of experiences into an artistic whole while, on the one hand, avoiding excessive subjectivity, solipsistic self-dramatization, and sentimentality – 'These are my feelings and therefore they're important' – or, on the other, losing the full texture of emotional immediacy through too impersonal an approach. He solves the problem, in part, by beginning the book with a sequence narrated in the third person and following it with one shifting among 'I,' 'you,' and the implicating 'we.' Several poems even omit the subject and leave us with the impression of a pure, unmediated, if anonymous voice. Similarly, by omitting the names of the main characters Ondaatje generalizes the potential significance of the events so that what we read becomes extended into something more than simply a chronological account of a particular set of experiences involving a specific group of people. The sources of the story may be as obviously autobiographical as those of D.H. Lawrence's *Look! We Have Come Through!* or Lowell's *History,* but the end result is a work of consummate poetry enacting a life and love story transcending the individuals originally involved in it. It's worth recalling that Bertrand Russell's response to Lawrence's poetic sequence about his love for Frieda Weekley was along the lines of So they've come through, but why should we care? The answer is obvious: because Lawrence transformed their love affair into art, it has become ours. As well, we no longer read it simply for the tale but also in order to linger over the telling, the sheer artistry of the thing. This is also why we *reread* it. The same is true of *Secular Love* – note the adjective, by the way, semantically allied with 'profane,' phonetically with 'sacred' – a book rich in human experience, carefully structured and beautiful crafted. When we finish the book, we inevitably think, 'Such overpowering love is not for all of us, but it tests the boundaries and so is revelatory; it is a human possibility, and must be part of any theory of the human condition.'[4]

The publication in 1982 of the frankly autobiographical, if often fictional, *Running in the Family* seemed to confirm the impression that
Ondaatje's work had, over the past decade, been moving slowly
towards a more direct engagement with his intimate experiences and
memories.[5] In a manner of speaking, *Running in the Family* is his equivalent of the early family-oriented sections of Lowell's *Life Studies*; *Secular Love*, by contrast, is the ruthless and unembarrassed engagement
with the self, an event as unavoidable in Ondaatje's present as his parents' troubled marriage in his distant past. It's impossible to be certain
about such matters, but I can't help thinking that he was able to write
Secular Love only because in *Running in the Family* he had finally confronted the most important figure in his life. Having dealt comprehen-
sively and unsparingly with the marriage and divorce of Philip
Mervyn Ondaatje, he turned to the breakdown of the marriage of
Philip Michael Ondaatje. The author's note to *Secular Love* tell us that
Ondaatje worked on the sequence before the memoir was finished
(128). Not surprisingly, the book's title, taken from the poem 'Women
like You' in the memoir, points us back to the tragic father even as we
read about the son. If *Running in the Family* was an experimental autobiography in prose, the four very different, though interrelated, sections of *Secular Love* show Ondaatje struggling to find a confessional
style and a poetic form to tell the story of the breakup of a marriage
and a family as a result in large part of the narrator's love affair with
another woman. This may be the one story and one story only of our
time, but as Tolstoy reminded us long ago, 'each unhappy family is
unhappy in its own way.'

The book is made up of four chronologically arranged sequences
telling the story of the breakup of a marriage and a way of life, the
poet's own near breakdown, and finally, after what one section calls
'Rock Bottom,' his recovery and return through the love of the other
woman. Despite changes in style and variations in tone and viewpoint,
the book should be read as a poetic journal, rather than as a collection
of discrete lyrics. One always senses the trace of a tacit sequential narrative. The first section, 'Claude Glass,' shows the poet at the beginning of the events, and 'Escarpment,' the last poem of 'Skin Boat,' the
fourth section, offers a sense of closure. The night and delirium of the
opening give way to daylight and clarity. Some of the poems, such as
the lovingly nuanced and nearly elegiac 'To a Sad Daughter,' can be
read by themselves, yet the volume is so closely organized, with so
much of the overall emotional and artistic effect depending on repeti-

tions and echoes of sound, image, situation, and emotion, that the poems often seem more like the chapters of a novel than parts of a collection. Another equally significant context is provided by Ondaatje's earlier work, and sections of *Secular Love* often seem like palimpsests of earlier texts such as 'Light.' Having made a claim for the book's unity, however, I want to emphasize that one only senses this in retrospect or on a second reading. The first time through it left me with the impression that I was reading the sort of biography Valéry describes when speculating about a new, perhaps impossible variant in the genre: 'I don't know ... if anyone has ever tried to write a biography and attempted at each instant of it to know as little of the following moment as the hero of the work knew himself at the corresponding instant of his career. This would be to restore chance in each instant, rather than putting together a series that admits of a neat summary and a causality that can be described as formulaic.'[6]

Some perspective and distance on the events is provided by the several epigraphs. The general opening epigraph from Peter Handke's *The Left-Handed Woman* simultaneously warns us about the unexpected stylistic and experiential openness, even rawness, of *Secular Love* and offers an implied judgment on Ondaatje's earlier work: 'Your trouble, I believe, is that you always hold back something of yourself. You're not shameless enough for an actor. In my opinion you should learn how to run properly and scream properly, with your mouth wide open. I've noticed that even when you yawn you're afraid to open your mouth all the way' (7). As in some of the epigraphs in the earlier collections, this is a warning about what to expect and what not to expect. It's as if Ondaatje is using Handke to remind us that even as he moves towards ostensibly confessional material, he's not only an actor but a reticent one, unwilling to reveal everything. The epigraph also reminds us that in poetry, as in any art, holding back or opening up is obviously a matter of degree as well as of technique; by holding back the clutter of irrelevant detail and by compressing events and characters, the writer can often create a greater impression of self-exposure and openness. *Secular Love* shows a writer who has found a style and a form that allow openness without sacrificing the economy and selectivity necessary for art. For instance, the book emphasizes the poet's daughter but not his son. A crucial aspect of that style is Ondaatje's delicate management of what I call the book's two voices or points of view: the first is that of Ondaatje the character in the story; the second, of Ondaatje the poet and creative voyeur who watches his own life and recreates it as art. This is the slightly guilty voice of the man who observes life even as he lives it, always in the hope of turning 'these giant scratches / of pain' (36) into art; who, when he writes that 'I fear / how anything can grow from this' (77), knows that in addition to the growing suffering and pain there is also the potential poem. This is the voice that knows that for the poet 'il faut que tu te voies mourir / Pour savoir que tu vis encore' (Paul Éluard).[7] Although at one point we read, 'There are those who are in / and there are those who look in,' we know that this distinction doesn't apply to Ondaatje – he's both. Perhaps one of the reasons he refers both to Federico García Lorca and Francis Ponge is that the former is one of those poets who are 'in,' while Ponge is among those who merely 'look in' and therefore offer an effective alternative to Gottfried Benn's warning 'You are using you own skin for wallpaper, and nothing can save you.'[8]

'Claude Glass,' the opening section, has its own epigraph, a dictionary definition of the title:

claude glass: a somewhat convex dark or coloured hand-mirror, used to concentrate the features of the landscape in subdued tones.
   'Grey [sic] walked about everywhere with that pretty toy, the claude glass, in his hand, making the beautiful forms of the landscape compose in its luscious chiaroscuro.' *Gosse* (1882)   (11)

Ondaatje or his source take this definition from the *OED*, though he changes Claude-Lorrain glass into 'claude glass.' The example is from Edmund Gosse's biography of Thomas Gray, though it is also worth recalling *Father and Son*, Gosse's classic 1907 memoir of his troubled relationship with his Calvinist father. I read this allusion as a reminder not only that *Secular Love* is art but that its view of the past is coloured, darkened in this case, by the poet's subjectivity. In other words, there are other ways of interpreting and writing about what happened. The first section, set at night, is pervaded by images of merging, drowning, darkness, disappearance, and drunkenness. This is the book's dark night of the soul, the son's rewriting in personal terms of the father's breakdown in 'Letters & Other Worlds' and *Running in the Family.* At once, it's an apology, an *hommage*, and the beginning of another story in which the central character – described here only as 'he' – is shown at a party on a farm, surrounded by family and friends, and inexplicably but inexorably drinking himself into oblivion. A disturbing point of departure for the love story to follow, it sketches in a suggestive emotional landscape of unfocused discontent and undefined anxiety and pain. It leaves the reader wondering why the central figure feels like an intruder, drinks so heavily, imagines drowning, and longs for the darkness of the surrounding fields. The answers can be inferred from the mood and from some of the details that inevitably recall his divorced parents. For anyone who has read *Running in the Family*, it is difficult not to see the father's behaviour there echoed or recalled in the son's in the poem's opening lines:

> He is told about
> the previous evening's behaviour.
>
> Starting with a punchbowl
> on the volleyball court.
> Dancing and falling across coffee tables,
> asking his son Are *you* the bastard
> who keeps telling me I'm drunk?
> kissing the limbs of women
> suspicious of his friends serenading
> five pigs by the barn
> heaving a wine glass towards garden
> and continually going through gates
> into the dark fields
> and collapsing.
> His wife half carrying him home
> rescuing him from departing cars,
> complains this morning
> of a sore shoulder.   (13)

If one reads these lines immediately after reading *Running in the Family*, it is tempting to think that 'he' must refer to Mervyn Ondaatje. But while the subject is the son, various images from the memoir as well as from 'Letters & Other Worlds' make the father the section's absent presence. References to letters, drowning, dark fields, and the closing couplet's 'absolute clarity' bring the distant past into the present by means of textual self-quotation. Another small linking detail: the son serenades five pigs; the father held five black dogs suspended by the leashes. And since *Secular Love* begins with the breakup of a marriage and of a family – note the early references to the wife and children – it's appropriate that 'Claude Glass' also calls to mind Doris Gratiaen

Ondaatje by alluding to 'Light,' her elegy. I'm thinking here of the home movie shown in 'Claude Glass' and the photos in the elegy.

> On the front lawn a sheet
> tacked across a horizontal branch.
> a projector starts a parade
> of journeys, landscapes, relatives,
> friends leaping out within pebbles of water
> caught by the machine as if creating rain.   (16–17)

Somewhere behind this image is the memory of the opening stanza of 'Light':

> Midnight storm. Trees walking off across the fields in fury
> naked in the spark of lightning.
> I sit on the white porch on the brown hanging cane chair
> coffee in my hand midnight storm midsummer night.
> The past, friends and family, drift into the rain shower.
> Those relatives in my favourite slides
> re-shot from old minute photographs so they now stand
> complex ambiguous grainy on my wall.   (*TTK*, 105)

The effect of these echoes is to situate the present story in the richly layered cross-currents of the family history, with its inheritance of other 'secular loves,' including those, like Ondaatje's parents,' that ended in divorce. When the sheet on which the home movies are being shown 'collapses like powder in the grass / pictures fly without target,' one suspects that the scattering of the images hints at the confusion in the speaker's mind, almost as if the breakup of the family pictures anticipates or reflects his own thoughts and feelings about his immediate family. At moments like this, one feels the etymological pressure of *saeculum* – the period of one human generation – within 'secular.' The adjective now has the spatial force of 'belonging to the present or material world' (*OED*) and the temporal implication that love is time-bound.

In a very suggestive shift, the white sheet reappears when 'At 4 a.m. he wakes in the sheet / that earlier held tropics in its whiteness' (18). It's not yet a winding sheet, but the suggestion of death and dying, introduced with the mention of a 'friend who said he would find / the darkest place, and then wave' (14) and the comment 'This is the hour /

when dead men sit / and write each other' (17), is now capped with the closing oneiric vision of a house slowly invaded by the neighbouring river. Paradoxically, drowning is described here in positive terms, a metaphor for the sleep available to everyone except him since he knows what they don't – that he's leaving. It is one of several constitutive images of doubling and separation in this first part. It's tempting to think that this drowning scene is a refashioning of scenes of drowning in 'Heron Rex,' *Coming through Slaughter*, or 'The Passions of Lalla' in *Running in the Family*. But it's possible that they all may owe something to a passage from William Faulkner's *Absalom, Absalom!* quoted in the thesis on Edwin Muir: 'The destiny of Sutpen's family which for twenty years now had been like a lake welling from quiet springs into a quiet valley ... and in which the four members of it floated in sunny suspension, felt like the first subterranean movement toward the outlet ... and the four peaceful swimmers turning suddenly to face one another, not yet with alarm and distrust but just alert, feeling the dark sea, none of them yet at that point where man looks at his companions in disaster and thinks *when will I stop trying to save them and save myself?*'[9]

The transition to 'Tin Roof,' the second section of the book, is made with another monitory epigraph, this time from Elmore Leonard, in which a male speaker tells a woman, 'I'm trying to tell you how I feel without exposing myself' (21). It's almost as if the writer feels himself pulled in two directions. On the one hand is his reluctance to write confessionally; on the other is the complex need to write as openly as possible about the fate of love. The section is made up of individual, often quite spare lyrics connected by the first-person speaker, subjective syntax, recurrent images, the setting, and his situation. He is now living alone in a sparsely furnished cabin somewhere on the Pacific Rim – probably Hawaii – trying to come to terms with what has happened. It isn't clear yet whether he has left his wife and family, but we are given a handful of details about the other woman: 'Here's to / the long legged / woman from Kansas / whispering good morning at 5, / dazed / in balcony moonlight' (38). For the most part, however, she, like the family, remains an absent presence, image, and memory that the speaker isn't quite certain he can cope with, since remembering in his situation is an act with inevitable moral complications.

Writing about his situation, he regularly finds himself envying a slightly idealized Rainer Maria Rilke – his life was less calm than Ondaatje implies – who becomes almost a tutelary angelic spirit, a poet capable of the calm and wisdom unavailable to the speaker. He reappears in Rainier beer (27), with 'the bird whistling *duino*' (31), and with a line from *Duino Elegies* (II.30) that serves as a title for a poem (50). In a refrain that brings some unity to the section, the speaker longs to be able to write *and* be happy. The early parenthetical comment – '(Do you want / to be happy and write?)' (27) – reappears ten pages later as another parenthetical sentence: ('Ah you should be happy and write') (37). The last poem in the section begins by referring to Rilke's 'calm' (43) but concedes a few lines later, in a quotation from one of his letters, that even the dead '"howl[ed] at the moon / with all my heart."' Even the angels of the *Duino Elegies* can offer no sense of transcendence since the speaker, conflating them with the woman he loves, is ambivalent about whether they are 'seraph or bitch' (23) or 'angel' or 'witch' (37). The best he can hope for is luck, not tranquillity or happiness: 'No I am not happy / lucky though' (37). Hovering somewhere behind the musings on the choice between happiness and writing are the well-known lines from Yeats's 'The Choice': 'The intellect of man is forced to choose / Perfection of the life, or of the work, / And if it take the second must refuse / a heavenly mansion, raging in the dark.'

We read the second section's lyrics always aware of the opening poem's startling closing couplet: 'This last year I was sure / I was going to die' (23). It both calls to mind Sylvia Plath, Anne Sexton, and John Berryman and recalls a major motif in 'Claude Glass' before taking on different permutations in this section. References to falling to pieces or breaking down will climax in the calm words about suicide that also inevitably look back to 'Heron Rex,' 'White Dwarfs,' and Buddy Bolden.

> so one is able now
> in ideal situations
> to plot a stroll
> to new continents
> 'doing the Berryman walk'
>
> And beneath the sea
> there are
> these giant scratches
> of pain
> the markings of
> some perfect animal

who has descended
burying itself
under the glossy
ballroom   (36)

The impersonality of these lines, like the second-person pronoun with which the section opens, is a good example of how Ondaatje maintains some detachment and control over material that otherwise might be overwhelming. Suicide here is presented obliquely, first through the image of John Berryman stopping on a railway bridge, waving to distant strangers, and then jumping, and then almost too metaphorically as 'some perfect animal' that has escaped pain by burying itself (and, it is worth noting, has left behind a record of its life – 'these giant scratches / of pain'). This is Buddy Bolden territory, but the speaker is Ondaatje.

If death is one possibility, renunciation offers another, and Ondaatje explores it in a bittersweet and darkly playful poem, the penultimate one of the group, in which he reimagines his situation by way of some of his favourite movies. Casting himself as Humphrey Bogart and his lover as Ingrid Bergman, he imagines Rick six months after he renounced Ilsa.

I see him lying under the fan
at the Slavyansky Bazar Hotel

and soon he will see the truth
he'll see it in the space
between the whirling metal.

　　　Stupid fucker
he says to himself, stupid fucker
and knocks the bottle
leaning against his bare stomach
onto the sheet.   (40)

Having committed himself to the woman from Kansas, the speaker now imagines himself as a Bogart (or 'Rick') who, after Ilsa's departure, realizes that he has made the mistake of his life in letting her go. Since there is no 'Slavyansky Bazar Hotel' in the film *Casablanca*, it's worth pausing over this detail. There is, however, such a hotel in Moscow in Chekhov's 'The Lady with the Little Dog,' and it is where the story's adulterous lovers meet when Anna Serghéyevna comes to Moscow to visit Dmitry Dmitrych Goorov. In contrast to Rick, the two, though married to others, find almost complete fulfillment at the Slavyansky: 'Anna Serghéyevna and he loved with the love that only the closest affinity can achieve, the love of husband and wife, of tender friends ... [they] felt that this love of theirs had changed them both.'[10] The allusions to the film and the story create a complex web of adulterous references and comparisons in which the situation of the poem's two lovers is juxtaposed to and therefore compared with the following relationships: Rick and Ilsa in the film; Rick and Ilsa as they might have been; Anna and Dmitry as they are; Anna and Dmitry as they might have been, had they separated from their partners; the poet's former relationship with his wife.

Having imagined himself as he might be if he renounced this love, the speaker then turns, in a complex shift the full moral and emotional force of which isn't felt until the last line, to another film, *Trapeze*. Our first response is that this is another example of a romantic triangle – Burt Lancaster, Tony Curtis, and Gina Lollobrigida. But Ondaatje adapts the image of the acrobats – already associated with the Ondaatjes in *Running in the Family* – in a surprising way.

> What about Burt Lancaster
> limping away at the end of *Trapeze*?
> Born in 1943. And I saw that six times.
>
> ....
>
> So how do we discuss
> the education of our children?
> Teach them to be romantics
> to veer towards the sentimental?
> Toss them into the air like Tony Curtis
> and make 'em do the triple somersault
> through all these complexities
> and commandments?   (41)

Nothing in the poem prepares us – 'how do *we* discuss' – for the return of the children or for the moral authority of 'commandments,' the breaking of which makes a romantic way of life possible, but which also introduces dangerous complexities in one's relationship with one's children. Anyone tossed 'into the air' might fall, as we are reminded by Lancaster's limp.[11] The poem ends with a question mark

– after all, we know that there is no adequate answer – but Ondaatje will return to the situation in one of the book's finest lyrics, 'To a Sad Daughter.'

The section itself is equally open-ended. The previously mentioned closing lyric – 'Oh Rilke, I want to sit down calm like you' – is dominated by the wish for order – the map image – and peace and for a poetry embodying these.

> I wanted poetry to be walnuts
> in their green cases
> but now it is the sea
> and we let it drown us,
> and we fly to it released
> by giant catapults
> of pain loneliness deceit and vanity   (43)

The past tense of the opening verb alerts us to what we won't find at this point in *Secular Love*, while the implied passivity of 'let' and 'fly' shows the self overwhelmed by the four feelings and attitudes unsparingly hammered home at the close. I find it difficult not to think that 'vanity' is a judgment on himself – the man judging the poet – for writing about these aspects of his life.

The next section of the book, the two-part 'Rock Bottom,' is both the dark night of the soul and the turn towards the speaker's new life. The first-person lyrics offer various perspectives on the situation, varying in mood from the nearly despairing to the humorous. The section's disjunct poems hang together as tenuously and desperately as the self that speaks them. They seem to function like a journal in which the writer tries not only to record and make sense of what is happening around him but to control the events by reimagining them as poetry. Reading them, I kept thinking of Jorie Graham's previously quoted 'Mother of Vinegar,' in which she suggests that 'contained damage makes for beauty.' My sense is that, for the most part, Ondaatje's concern is with containment, with achieving a momentary stay against confusion. The poems repeatedly hint at order, mapping, focus, and peace even as they show a self with a tenuous hold on reality and occasionally even on the verge of dissolution. They are almost apotropaic gestures against the confusion and pain that the speaker knows are inevitable. At one point he reminds us that sometimes poetry can make something happen:

Reading Neruda to a class
reading his lovely old
curiosity about all things
I am told this is the first time
in months I seem happy.
Jealous of his slide
through complexity.
All afternoon I keep
stepping into his pocket

        whispering
instruct and delight me   (78)

As so often, the lines seem simpler than they are. We are so accustomed to the speaker's almost uninflected voice and the poetry's refusal of coloratura effects that it's easy to overlook the ways in which the poems 'delight' one. Notice in the above quotation how the prosaic quality of the grammatically complete first sentence gives way to the easy music and understated figurative language of the remainder of the verse. Particularly impressive and effortless is the use of l's and s's to hold the lines together: 'curiosity ... jealous ... slide ... complexity ... whispering.' The closing phrase – 'instruct and delight me' – may simultaneously be a disguised question. Since it's another way of saying *utile et dulce*, I wonder whether he's concerned about *his* poem's effect on his readers: can poetry of this kind 'instruct and delight'? In lines such as these one senses an attempt to impose order on and to find beauty in material that is resistant to both expectations. Though a decade has passed since *Rat Jelly* (1973), some of the questions raised in that collection – especially in the title poem and 'King Kong meets Wallace Stevens' – are still pertinent. In fact, the dark and fragmented opening poem of 'Rock Bottom' looks over its shoulder, so to speak, both at 'Rat Jelly' and 'Letters & Other Worlds' (and, by implication, *Running in the Family*).

2 a.m. The moonlight
in the kitchen

Will this be
testamentum porcelli?
Unblemished art and truth

whole hog the pig's statement
what I know of passion
having written of it
seen my dog shiver
with love and disappear
crazy into trees

        I want

the woman whose face
I could not believe in the moonlight
her mouth forever as horizon

        and both of us
grim with situation

now
suddenly
we reside
near the delicate
heart
of Billie Holiday   (47)

The sardonic humour of 'Rat Jelly' is replaced here by irony and the near self-contempt evident in 'the pig's testament.' More precisely, it's the testament of a *porcellum*, or little pig. There must be a hint here – and it's strengthened by the echo of *Running in the Family* in 'disappear / crazy into trees' – of a big pig, so to speak, of the father. His testament we have already read in 'Letters & Other Worlds' and in the memoir. In both generations the question remains whether one can make 'unblemished art' out of 'truth / whole hog'? The book as a whole seems to answer that one can't. The closing reference to Billie Holiday is also a reminder about the connection in certain kinds of art – think of *Coming through Slaughter* – between truth, suffering, and creativity. The singer sang the truth about 'passion' in her art but, like Bolden, might be said to have died of it. Unlike Neruda, neither she nor the poet can 'slide / through complexity.'

In this case, the complexity includes both his pain and his wife's, and it is a measure of the complexity and honesty of the self-presentation that he repeatedly sees beyond himself. The reference to 'both of us / grim with situation' anticipates the more specific delineation in 'Speaking to you':

Everyone has learned
to move carefully

'Dancing' 'laughing' 'bad taste'
is a memory
a tableau behind trees of law

In the midst of love for you
my wife's suffering
anger in every direction
and the children wise,
as tough shrubs
but they are not tough
– so I fear
how anything can grow from this   (77)

To be frank, I'm not sure what 'bad taste' refers to, or what Ondaatje is getting at with the suggestive figure of 'a tableau behind trees of law,' unless the first line recalls events between the lovers that are now simply a memory screened 'behind trees of law,' that is, behind the 'commandments' and the legal working out of his situation? If the 'tableau' does indeed refer to the lovers, then it anticipates the temporary sense of order that the section closes with in '(Ends of the Earth).' Here the woman from Wichita – note the echo of 'seraph or bitch' (23) and 'angel to witch' (37) – and the man from Canada reduce the compass of the world to make their lives manageable in a trope that brings Donne to mind:

We grow less complex
We reduce ourselves   The way lovers
have their small cheap charms
silver lizard,
a stone

Ancient customs
that grow from dust
swirled out
from prairie into tropic

Strange how the odours meet

How, however briefly, bedraggled
history
            focusses   (83)

Here history is reduced to or focused around the story of their love
affair. For the moment, nothing else exists. This is as strong an affirmation as the book makes before what might be called the 'look, we have
come through' poems of the fourth section, 'Skin Boat.'
    The final section is more open and varied in styles and concerns than
any of its predecessors, as if indicating that the speaker is able again to
turn his attention to aspects of his life other than those connected with
the love affair. That each poem has a title and many end with a period
is another sign of recovery in so far as it indicates a return of some
detachment and control. The events and lyrics in the earlier sections
seemed to flow into and out of one another as if indicating that the
speaker, the fragile controlling intelligence and voice, couldn't keep
them separate, but was overwhelmed by what was happening to him in
life and in mind. There are fewer hoverings, doubts, and doublings back
in the final section than in the first three, even though it does attempt tentative summaries and conclusions to several of the book's major concerns. It is also the section in which the woman from Kansas is most
prominent. Two of the poems – 'Her House' and '7 or 8 Things I Know
About Her / A Stolen Biography' – offer an eccentric, capsule biography
as idiosyncratic in its genre as *Running in the Family.* Nowhere does the
section offer a full-length portrait; instead we get glimpses of shoulders,
legs, mouth, hair, and the 'skin boat' that is her stomach. The poet
chooses to record only what is important to him, though he makes it clear
that his acceptance of her previous life and his love are unconditional.

Kissing the stomach
kissing your scarred
skin boat. History
is what you've travelled on
and take with you

We've each had our stomachs
kissed by strangers
to the other

and as for me
I bless everyone
who kissed you here   (81)

A scar, as we know from even the earliest poems, is one of Ondaatje's signature words, like chaos, nets, drowning, darkness, wounds, a dark room, and ceremony. It is literally memory incarnate, an inscription that recalls an event in one's life that has left its runic mark. His scars are found poems in which the gaps between past and present and events and words have been elided.

The woman's introduction into the narrative and the confirmation of their love seem to liberate the speaker to affirm other important relationships, other kinds of love. 'Pacific Letter' and 'The Concessions,' for instance, celebrate the love of friends: 'I do not know what to say / about this kind of love / but I refuse to lose it' (111). The gentle, genial 'Pacific Letter' similarly celebrates friendship and, by the way, shows Ondaatje's ability to deal with the domestic emotions of the middle range. It recalls, 'After separation had come to its worst / we met and travelled the Mazinaw with my sons / through all the thirty-six folds of that creature river / into the valley of bright lichen' (100). (The 'thirty-six folds' are from Pound's 'Exile's Letter.') Two Sri Lankan poems that had previously appeared in *Running in the Family* – 'The Cinnamon Peeler' and 'Women like You' – broaden the context of the discussion of passion and love to imagined situations in ancient and modern Sri Lanka in a style that is at once colloquial and hieratic. As well, they call attention to the relationship between the memoir and *Secular Love*. 'Proust in the Waters' and 'Birch Bark' – two of the last three poems – celebrate a unity in and with the landscape and envision a preconscious and pre-verbal way of being in the world in which one strives 'to know the syllables / in a loon sentence' (122). Most poignant is the love poem 'To a Sad Daughter,' which inevitably reminds us of what preceded this final section's poems of fulfillment.

Also worth noting in this context is the increase in references to various kinds of songs, but especially love songs such as 'Prisoner of Love' and Bessie Smith's 'Any Woman's Blues,' which refract this particular version of 'secular love' through earlier ones. Rock songs, blues, folk songs, ballads, and waltzes as well as singers such as Dewey Wilson, Frank Sinatra, Billie Holiday, Bessie Smith, and Fats Waller are all part of a richly layered set of cultural references giving the central story a cultural history, depth, and resonance. They accomplish on the aural level what the references to films achieve on the visual. By introducing fragments of other love stories, they not only comment implicitly on this one, but they also distract the reader, however momentarily, from the nearly claustrophobic and potentially solipsistic narrative of the first three sections.

A similar broadening of perspective occurs in 'Women like You' (90–2), in which the speaker's lover seems present only in the second person singular and is presented from the perspective of the Sigiri Graffiti in Sri Lanka. The poem combines sentences from several of the graffiti, inscribed on a cliff face below depictions of women, with the speaker's own words that simultaneously evoke the graffiti, describe the paintings, and celebrate his love for her. Since the cover reproduces a section of the paintings, the poem has an ekphrastic dimension. Lovers past and present are compared in a contemporary love poem that draws on ancient verses written with 'an alphabet / whose motive was perfect desire.' The motif will return in the book's final movement. Through the haiku-like middle section there is an ambiguity about the referent of the 'you' that allows one to read the stanzas as being addressed either to the women on the Sri Lankan cliff or his lover or both.[12]

Seeing you
I want no other life
and turn around
to the sky
and everywhere below
jungle, waves of heat
secular love

Though Sigiriya isn't quite a holy place, there is a teasing combination of the sacred and the profane in the unusual use of 'secular' in this context that lends the scene and the passage an aura it would otherwise lack. With impressive, if spare, word-painting, Ondaatje evokes these figures with a handful of sometimes borrowed words – 'the golden / drunk swan breasts / lips / the long long eyes' – as a prelude that amounts to a prayer-offering which looks towards the women painted on the cliff face and backward to his absent lover.

I bring you

a flute
from the throat
of a loon

so talk to me
of the used heart

There is an almost Eastern sense of form as something organic developing out of the aural and rhythmic relationships not only between words ('you ... flute ... throat ... 'loon') but also between the protracting and pregnant silences of white spaces. I doubt that I'm the only reader who also hears *lonely* in 'loon' and *abused* in 'used.'

Two earlier poems, slightly indebted to Pound, remind us that Ondaatje is working in a long poetic tradition in which poems in English grow out of lines or fragments of Asian originals. The author's comment on 'The River Neighbour' and 'Pacific Letter' is worth keeping in mind when reading his own imitations: 'Two poems ... are based on Rihaku – Tu Fu – Pound poems. They are not so much translations as re-locations into my landscape, the earlier poets making their appearance in these poems' ([128]). I suspect that like his other 're-locations,' including those in *Handwriting* (1998), these also owe much to the example of W.S. Merwin's translations of classical Sanskrit love poems.[13] The better-known and much anthologized 'The Cinnamon Peeler' is a good example of a different use of an Eastern setting and material. Important here is the nearly timeless, universal story of frustrated desire and love painted with a South Asian palette that mirrors the speaker's love for 'the long-legged woman from Kansas.' That the status of the love affair is problematic is suggested by the verbs in the poem's first line: 'If I were a cinnamon peeler / I would ride your bed' (88). If you *weren't* married, we *would* be together even now?

'To a Sad Daughter' (95–7) is a very different kind of love poem, tense with memory, affection, and anxiety. It is the only poem in this closing section to recall, if only obliquely, the separation and the breakup of the family; these are the withheld, unspoken events that on first reading we expect to appear at some point in the lyric. The presence of 'daughter' in the title and the mention of 'cuts and wounds' in the first stanza raise the expectation that the specifics of this family romance can't be avoided. When they don't appear, I suspect that we feel both disappointment and relief. Yet in retrospect it's obvious that

Ondaatje doesn't have to refer to the poem's 'history,' since he can take it for granted that, whether mentioned or not, it will inform every reading. Keeping the past in reserve, so to speak, is more effective than making it explicit. As well, rereading the poem, we become aware that the past is there in images within it: *Casablanca*, swimming and drowning, blood, ceremonies, breaking down, masks.

The poem is a confessional dramatic monologue of concern and advice. Though calm and restrained, it is tense with anxiety because of the implied family situation, which adds an even more ominous dimension to the images of darkness, violence, breaking, blood, and threat. Even a seemingly trivial detail such as the fact that the sixteen-year-old daughter is 'sleeping in [a] tracksuit' carries the possible implications that she's distraught to the point that she no longer changes for bed and/or that she wants to flee the situation. The tracksuit isn't mentioned again, but I assume that most readers recall it when a page later the father advises her, 'If you break / break going out not in.' The sentence becomes even more sombre when we recall from earlier in the poem that he and she share 'purple' moods and that he tends to 'ride / the ceremonies / until they grow dark.' The slightly later comment that 'each / one we know is / in our blood' is potentially equally ominous when we think of the bloodlines running from *Running in the Family* through *Secular Love*. Farther back in time we also recall that Ondaatje had juxtaposed in *Rat Jelly* a poem about comforting his son 'sweating after nightmares' ('Griffin of the night') and his elegy for his father. At every turn in the poem, the speaker's calm tone is undermined by images carrying menacing associations from his other work. For example, when he affirms, 'I'll sell my arms for you, / hold your secrets forever,' I recall Buddy Bolden's anxieties about his children and his desire to stretch out his right arm into the fan circling overhead in N. Joseph's Shaving Parlour (*CTS*, 47).

But the speaker is also anxious about his daughter's attitude to him. He doesn't say so, but it can be sensed in two of the images he uses to present himself. The first is of 'the belligerent goalie' in the hockey poster (Ken Danby's *At the Crease*, [1972]?) above her bed.[14] It reappears a few stanzas later as an 'angry' goalie and then closes the poem in the following lines: 'Your goalie / in his frightening mask / dreams perhaps / of gentleness.' The speaker is never directly identified with the goalie – though he is a 'sentinel' in 'Claude Glass' – but the imagery associates him with the creature from the black lagoon, which in turn is associated with 'angry goalies':

One day I'll come swimming
beside your ship or someone will
and if you hear the siren
listen to it. For if you close your ears
only nothing happens. You will never change.

I don't care if you risk
your life to angry goalies
creatures with webbed feet.
You can enter their caves and castles
their glass laboratories. Just
don't be fooled by anyone but yourself.

If I read these lines correctly, they imply that the daughter is afraid of the father at this point, even though he's on some level a defender of the goal (= home) and a friendly, if repulsive, creature (from the black lagoon). If he's a goalie, then we know that he has deserted his goal, which figuratively includes her room. And despite his love, he seems aware that he might seem to represent a danger to her ('if you hear the siren'); otherwise why would the siren go off? But 'siren' also brings the suggestion of the sirens singing to Odysseus and prepares us for his warning that 'if you close your ears / only nothing happens.' It's possible to interpret his advice that she be open to change and that she 'Want everything' as an implicit justification of his recent action of deserting the goal. This richly textured poem contains one other reminder of what he has left behind in a stanza that recalls one of Ondaatje's early poems about his first wife, 'Billboards,' in which he sits at the same table as his wife previously sat and writes with a pen that still carries her smell. In 'To a Sad Daughter' this image becomes 'One afternoon I stepped / into your room. You were sitting / at the desk where I now write this.' In the earlier poem he imagines his wife's world; in this one he recalls his daughter's before he irrevocably changed it. In the midst of familial chaos, she was 'busy with mathematics' – busy, in other words, trying to maintain a space of ordered clarity.

The references to death in the final stanza pertain as much to him as they do to her, even though he says that it is something 'you fear now, greatly.' Similarly ambiguous is the assertion 'Memory is permanent,' which, if probed, reminds us that not only will they not forget the love between them but also that they will be unable to forget how his desertion threatened it. In this respect the poem is a gesture by a gentle father who seems to be wearing a 'frightening mask' – he has changed – even as he prays for 'gentleness' for and from his daughter. If Ondaatje does indeed introduce himself and his emotions into the poem through these tropes, I suspect he does so in order to avoid what might seem like a self-dramatizing and perhaps sentimental self-regard. Instead of a subjective and direct statement about his feelings, he enacts those attitudes, feelings, and judgments in metaphors charged with ambiguity and ambivalence.

This is the most intense and emotionally ambivalent of the poems in 'Skin Boat.' Those that follow feel like a peaceful stretch of water after one that always seems on the verge of turning into rapids. The wry, playful humour of 'Translations of my Postcards' signals the shift, as does the inevitable Ondaatje dog poem, 'A Dog in San Francisco.' The various lyrics are still recognizably part of a sequence, but they also have a greater formal integrity and aren't as dependent on the poems around them for their meaning. The understated closing poem, 'Escarpment,' is set up by two landscape poems – 'Proust in the Waters' and 'Birch Bark' – each of which hints at a prelinguistic state of being in which the self and landscape fuse. 'Proust in the Waters' (122–3) seems to me perfect except for its title. It evokes a peaceful nighttime swim during which the unidentified swimmer muses on the possibility of knowing 'the syllables / in a loon sentence / intricate / shift of preposition / that signals meridian / west south west.' Earlier lines recall other scenes with water imagery and drowning; the crucial difference here, however, is that the swimmer imagines both the dive and the confident return from the depths: 'We love things which disappear / and are found / creatures who plummet / and become / an arrow.' I assume that the creatures – including the speaker, who never uses the first-person pronoun – 'become / an arrow' because, like him, they know their target or goal. That the swimmer reaches his goal is apparent from the brief and anonymous exchange of words that closes the lyric: '*Where are you?* / *On the edge* / *of the moon bar.*'

'Birch Bark' (124) – dedicated to George Whalley – brings back the memory of earlier storms and reaffirms affection and friendship in a peaceful canoe ride. Its closing phrase – 'after storm' – could easily be the epigraph to 'Escarpment,' the book's last poem. In *The Cinnamon Peeler* Ondaatje reverses the order of the last two poems. Since I prefer the original version, I'll treat 'Escarpment' as the book's terminus. The sequence closes, as it opened, with a framing prose piece (125–6), which seems to me one of Ondaatje's finest prose poems; where the first focused on the woman, this one shows the two of them exploring a creek 'which has no name.' Like the book's first section, this one is narrated in the third person, and it opens with the male character awake at four in the morning, a scene that recalls a similar sleepless night at the book's start. This one is different, however, because it shows him recalling the previous day's walk through the local countryside and in 'the body' of the river. And though the poem doesn't refer to the past or to the earlier scenes, several echoes and allusions inevitably bring them to the margins of the text and of the reader's mind. It is almost too fortuitous that he 'walks through in an old pair of Converse running shoes' – in 'Walking to Bellrock' they were Adidas – since this is a scene of implicit converse between past and present which is also a converse (exact opposite) of the past. In sentences whose halting trajectory mimics the clotted riverbank and his stumbling progress, we watch as he explores the water while remaining aware of her presence nearby. Though they are finally together, we are subtly reminded that, in a manner of speaking, they are in an unmapped country. The creek is without a name – he thinks of calling it 'Heart Creek? Arm River?' – and musing on it, he also begins to want 'a name for them, something temporary for their vocabulary. A code.' The idea is quietly reiterated in the fact that when they sit together, they talk about 'relatives, books, best friends, the history of Lewis and Clark.' Similarly, the pattern that the sun creates on the shore is a 'crossword.' Though separate, they remain mysteriously joined; she may be absent, but we know that he is thinking that 'there are not many ways he can tell her he loves her.' But she is also a felt presence because the poem subtly insinuates a connection between the landscape, especially the river, and her body. Three times the narrator describes the river as a 'body,' and the twice-mentioned 'cedar root' that saves him from being swept away is twice compared to 'her forearm.' The passage doesn't say that she has saved him, but it does remind us of earlier scenes in which he felt loss and had intimations of drowning, especially a stanza in 'Rock Bottom' in which he tells her, 'At night / I give you my hand / like a corpse / out of the water' (52). The cumulative effect of all this is to leave one with a sense of an ending offering formal and thematic completion – affirmation, confirmation, and a quality of what might be called secular grace.

To recall Lawrence and Frieda, they have come through.

CANON II

One of the more interesting moments in Ondaatje's interview with Eleanor Wachtel occurs in the following exchange:

> EW: You don't write much about Canada, except for your last novel and some of your poetry. Does that say something about your sense of self here?
>
> MO: I think I write quite a lot about Canada. I don't write essays or portraits of Canada, but a lot of what I felt about the country went into *In the Skin of a Lion*, and most of my poetry is about the landscape around me, the people and emotions around me. I don't sense that I'm avoiding it.
>
> EW: Do you feel Canadian?
>
> MO: I feel Canadian. As a writer I feel very Canadian. I became a writer here.[1]

Ondaatje may feel 'very Canadian,' but the fact remains that, with the one named exception, all his longer works and two of his sequences of poetry are not set in Canada. It's as if his imagination needs stories and landscapes that on some deep level mimic his sense of estrangement and displacement in a way that Canada, with which he is now familiar, can't. This doesn't make him any less Canadian than a writer such as Rudy Wiebe, whose work almost always deals with Canadian subjects, though it does mean that he's a different kind of Canadian writer, with his own rooms in a different wing of the mansion of CanLit.

In future discussions of the canon he will be among those writers whose work doesn't reflect the national-referential aesthetic that was central in defining the canon until the early 1970s, whose last signifi-

cant body of work is Al Purdy's poetry and whose last critical monu-
ment is *Survival*. It's arguable that Ondaatje's critical success with *The
Collected Works of Billy the Kid*, *Rat Jelly*, and *Coming through Slaughter*
was the moment when the definition of the Canadian canon became
problematic. Almost single-handedly, he introduced postmodernism,
post-colonialism, and multiculturalism into the discussion. I'm not
suggesting that there were no other writers whose work was considered 'pomo' or 'poco' in the late sixties and through the seventies. I'm
simply saying that none had produced a body of work of sufficient
originality and stature to cause a seismic shift in the Canadian field.
Atwood seems to have sensed something of this when at the height of
her nationalist phase she defended omitting Ondaatje from *Survival* –
though she discusses his anthology of animal poems *The Broken Ark* –
on the grounds 'It seems to me dangerous to talk about "Canadian"
patterns of sensibility in the work of people who entered and/or
entered-and-left the country at a developmentally late stage of their
lives.'[2] In other words, if Ondaatje is a 'Canadian' writer, his ways of
being and writing 'Canadian' will be different from Purdy's, Wiebe's,
or Atwood's. Neither in 1972 nor thirty years later could his work find
a place in *Survival*. The stress of the national, whether social or historical, simply isn't there.

   That Ondaatje is aware of this difference, especially in his early
work, seems to me indicated by his playful inclusion of Canadian content both in *The Collected Works of Billy the Kid* and *Coming through
Slaughter*. If challenged about the Canadianness of the former, he can
always point to the following from Billy's newspaper interview: 'Dancing I like. I'm a pretty good dancer. Fond of music too. There's a Canadian group, a sort of orchestra, that is the best. Great. Heard them often
when I was up there trying to get hold of a man who went by the name
of Captain P——.* Never found him. But that group will be remembered a long time' (84). This is the book's Canada Council moment.
Referring to bp Nichol, the Guy Lombardo of sound poetry, Ondaatje
bows in the direction of Canadian content, reassuring those, like the
Conservative member of Parliament, who doubted his suitability for a
Governor General's Award. He repeats the gesture of a national signature in *Coming through Slaughter* with Buddy's 'elaborated long seduc-
tions usually culminating in the story of Miss Jessie Orloff's famous
incident in a Canadian hotel during her last vacation' (12). It's as if he's
saying, If you want this sort of obvious Canadian content, I'll give it to
you, but let's get it over early, the way that Hitchcock drifts through an

early scene in a film. What he doesn't reveal is that Miss Jessie Orloff is a screen for Jayne Mansfield.

Ondaatje's situation as a Canadian writer whose work has achieved canonical status becomes slightly more complicated if we notice that his fiction is now being taught on courses devoted to Sri Lankan fiction in English. And after *Handwriting* it won't be long before he begins to appear in anthologies of contemporary Sri Lankan poetry. Yet whether thought of as Canadian or as Sri Lankan, he's an isolated and nearly autochthonous figure in both cultures: influenced by writers in neither country and without obvious influence on the next generation.

I'll leave it to the literary historians to sort it out. To paraphrase Voltaire on God, *C'est leur métier.*

Handwriting

The Poetry of Return

There are partings which are like deaths.

François Truffaut[1]

Asia. The name was a gasp from a dying mouth. An ancient word that had to be whispered, would never be used as a battle cry. The word sprawled. It had none of the clipped sound of Europe, America, Canada. The vowels took over, slept on the map with the S. I was running to Asia and everything would change.

RF, 22

Fourteen years separate *Secular Love* and *Handwriting*, and it would be difficult to name two volumes of poetry published in succession by the same author that differ as obviously and as much as these do. *Handwriting* shows that Ondaatje has wrestled with his early figuratively congested style to produce lyrics that are as spare, short, and lapidary as Sanskrit love poems or the Sigiri Graffiti. The difference is as dramatic as that between early and late Montale or Merwin. Where *Secular Love* has obvious affinities with the tradition of poetry in English, its successor alludes, from the opaque title of its first poem on – 'A Gentleman Compares His Virtue to a Piece of Jade' – to a completely different tradition. Where the former shows Ondaatje at his most subjective, romantic, and nearly confessional, the latter reveals an impersonal, classical, almost hieratic poetry in which the poet's self has disappeared either into a communal voice – 'we' – or into anonymity. Still, there are some connections and residual traces of the earlier work. The Sri Lankan poems in *Running in the Family* and *Secular Love* can now be seen as hinting at the direction Ondaatje's poetry would take. The book's title looks back to a comment in *Running in the Family* that the mother's handwriting had changed at thirty, 'as if at the age of thirty or so she had been blasted, forgotten how to write, lost the use of a habitual style and forced herself to cope with a new dark unknown alphabet' (150). There's also what I call his Francis Bacon moment, the telltale scene of 'Someone with fever / buried / in the darkness of a room' (13) that we have encountered in *The Collected Works of Billy the Kid, Coming through Slaughter, Running in the Family,* and *Secular Love.* And finally, though it is differently inflected, there is the continuing interest in the play between order and chaos, figured in *Handwriting* as maps and land, art and war.

Reading *Handwriting*, I almost have the impression that Ondaatje re-educated and reinvented himself as a poet in the years after *Secular Love* by immersing himself not only in Sri Lankan life and history (the signs of this encounter are also obvious in *Anil's Ghost*) but also in the classical traditions of Sanskrit, Sinhalese, and Tamil poetry and culture. Their influence can be seen in the subject matter, texture, and voice and even in the diction, where many of Ondaatje's earlier signature words now play a subordinate role to words drawn from Sri Lankan culture and history. It's therefore arguable that the Sinhalese Sigiri Graffiti, quoted earlier in 'Women like You,' are more relevant for a reading of *Handwriting* than are Stevens or Yeats or any contemporary poets writing in English. As a result, *Handwriting* is in many respects the most difficult of Ondaatje's books of poems, but since the difficulties are different in kind from those encountered in the most challenging of the earlier lyrics such as 'Letters & Other Worlds,' 'White Dwarfs,' or 'To a Sad Daughter,' the reader isn't immediately aware of them. In the poems named, we tend to pause when confronted with a trope tense with connotation or with too sudden a shift in poetic thought. Though these kinds of cruces are also present in *Handwriting*, the new collection creates a new kind of difficulty by hinting throughout that its poems owe more to the Sanskrit, Sinhalese, and Tamil traditions of poetry than they do to those in English. The reader often senses the pressure of another tradition or another level of significance or reference without being able to define it. The following verses from 'A Gentleman Compares His Virtue to a Piece of Jade' (3–5) are representative:

The enemy was always identified in art by a lion.
And in our Book of Victories

wherever you saw a parasol
on the battlefield you could
identify the king within its shadow.
We began with myths and later included actual events

The past tense in these and other verses ('We believed in ...') warns us that this way of being-in-the-world has either passed or is under threat. The emphasis here is on the general and the typical. The speaker remains unidentified, as does the community and way of life he evokes and addresses. As Rochelle Vigurs points out, 'The narrative voice is restrained, there is no sure direction or argument, and the emotional shading is subtle.'[2] The poem's catalogue of allegorical details – the majority of the images recur in the book – meanders without any particular order or direction for three pages, but it is always concerned with the figurative and sensory nature of art, its materiality ('The archaeology of cattle bells'), and the precariousness of creativity. Its closing image is of 'That tightrope-walker from Kurunegala / the generator shut down by insurgents // stood there / swaying in the darkness above us.' Though we don't know it yet, to be an artist in this world is to walk a tightrope in darkness and perhaps *into* darkness in order to risk a poem like this one about 'the intimate life, an inner self.' The 'gentleman' who speaks this poem alerts us to this reality even as he draws us into and selectively describes a culture radically different from our own, while simultaneously teaching us how to 'read' it. Vigurs's response to the title opens up several possibilities:

> If one were to attempt to ascribe a 'flavour' to 'A Gentleman Compares His Virtue to a Piece of Jade,' nostalgia might do. The formal diction of the title suggests the narrator is a member of the educated elite. If he were a [Sri Lankan] Burgher of Portuguese descent he might call his feeling, as he compares his virtue to a piece of jade, *saudade*, which translates loosely as nostalgia for the grandeur of the past, a kind of bittersweet melancholy, a pleasure from which one suffers. In contemplating his 'piece of jade,' the gentleman might be contemplating his own green island, its concurrent pleasures and sufferings captured, gem-like, simultaneously translucent and diffused ... [The poem] is a map to a distant country of the mind where poetic conventions and epistemological expectations will not be reliable guides.[3]

Reading a poem like this one reminded me of my first readings of

Arthur Waley's and Ezra Pound's translations. I knew that some aspects of the poems were simply inaccessible to me because I did not know anything about the conventions of classical Chinese poetry. I often sensed the pressure of a convention or a symbolism as elusive as it is felt. I'm not suggesting that Ondaatje's lyrics are translations in the narrow sense of the word. But the subject matter and the style do suggest that he is trying to get as close as he can, without knowing Tamil or Sinhalese, to the literary and cultural traditions he left behind when he emigrated, and to translate them for readers even less knowledgeable than he is.

We have to imagine the ambiguity of his situation after his return to Sri Lanka in 1978. We have to picture a writer who, having established himself in one language and in a particularly dominant literary tradition, now wants to belong as well to another culture and literature. Having finally returned, though as a visitor, he now finds himself wanting to write not only about the place that used to be his home but also from within it. But without access to either of the native languages, the best he can do is to forge a style *in English* that will evoke the now *foreign* language, poetry, and culture.[4] If one didn't know Ondaatje's other work, one might almost think that the book has been written by a Sri Lankan writer completely fluent in English. Interestingly enough, Ondaatje gives us an example, halfway through the book, of what a poem by such a bilingual poet might look like in "'All those poets as famous as kings'" (29):

Hora gamanak yana ganiyak	a woman who journeys to a tryst
kanakara nathuva	having no jewels,
kaluwan kes kalamba	darkness in her hair,
tharu piri ahasa	the sky lovely with its stars

These lines seem transparent, yet one can't help wondering whether a greater knowledge of Indian and Sri Lankan love poetry wouldn't reveal layers of significance unavailable to a reader primarily accustomed to European love poetry. To what extent does the classical distinction between 'love-in-enjoyment' and 'love-in-separation' come into play here? Or the theory of the nine *rasas*, or moods or flavours? It's also worth noting that this is the final poem of the first section. Its title, like the book as a whole, counterpoints poets and kings and, by extension, peace and war. It may also be a tacit reminder of the distinction in the classical tradition of Tamil poetry between *akam*, the poetry of the 'inner world,' and *pur̲am*, the poetry of action in which kings can be praised.[5] '"All those poets as famous as kings"' is, of course, precisely the sort of poem Ondaatje cannot write because he has lost – an important trope in the book – his mother tongue. He reminds us of this loss in the poem about 'my ayah Rosalin.'

> The last Sinhala word I lost
> was *vatura*.
> The word for water.
> Forest water. The water in a kiss. The tears
> I gave to my ayah Rosalin on leaving
> the first home of my life.
>
> More water for her than any other
> that fled my eyes again
> this year, remembering her,
> a lost almost-mother in those years
> of thirsty love.
>
> No photograph of her, no meeting
> since the age of eleven,
> not even knowledge of her grave.
>
> Who abandoned who, I wonder now.   (50)

The ambivalent feelings towards his father – 'who abandoned who' – reappear here in his third Sri Lankan elegy, in which *vatura*, the 'last Sinhala word' he lost, is a near homophone for father. Like 'Letters & Other Worlds' and 'Light,' this is simultaneously an elegy for a person and for 'the first home of my life.' It's worth noting that the three poems are completely different in style. This one is organized on the basis of images or motifs that recur throughout the book: water, forest, grave, flight, and disappearance. The struggle between remembering and forgetting is enacted even on the level of sound in the interplay of the s's and r's in 'this year, remembering her, / a lost almost-mother in those years / of thirsty love.' The elegy reminds us that the book is dedicated to Rosalin Perera. The dedication takes the form of a quotation from Robert Louis Stevenson's dedication of *A Child's Garden of Verses* to his 'ayah,' Alison Cunningham.

For the long nights you lay awake
  And watched for my unworthy sake:
For your most comfortable hand
  That led me through the uneven land ...[6]

If, on the one hand, this quatrain is part of a long-delayed tribute to an ayah, on the other, it also reminds us of the poetic tradition that Ondaatje is leaving behind him in writing *Handwriting*. Once we pass the dedication, most of our assumptions about genre, poetic kinds, and symbolism become irrelevant. Since the poems are written in English, it's obvious that we're not completely at sea, but it's also obvious as early as the Sinhalese words in the table of contents – Anuradhapura, Siyabaslakara – that some of our old maps, guides, and assumptions about poetry and reading will be useless. After Stevenson, the sequence successfully evades European literature with the exception of a line from Van Morrison (35), an allusion to Henry James (5), a reference to Thomas Merton (13), and three accidental and irrelevant echoes of Hesiod ('works and days'), Wordsworth's 'Intimations of Immortality' ('The Story'), and Milosz's 'Ode to a Bird' ('Death at Kataragama').

'The Story' (60–6) is also one of the few occasions on which Ondaatje speaks in his own voice. Almost everywhere else, he disappears into an anonymous first- or second-person persona who introduces us to a communal mosaic dealing, often in 'miniature tableaux,'[7] with nearly two millennia of Sri Lankan life and history, the background, as it were to *Anil's Ghost*. The three parts juxtapose poems dealing with past and present, and individual lyrics often shift suddenly from one to the other, as if to emphasize the persistence of the past in the present. The past appears here, as it did in *Running in the Family*, as myth, legend, history, and aesthetic artefact. *Handwriting* swerves away for the most part from what could be called autobiographical concerns to a lyrical and multi-layered mosaic of a place and its layers of history. Though this complex sequence is by no means a *sandesa* or message poem, it has a similar topographical concern in that it names nearly twenty places on the island.

In *Running in the Family* it is the lost and buried father who was pulled out of the depths of memory and history. In *Anil's Ghost* an anonymous body is identified and thus, in a manner of speaking, resurrected into history. Here it is the entire culture and history of a people that is at stake, as the allusions to various eras and the periodic references to flight, soldiers, assassination, and war make clear: 'There were goon squads from all sides // Our archaeologists dug down to the disappeared / bodies of schoolchildren' (27). The recent violent history of Sri Lanka is part of the book's more comprehensive and often implied tapestry, as it was in *Running in the Family*. But as in the more explicitly political *Anil's Ghost*, Ondaatje avoids judgment, almost as if he recalls criticizing Edwin Muir in his thesis for being too moralistic and didactic in his war poems. His ideal is the 'neutral inevitability' he discerns in Yeats's 'The Second Coming' and 'Easter 1916.'[8] Thus while *Handwriting* refers to 'goon squads from all sides' and 'the sects of war' (11), it doesn't try to apportion blame or make judgments. Even when dealing with a specific contemporary event such as the assassination of the president, it does so in an impersonal pitch:

> The heat of explosions
> sterilized all metal.
>
> Ball bearings and nails
> in the arms, in the head.
> Shrapnel in the feet.
>
> Ear channels
> deformed by shockwaves.
> Men without balance
> surrounding the dead President
> on Armour Street.
>
> Those whose bodies
> could not be found.   (28)

I speak of an impersonal pitch instead of tone because it may be useful here to follow Geoffrey Hill's distinction between pitch (subject oriented) and tone (reader oriented). The voice and images evoke the scene for us, but in almost every instance they seem to turn back into the event. Though the scene is also described in some detail in *Anil's Ghost*, it seems less of an intrusion there because contemporary politics and history are part of that novel's climate. In *Handwriting*, by contrast, they always seem a violence against the fabric of the culture and the desires of the text. The poet deals with them, but only reluctantly.

Here, as in *Anil's Ghost*, the artist only seems to lose to the soldier in the debate between art and war or life and death since his art, however perishable its materiality, usually survives the depredations of violence. The third section of 'Burial 2' (23) affirms this:

> The poets wrote their stories on rock and leaf
> to celebrate the work of the day,
> the shadow pleasures of night.
> *Kanakara*, they said.
> *Tharu piri* ...
>
> They slept, famous, in palace courtyards
> then hid within forests when they were hunted
> for composing the arts of love and science
> while there was war to celebrate.
>
> They were revealed in their darknesses
> – as if a torch were held above the night sea
> exposing the bodies of fish –
> and were killed and made more famous.

I assume that the poets wrote 'on rock and leaf' because they wrote love poems on the Mirror Wall of the Sigiriya Rock as well as in palm-leaf books. The first stanza hints at their words (*Kanakara*) with part of a poem that will appear six pages later. Ironically, this love poem itself constitutes a provocation and offence during a time when others insisted that 'there was war to celebrate.' Like *Handwriting*, the poem resists the compulsions of politics and ideology to concentrate on what Ondaatje variously calls gesture, ceremony, choreography, 'the intimate life,' courtesy, or, more inclusively, art. The book's heroes are the various craftsmen, artists, and 'handwriters' who create rather than destroy, whose work offers what Denis Donoghue calls the 'aesthetic space' in which 'the immediate pressures of ethical and political decisions are deferred'[9] and in which, as at the end of *Anil's Ghost*, a comprehensive vision of individual and communal life is offered. There is something of this in 'The Medieval Coast' (20), which is short enough to quote in full.

> A village of stone-cutters. A village of soothsayers.
> Men who burrow into the earth in search of gems.
>
> Circus in-laws who pyramid themselves into trees.

Home life. A fear of distance along the southern coast.

Every stone-cutter has his secret mark, angle of his chisel.

In the village of soothsayers
bones of a familiar animal
guide interpretations.

This wisdom extends no more than thirty miles.

The general location of the village is indicated by the two poems that surround it; the historical period is announced by the title. The stone-cutters, soothsayers, and circus in-laws are part of the book's gallery of artists – each with his version of a 'secret mark' or handwritten signature – who give expression to what Lawrence called the spirit of a particular place, be it a coast, an island called Sri Lanka, or even a country called Canada. In a book in which art is threatened with destruction, the stonecutters represent a privileged guild since their work will probably outlive anything committed to paper or palm leaves.

Art and artists are at risk throughout the book, and one of the most moving poems records 'What we lost' because of the violence and chaos of war. Its casual catalogue lists 'The interior love poem,' 'The rule of courtesy,' 'Gestures between lovers,' 'The small boats of solitude,' and 'Lyrics that rose / from love / back into the air,' as well as knowledge of 'how monsoons / ... / would govern behaviour.' It concludes, in a sentence simultaneously clear and elusive, 'All this we burned or traded for power and wealth / from the eight compass points of vengeance / / from the two levels of envy' (24–5). The book itself can be read as a challenge to 'power and wealth' and 'the sects of war' that treat its presence and vision as irrelevant and that threaten the existence of aspects of life unrelated to 'power and wealth.' Only images related to art and culture outnumber the images of war in the poems.

The first and third sections are separated by an interlude, the volume's longest poem, 'The Nine Sentiments (*Historical Illustrations on Rock and Book and Leaf*).' Here 'power and wealth' and the violence they engender are ignored, and the focus is on the nine sentiments or emotions of Indian love poetry. Ondaatje lists them in his notes as follows: 'romantic / erotic, humorous, pathetic, angry, heroic, fearful, disgustful, amazed and peaceful' (78). Daniel Ingalls's explanation of the relationship between an emotion and the mood (*rasa*) it may create in a play or poem is worth quoting at some length since it hints at an emotional and aesthetic complexity absent from Ondaatje's note. It also raises the question of how much of the theory of the sentiments is relevant to a reading of Ondaatje's eleven-part poem.

> The critics spent much effort in analysing what I have called mood. The theory was applied originally to the theatre and came only later to be applied to all forms of literature. It begins by classifying the human emotions (*bhâva*) into eight, or according to some critics nine, basic or stable (*sthâyin*) types: sexual excitement, laughter, grief, anger, energy, fear, loathing, and wonder, to which some add, as ninth, peace. These emotions are stable only in relation to some thirty-three transitory experiences, such as embarrassment, reminiscence, worry, and so forth. The effort of the dramatist or poet is to transmit a sort of decoction of these stable emotions to his audience. He does so by employing certain means: the characters of his play or poem, the stimulants, such as rain clouds or sandalwood or bees when the mood is erotic, victories and triumphs when the mood is heroic; and so on. The decoction which the audience receives is what I have called mood. A more literal translation of the Sanskrit *rasa* would be flavour or taste. The moods bear names corresponding, with some small but interesting differences, to the names of the basic emotions from which they are derived. They are the erotic, the comic, the compassionate, the cruel, the heroic, the terrifying, the horrid (or loathsome), the marvellous, and the peaceful. The mood is not the original emotion itself or we should not enjoy hearing sad poetry like the *Râmâyana* ... A mood ... since it is created by an artist, may be purified and sustained and can be combined with other moods in an artistic fashion. Again, the emotion is personal whereas the mood is universal.[10]

This commentary reminds us of these poems' full cultural context, one unavailable to most of us. A rough equivalent would be a Sri Lankan without English who reads a Sinhalese imitation of a Shakespearean sonnet without any knowledge of Shakespeare, the sonnet tradition, or its conventions. To return to Ondaatje, to be frank, I'm not always sure which sentiment or mood is prevalent in which poem. The first and second, for instance, are equally romantic/erotic. The first reads as follows:

All day desire
enters the hearts of men

Women from the village of ____
move along porches
wearing calling bells

Breath from the mouth
of that moon

Arrows of flint
in their hair   (33)

As I said above, this is the first of an eleven-lyric sequence, and most of its concerns and images will be recalled before the sequence ends with 'Where is there a room / without the damn god of love?' As Vigurs has pointed out, this couplet echoes lines from 'a poem by Bhartrihari, a fifth century philosopher-poet who wrote, '"Damn her, damn him, the god of love, / the other woman, and myself!"''[11] The approach in the poem, as throughout, is imagistic, though there is usually a gently implied narrative; the diction and syntax are simple and direct; whatever music there is – 'from the mouth / of that moon' – is unemphatic. The work of poetry is also done by the enjambment, by the lack of connectives, and by the way the lack of punctuation creates a space for silence to seep in and expose the individual image, the silent white acting as a setting rather than a frame. This is obvious in these lines from the third poem in the sequence:

One sees these fires
from a higher place
on the cadju terrace

they wander like gold
ragas of longing
like lit sequin
on her shifting green dress   (35)

'Cadju' and 'ragas' (the sound evokes the sense in 'like gold / ragas of longing') remind us that we are on foreign ground, strangers in a strange land. With the exception of Anne Michaels, I can't think of another contemporary Canadian poet capable of risking the shift from the strong and musically evoked simile of the second verse to the equally striking visual simile in the third. Like most of the book, the poem offers the reader none of the familiar signposts either of the canon or of contemporary poetry in English. The closest it comes is in the identical metre of the last two couplets of the first quotation, each of which is a trochee followed by an iamb and an anapest, a small trick of the metrical knife that Ondaatje occasionally uses to tighten up an ending, to bring a poem to a point ('Step' is another example).

A more obvious link to the Eastern traditions than the elusive nine sentiments exists in images that look back to classical Indian and Sri Lankan love poems: the lotus, ankle bracelets, bells, the 'three folds on their stomachs,' the arrow of love, and pools. These ramify among the eleven poems and the other two sections, forming a tessera of subtle and often subterranean connections holding the disparate and ostensibly unrelated parts of the book together. 'The Nine Sentiments' closes with a poem whose dominant sentiment seems to be anger and resentment at the fact that the answer to its last question is a negative: 'Where is the suitor / undistressed / one can talk with // Where is there a room / without the damn god of love?' (43). The entire second section ends on a question mark and with an implied negative. It's as if Ondaatje wants to reassert a slightly more sombre tone before returning to poems in the third section dealing with losses different from those caused by desire and love.

The transition is made in 'Flight,' the first poem of the third section, in which Ondaatje reintroduces himself into the text in a scene bringing the past into the present and the personal into the public by juxtaposing two very different flights from Ceylon or Sri Lanka: 'In the half-dark cabin of Air Lanka Flight 5 / the seventy-year-old lady next to me begins to comb / her long white hair, then braids it in the faint light. / ... / Pins in her mouth. She rolls her hair, / curls it into a bun, like my mother's' (47). This is followed by 'Wells,' a triptych, the central section of which is the already discussed elegy for Rosalin Perera, while the first and third sections celebrate return and survival. It's not clear to me that the third part is unified by any one set of concerns, though several poems, including the last six, deal with different kinds of disintegration, dissolution, and disappearance as well as ways of resisting or overcoming them.

'Death at Kataragama' (55–7) is the first and in many ways the most startling and original. On the one hand, it recalls Ondaatje's various animal poems; on the other, it seems to echo the scene in *Coming through Slaughter* where the narrator, ostensibly Ondaatje, wonders why he is drawn to Buddy Bolden and his self-destructive life and art.

In this piece of prose the narrator-writer begins with a paragraph describing what seems to be the writing of one of the poems in *Handwriting*:

> You hear sounds of a pencil being felt for in a drawer in the dark and then see its thick shadow in candlelight, writing the remaining words. Paragraphs reduced to one word. A punctuation mark. Then another word, complete as a thought. The way someone's name holds terraces of character, contains all of our adventures together.

These lines seem to describe poems characterized by omission, compression, implication, and what the architect John Pawson has called 'the omission of the inessentials';[12] in other words, poems like the ones that we have been reading. But we haven't heard previously the note of urgency that pulses through the lines in the desire to compress the written accounts of experience to the point that language itself disappears. That note sets up the speaker's startling desire in the second and third paragraphs to merge his 'soul' with and disappear into a 'a woodpecker I am enamoured of I saw this morning through my binoculars.' Here, as in 'Beaver' (*RJ*, 47), the impulse behind this characteristically romantic desire seems to be a dissatisfaction with human life as well as with imaginative writing as a means of apprehending reality. He admits, 'I no longer see words in focus. As if my soul is a blunt tooth. I bend too close to the page to get nearer to what is being understood. What I write will drift away. I will be able to understand the world only at arm's length.' Recognizing that becoming a woodpecker 'could be a limited life,' he nevertheless admits that had it 'been offered to me today, at 9 a.m., I would have gone with him, traded this body for his.'

The desire is then reiterated in a memory of an almost visionary encounter with 'ten water buffalo when I stopped the car': 'the haunting sound I was caught within as if creatures of magnificence were undressing and removing their wings. My head and almost held breath out there for an hour so that later I felt as if I contained that full noon light.' The water buffalo, heavy, wet, and muddy, are nevertheless almost Rilkean angelic visitors – 'their wings' – reminding him of modes of being different from his own. Each scene is followed by a paragraph about death reminding him of what is entailed in the loss of self. In both instances we have an intense longing for self-oblivion inseparable from and perhaps caused by an acute, sometimes desperate awareness of self. The speaker implies that even when he writes about others with negative capability, he always does so self-consciously, even as he enters 'another's nest, in their clothes and with their rules for a particular life.' What he wants here is a spontaneous, 'quick decision' or 'sudden choice' to escape himself by entering what Yeats calls 'the labyrinth of another's being' ('The Tower'). Woodpecker or water buffalo, 'I would give everything away for this sound of mud and water, hooves, great wings.'

The bad faith inevitable in this kind of writing is obvious in the fact that the desire for an unconscious mode of being and unity with the non-human can be described only in language. The poem itself, like Lawrence's 'Snake' or 'Bat,' is already complicit in the speaker's eventual failure. What he desires is impossible for any man or woman, and perhaps especially so for a writer. But the desire itself to enter into being or Being or to achieve a unity between subject and object, language and reality, may help us understand why so many of the book's arts – from statues to bells to stilt-walkers – are non-verbal. In this poem's penultimate clause he refers to 'that book I wanted to make and shape tight as a stone.' The implications of the final simile have been sensitively developed by Marnie Parsons in her review of the book. Her very perceptive commentary is worth quoting at some length:

> *Handwriting*'s half-title page has, according to the notes at the end of the book, 'an example of rock art, possibly a variation of a letter of the alphabet,' and in 'Death at Kataragama,' the speaker refers to 'that book I wanted to make and shape tight as a stone.' The whole book unfolds from those two details. Details as simple as that rock art, the possible variation of a letter represented in pale gold against the stone grey of the book's hard cover. It stands, alone, as speaking for the entire book, this trace of handwriting into which Ondaatje pours himself in order to uncover his kinship with letter, language, story, art, with the history of the infinitely rich country of his birth.
>
> This book wants to be stone – it is thick with carved stones, cut gems, jade and rock. It wants to be rock that Ondaatje carves as testament to his kinship with the makers and lovers who people the Sri Lanka of this book. Poets, forerunners quite different from those he wrote about in *Running in the Family*, permeate the text ... Their poems and manuscripts, whole libraries buried 'under the great medicinal trees / which the invaders burned' (21), are in some small way recovered in these poems, or

recalled – another silence made palpable – and, in at least one instance, transmuted to jade.[13]

Two different kinds of recovery and recollection occur in the next two poems. The first, 'The Great Tree' (58–9), is a complex, multi-layered, and nearly calligraphic poem about two Chinese artists of the fourteenth century, the poet-calligrapher Yang Weizhen and the Taoist painter Zou Fulei. Both in overall conception and details, the poem is based on information about Yang Weizhen's 'Colophon to the Painting "A Breath of Spring" by Zou Foulei' in the exhibition catalogue *From Concept to Context – Approaches to Asian and Islamic Calligraphy*.[14] The catalogue describes the relationship between the two artists as follows:

> Yang Weizhen, a renowned scholar-poet and calligrapher, was a close friend of Daoist painter Zou Foulei. Yang was inspired by Zou's painting of a plum branch [*A Breath of Spring*], and few of his other calligraphic works match the quality of his colophon on the Freer handscroll. Yang's untrammelled and unrestrained colophon is well suited to Zou's powerful painting. His poem and postinscription praise Zou Fulei and Zou's brother, and record his meeting with them. The colophon supplies the only firsthand material concerning Zou Foulei, for whom biographical details would otherwise be lost.

Ondaatje transforms the entry and the colophon into a poet's elegy for a painter that is simultaneously a meditation on various things, including the survival of art, the dialogue between the arts, and, implicitly, Ondaatje's own uses of the past, both Chinese and Sri Lankan. His relationship to the quotations from Yang Weizhen (spelled 'Weizhem' by Ondaatje) and the Sri Lankan fragments he uses and imagines in the book is analogous to Yang Weizhen's use of Zou Fulei's painting in his elegy: 'each sweep and gesture / trained and various / echoing the other's art.' In case we don't make the connection, the poem's last couplet anticipates 'Last Ink,' the title of the book's last poem: 'A night of smoky ink in 1361 / a night without a staircase.' The relationship between the two Chinese artists recalls Ondaatje's relationship to bp Nichol in the elegy 'Breeze,' the last poem in *The Cinnamon Peeler*, in which he resists the fact of the other's death by asserting, 'We sit down to clean and sharpen / the other's most personal lines,' and vows, 'From now on / no more solos' (*CP*, 194). A decade later these lines resurface as 'each sweep and gesture / / echoing the other's art.' Incidentally, the title, 'The Great Tree,' is taken from Yang's colophon ('The Sage of the Great Tree is in deep dreaming') and applied, I assume, to the plum tree in the painting.

The next poem is 'The Story,' a four-part poem as elusive as any in the collection. References to 'that bus ride in winter' (60) and 'the speed of the city' seem to locate the first and third parts in the present. References to an unspecified king and queen, warriors, and 'blades of poison' create the impression that the second and fourth lyrics are the stuff of legend and belong perhaps to an unspecifiable past. It's worth noting as well that there are no indications in any of its lyrics that the poem is directly connected with Sri Lanka. Such an association depends entirely on the poem's place in *Handwriting*. The connection between past and present is thematic: each 'story' is concerned with remembering and/or reimagining a lost past. The first-person speaker of the first and third lyrics begins by suggesting apodictically, 'For his first forty days a child / is given dreams of previous lives. / Journeys, winding paths, / a hundred small lessons / and then the past is erased' (60). The anonymously narrated second and fourth lyrics seem to contradict this with a story in which a prince mysteriously recalls something that his father did while the son was still in the womb. Both parts of the poem seem to be about fathers and sons, about exile and loss, and about the possibility that what has been lost and forgotten may be recovered. In both stories the recovery includes an inadvertent or accidental legacy handed from one generation to the next. Thus the first-person speaker's early 'departures from family bonds / leaving what was needed' has resulted, if the speaker is indeed Ondaatje, in some of his best work. Similarly, the king's prediction that 'There will be a war' and that 'In the last phase seven of us will cross / the river to the east' (61) is fulfilled by his son and six others, and one of his unconscious acts may have the result of saving his son's life. In the fourth section the future tense is replaced by the present, which persists until the seven are victorious. The story breaks off momentarily at this point, and we are told that 'what should occur now is unremembered.' But what is 'unremembered' can be reimagined, as imagination becomes a form of memory, just as in 'The Cinnamon Peeler' what is desired – 'If I were a cinnamon peeler' – becomes momentarily real because of the play of grammar and a counter-factual statement: 'We remember it as a tender story, / though perhaps they perish. / The father's lean arm across / the child's shape, the taste / of the wisp of hair in his mouth ...' (65).

The narrator begins by recalling that in the second lyric the father had bitten off a piece of his sleeping, pregnant wife's hair and braided it with his own. And though he says that 'perhaps they perish' and then makes it more definite with 'they will die without / the dream of exit' (66), he ends his narrative with a third ending in which 'They take up the knives of the enemy / and cut their long hair and braid it / onto one rope and they descend / hoping it will be long enough / into the darkness of the night' (66). The dead father's legacy to the son is the subconscious memory of the braided hair, which the son doesn't even recognize as a memory but which nevertheless may save seven lives. The descent into the darkness on a rope, which may or may not be long enough, is the perfect visual and dramatic equivalent of what I take to be the first-person speaker's prayer for his grandson in section three. Incidentally, I find it impossible not to think of 'To a Sad Daughter' while reading these lines, whose speaker may be the poet addressing the child in the story.

> With all the swerves of history
> I cannot imagine your future.
> Would wish to dream it, see you
> in your teens, as I saw my son,
> your already philosophical air
> rubbing against the speed of the city.
> I no longer guess a future.
> And do not know how we end
> nor where.
>
> Though I know a story about maps, for you.   (63)

It's not clear to me what 'story about maps' he intends, unless he means the story of the king, queen, and prince, which is implicitly linked in the first poem with maps: 'Some great forty-day daydream / before we bury the maps' (60). If that's the link, then the numinous, legendary story is part of the recalled and imagined map of the past that the speaker – Ondaatje? – wants to hand on to the child being addressed. One of the poem's implications seems to be that while we can't know the future – we all descend a rope in and into darkness – we can remember, know, and imagine the past. And poetry is one of the arts that can do this while also establishing a relationship between past and present. Beginning in what has been mysteriously forgotten and ending with what can only be imagined, the poem offers a vision of wholeness which, however provisional and aesthetic, nevertheless represents a valid attempt to make sense of the swerves and lacunae of private and public histories.

'Step' (69–71), the book's penultimate poem, turns our attention to a different kind of 'art,' knowledge, or map, but one also capable of survival, perhaps even transcendence. I refer to Buddhism, references and allusions to which have punctuated the sequence. The presence of Buddhism in any book dealing with Sri Lanka is natural and inevitable if we keep in mind C.H.B. Reynolds's comment that 'it has been claimed that without Buddhism the very language of the Sinhalese might never have developed. Certainly the teaching of Gotama the Buddha and his revered personality so impressed themselves on the imagination and way of life of the Sinhalese that it became the major theme in their culture.'[15] The two-part poem begins with a description of a monk's funeral pyre before shifting to a meditative section devoted to a monastery and the contemplative life. As with the other poems in the book's final movement, the point of departure is disappearance.

The ceremonial funeral structure for a monk
made up of thambili palms, white cloth
is only a vessel, disintegrates

completely as his life.

The ending disappears,
replacing itself

with something abstract
as air, a view.

The section ends with a return to mundane concerns – 'a lazy lunch' – and the subsequent 'disarray of grief.' To this point, the poem recalls the last line of 'House on a Red Cliff,' its immediate predecessor: 'Last footstep before formlessness' (68). As so often in Ondaatje, lyrics echo one another, repeat images and situations, and achieve a subtle harmony and mosaic as understated as a chime: the poem's last verse looks back to 'Last footstep': 'the pillars once let you step / to a higher room / where there was worship, lighter air'; 'Last footstep' recalls the rope descending 'into the darkness of the night' in 'The Story'; and *that* image in turn builds on the closing couplet of 'The Great Tree': 'a night of smoky ink in 1361 / a night without a staircase[.]' Throughout, the work of art is an attempt to overcome or to offer a tentative answer to formlessness and disintegration, to offer form, 'array,' and shelter in place of chaos.

But in its second section 'Step' goes further in a subdued, reflective lyric about 'thirty women in white' who 'meditate on the precepts of the day' in a ruined 'forest monastery.' This spiritual poem gathers up some of the images that appeared in earlier love poems – 'The sensuous stalk / the sacred flower,' 'physical yearning' – while putting them to a completely different use. In their contemplative life, the thirty women stand contrasted to the sensual and worldly women in 'The Nine Sentiments': 'They walk those abstract paths / their complete heart / their burning thought focused / on this step, then *this* step.' Both lovers and nuns focus intensely on the moment, but the devotion of the latter will lead to 'another level':

How physical yearning
became permanent.
How desire became devotional
so it held up your house,
your lover's house, the house of your god.

Spiritual longing and desire lead both to order and a revelation that answers the first section's 'disarray of grief' and the disintegration of the body on the funeral pyre. Having read the second lyric, we now understand the full force of the first poem's opening line: 'The ceremonial funeral structure for a monk.' Buddhism, like poetry, is a ceremony or set of ritual gestures that tries to make sense of transience, formlessness, and disarray. The gently ambiguous closing quatrain simultaneously affirms its vision while leaving me with the impression that the speaker, like Philip Larkin in 'Church Going,' admires it without belief because for him these are empty symbols drained of their full significance: 'And though it is no longer there, / the pillars once let you step / to a higher room / where there was worship, lighter air.' The adverb 'once' and the past tense seem to me to undermine subtly the harmony and sense of completion produced by the quatrain and the resonant dactylic rhyme – 'longer there / lighter air' – to suggest that the 'higher room' or mode of spiritual being is not available in the modern era. However attractive we may find the consolations of religion, a more accurate trope of our condition is the figure descending a rope in darkness. The nuns belong in the world of Eliot's 'The Dry Salvages.'

> ... But to apprehend
> The point of intersection of the timeless
> With time, is an occupation for the saint –
> No occupation either, but something given
> And taken, in a lifetime's death in love,
> Ardour and selflessness and self-surrender.[16]

Ondaatje's narrator, by contrast, could have spoken the demystifying words heard by the woman in Stevens's 'Sunday Morning': 'She hears upon that water without sound, / a voice that cries, "The tomb in Palestine / Is not the porch of spirits lingering. / It is the grave of Jesus, where he lay."'[17]

In one of his livelier footnotes, Freud tries to console us by pointing out, 'As the poet says, though life may be tragic, there is always brandy.' 'Last Ink,' the three-part lyric that is *Handwriting*'s last poem and its coda, substitutes 'art' for 'brandy.' The first section is a meditation on art that borrows its imagery from 'The Great Tree.' The second section develops the concern with art by focusing on how the artist expresses his love for a woman – first mentioned in the last line of the first section – on a seal, scroll, paper, and jade. The brief final section is almost an 'envoi' that in a now familiar gesture brings Ondaatje back into the picture – 'My body on this hard bed' – while summing up the poem and announcing the end of the book – 'Last ink in the pen' (74).

After an enigmatic and not completely successful opening that introduces the theme of love, the poem shifts to a scene emphasizing the fortuitousness of art.

> In certain languages the calligraphy celebrates
> where you met the plum blossom and moon by chance
>
> – the dusk light, the cloud pattern,
> recorded always in your heart
>
> and the rest of the world – chaos
> circling your winter boat.   (72)

I take the 'winter boat' to be a metaphor for the aging poet. The chance meeting with the plum blossom and moon is then transformed into a representation 'on a scroll or nudged / ... onto stone / to hold the vista of a life' (72). In the next verse we learn that the life referred to is the artist's own, and it includes 'The memory of a woman walking down stairs' (73). So far the images, events, and concerns are nearly timeless, though anyone familiar with *Secular Love* may be tempted to identify the woman with the anonymous woman of that sequence. The poem could be taking place almost anywhere – 'In certain countries,' 'In certain languages' – though the title of the work, 'Night of the Plum and Moon,' suggests Asia.

The poem's impersonality – 'you' is still the dominant pronoun – is maintained throughout the second stanza, which now includes the unnamed woman in the chance meeting with the plum blossom and moon. The impetus behind the work of art is now acknowledged as desire for her.

> When you first saw her,
> the night of moon and plum,
> you could speak of this to no one.
> You cut your desire
> against a river stone.
> You caught yourself
> in a cicada-wing rubbing,
> lightly inked.
> The indelible darker self.   (73)

The sombre implications of the last line are then picked up in the instructions of 'the Masters,' who said, 'A seal ... / must contain bowing and leaping, / "and that which hides in waters "' (73). The section then describes a 'scroll' with a narrative that seems a condensation of the events of *Secular Love*, as if Ondaatje is trying to put that book into perspective while bringing its successor to a close.

> Yellow, drunk with ink,
> the scroll unrolls to the west
> a river journey, each story
> an owl in the dark, its child-howl
> unreachable now

– that father and daughter,
that lover walking naked down blue stairs
each step jarring the humming from her mouth

I want to die on your chest but not yet,
she wrote, sometime in the 13th century
of our love   (74)

As so often in this book, I find myself moved by the poetry without being able to offer an adequate paraphrase, one that makes sense of all of its parts, or being able to answer the questions that the lines provoke. I suspect, however, that the poem looks over its shoulder back to *Secular Love*. Why does the scroll unroll to the west? Why is the 'child-howl / unreachable now?' Which lover walked 'naked down blue stairs?' And why are the stairs blue, unless it is to prepare us for the section's closing line, in which she is 'caught in jade / / whose spectrum could hold the black greens / the chalk-blue of her eyes in daylight'? The love is in its '13th century' because, I assume, he feels as if they have been in love forever. It's a line Donne or Cole Porter might have written.

The brief third section opens with a summary of their love as 'Our altering love, our moonless faith' (74). I take 'altering' to be synonymous with changing and growing; and their 'faith' in each other is 'moonless' because changeless, without the periodicity of the moon. The image is charged with local and more general associations. The potentially negative adjective 'moonless' inevitably reminds us of moonlit nights like the one of 'plum blossom and moon' with which the poem opened. And the moon has been one of the book's recurring images whose significance has been incremental. The next line – 'Last ink in the pen' – introduces a sense of urgency about the completion of the poem that echoes the speaker's anxiety in the next line about his separation from his lover – 'My body on this hard bed':[18] 'The moment in the heart / where I roam restless, searching / for the thin border of the fence / to break through or leap' (74–5). If the fence signifies some sort of impediment to their love, it's not clear to me, on the evidence of the poem or of the book, what that is or why it exists. And does Ondaatje mean 'the thin border of the fence' or 'the border of the thin fence,' or does it matter? The final line, as grammatically incomplete as the other syntactic units in the section, takes us back to the Masters' advice on the previous page and is intended as a modifier of the lines just quoted: 'Leaping and bowing.' If we think of the conventional denotations and connotations of both gerunds, then leaping is associated with activity and joy, bowing with respect, passivity, submission, and sometimes grief. As a figurative summary of the book, the line strikes me as particularly apt. For the attentive reader, it also carries in its wake the memory of the line that follows it in the second section: 'A seal, the Masters said, / must contain bowing and leaping, / "and that which hides in waters."' As in *Anil's Ghost*, one of Ondaatje's major concerns in *Handwriting* has been with the recovery, whether real or imagined, of what has been lost, buried, sunk, or forgotten, whether literally or figuratively. It is rhetorically appropriate that the poem and the book end with an image that nudges the reader into noticing a lacuna, a missing trope that he or she must retrieve from memory. In the end, despite its sensuous love poems and affirmative celebration of 'finite things,' *Handwriting* answers Hölderlin's question 'what are poets for in a destitute time?' by pointing to elegy, a genre that mourns wounds and losses while simultaneously preserving, even resurrecting, their memory.[19]

In Eliot's words, 'Every poem an epitaph.'[20]

LAST WORD: ONDAATJE ON POETRY

Exile is a dream of glorious return.

Salman Rushdie[1]

1971 (Interview, *Manna*)

[*The Dainty Monsters*] wasn't written in that order, much more mixed up. Tho 'Peter' was, if I remember, the last poem written. The poem in that book which I wrote first was either 'Sows' or 'Song to Hitchcock and Wilkinson.' The section and the order of the poems was something very carefully structured when I was getting the book together. That was and still is very important to me. (20)

The recent fashion of drawing journalistic morals out of literature is I think done by people who don't love literature or who are not capable of allowing its full scope to be seen. I've seen this done to Margaret Atwood's *Journals of Susanna Moodie* which is really a fine *poem*, not an *essay* or statement. (21)

I wanted the poems in [*The Collected Works of Billy the Kid*] to have a very natural speechline and also for the poems to be very *tight* and *introverted*. A mental shorthand – person thinking very naturally and yet have the lines withdrawing and changing meaning depending on whether line B referred to line A or to line C. So a formal punctuation had to be removed and so it had to be suggested in the phrase or the way the line fell on the page. (21)

1975 (Interview, *Rune / Spider Blues*)[2]

At that time [of *Sons of Captain Poetry*] I was very interested in the possibilities of concrete poetry and I'd just finished the actual writing of
The Collected Works of Billy the Kid and there was a real sense of words
meaning nothing to me anymore, and I was going around interpreting
things into words ... I just felt I had to go into another field, something
totally visual. The film was quite a help cos it freed me from going
around and doing this kind of thing ... Also I wanted to write something on Nichol and I'd realized you couldn't really *write* about concrete poetry, that it had to be expressed in another form. (14)

My first drafts always seem horrendously awful and I've always been
amazed how I get from the first draft to the finished product. I'm a
great believer in rewriting. I suppose this is the effect of film on me
because no one can make a totally unconscious film. All art, for that
matter, is self-conscious. One has to admit that; one has to be on the
border where that craft meets the accidental and the unconscious, as
close as possible to the unconscious. (22)

There's a great deal of lying in poetry, by necessity. It's not a case of
being tactful or misrepresenting something but of making art; art is, to
a certain extent, deceit. And what disturbs me in having my work
interpreted as either physically or biographically right or wrong is that
there's an emotional or psychological rightness which, for me, is more
important than the other two. The epigraph in *Rat Jelly* from Melville's
The Confidence Man is like the one at the beginning of John Newlove's
Lies, 'accidentally telling the truth.' (23)

1980 (Interview, *Twelve Voices: Interviews with Canadian Poets*)

I think [the poet] has to remain silent after he's written the poem. I
think it only damages a poem to have the poet try to explain it. I can't
understand writers who do this. The statement that a poet makes in a
poem is just as much the *way* he says it as *what* he says. To ask someone
who's said something in a poem to paraphrase it or to expand that
statement can only destroy a poem, for me. It's the case of a poem
being looked on as a crossword puzzle; the reader wants to know
exactly what is meant. But I don't think the reader should ask the poet
exactly what he is saying.

What he wants to say he has *said*, and a poem is important in what it doesn't say as well as what it says. (137)

I hate the term 'artist,' I hate the term 'poet,' it has so many connotations of someone who is separate from the real world, someone who supposedly 'deserves' more, 'knows' more, than the man on the street. It suggests someone who is superior to any other craftsman that exists around us today, and I think this is a real problem of artists ... I like the term 'writer' simply because it's someone who does something, who is using words. (143)

1984 (Interview, *Spider Blues*)

There has been a great change in what 'structure' is in a poem or in a novel. Or 'design.' Or the 'context' of a novel. Where the narrator stands or sits. For example, how do you talk about the architecture in Salman Rushdie's *Midnight's Children*? It is something remarkable. (322)

What academics are obsessed with is who won the horse race or what it really means. But if you watch a replay you start discovering form. You don't watch the horse in front anymore – the leading horse representing 'content' – but it's the horse in fourth place saving himself. I think that writers think about and are interested in that kind of thing, the undercurrents of shape and tone as opposed to just the meaning. The way Rudy Wiebe says what really makes the Mad Hatter's tea party go is the dormouse!! Now that to me is wonderful and exact. More is said in that remark than in most critical articles. (324)

I wanted to call my new book of poems, *Secular Love*, 'a novel.' I structured it like one. For me its structure and plot are novelistic. Each section deals with a specific time period but the people in them are interrelated. But, of course, they are drawn in a lyric, perceived by a lyric eye. (324)

Although I guess you always do go back and write the same story. The least you can do is try to make it look like something else ... I think one tries to start each new book with a new vocabulary, a new set of clothes. Consciously or subconsciously we burn the previous devices which have got us here but which now are only rhetoric. (325)

At the conference on the long poem, George Bowering was talking about the derivation of the word 'order' as coming from 'to begin.' I don't know if that's true or not but it's interesting that in writing *Running* and *Slaughter* the two pieces I wrote to *order* the book were written last – but went in at the beginning. I'm always preoccupied over what should be left in and what should be left out. I love restructuring things. Then later there's a stage where you just want to make the book *look* as good as you can; and that's why I'm always interested in how a book is designed.

There's also the idea that a good poem or a good book is like a well-oiled machine – it has no superfluous parts. (327)

If everything we write turns out to be totally unfashionable or wrong-headed, the actual writing has still been a private satisfaction. I'm not sure what that satisfaction is but it has something to do with making something and putting it out there when you're finished – like a table or chair that's there and your role ends at that point. (330)

1990 (Interview, *Conjunctions / Essays on Canadian Writing*)[3]

I've always been convinced by mental or artistic landscapes. When I was growing up in England my image of America was essentially formed by songs by the Coasters. 'Poison Ivy,' 'Young Blood,' 'Yakety Yak.' (243)

Well, we've all travelled through the country that was Conrad. He is to twentieth-century fiction what Yeats is to twentieth-century poetry. He is full of political pitfalls and yet remains pretty central. I'd probably take Ford's work with me to a desert island before Conrad's. Conrad is not someone I return to, although there are many allusions to him in [*In the Skin of a Lion*]. Whom do I return to? Pound said – I don't remember his exact wording – that poetry had to get back the power that the novel had. Poetry should be able to do what the novel could. And then he and everyone else began a revolution, and people like Pound and Bunting and Niedecker, all these people gave a fantastic boost to poetry, but there were things they did in poetry that I don't think most novels have yet picked on – the scope, the simultaneity, the sharpness of language. There was an exploration that went on during that period of poetry earlier in this century which still hasn't reached the novel. (248)

1993 (Interview, *Writers and Company* / *Essays on Canadian Writing*)[4]

That need to move out of poetry into prose happened only with *Billy the Kid*; I needed to build that corral, that landscape and so forth, with prose. Since then I know when I'm writing poetry and when I'm writing prose. With [*In the Skin of a Lion* and *The English Patient*] I've been so intensely focused on them that the idea of writing poetry was diverted, or contained within the prose. David Malouf told me recently: 'Every novel has about a thousand lost poems in it.' I think that's true. My novels don't have that *Ben Hur* sense of looking down and encompassing the full scope. My book may have that kind of scope, but it's pieced together with little bits of mosaic. Each scene tends to be written from the point of view of that private poetic voice – not so much in terms of language but in how one sees things. (256)

2002 (Interview, *Where the Words Come From*)

I tend not to think of poetry as something preconceived. I don't sit down because I have an idea I want to get across, or even an emotion that I am clear about. I'm not quite sure what is going to happen. I might start a poem thinking about traffic but it could end up being about a sparrow, and then I'll rework it and rework it and it will turn into being about something else. For me the poem is discovered during the process of making it. (33)

I know in my earlier poems I was almost too casual, too lackadaisical. Wild and woolly, someone said. With *Handwriting* I really wanted to write the poems as if there was a limit to the number of words that could be used. You do have to work at being simple. I really wanted to take off, remove, all those extra clothes that were there in the earlier poems. (34)

And *Elimination Dance*, which was more like a joke than anything else – actually taught me a lot about humour and pacing and timing. (39)

[Going to university] I remember picking up an anthology by Brinnin and Read called *The Modern Poets* ... And I read all these poets I'd never heard of. I read Ted Hughes for the first time and Philip Larkin, I guess. It was mostly some English and some American. I went out and bought their books. Thom Gunn's *My Sad Captains*; Ted Hughes's *The Hawk in the Rain*. About the same time I was discovering W.B. Yeats and Robert Browning at university. And about that time I started reading the poets who were writing in Canada. And then later on it was William Carlos Williams and Robert Creeley. It took me a while to get to them, but they were also crucial to me. Williams's 'No ideas but in things' was an opening door. (40)

2002 (*The Conversations: Walter Murch and the Art of Editing Film*)

In writing, especially in poetry, you are always trying to find ways to forge alliances between unlikely things, striking juxtapositions, finding the right shorthand for ideas, metaphors. You see it in the influence of Spanish poetry, what in the West we call 'leaping poetry' – those sometimes surreal, sometimes subliminal connections that reveal a surprising path or link between strangers. The way a pun or even a misprint can work on a simpler level. There's the story about Auden writing the line 'The poets know the names of the seas' in a poem. It came back from the typesetter as 'The ports know the names of the seas,' and Auden realized that the misprint was better, and kept it. (34)

In literature, even in something as intimate as a poem, those early drafts can be just as wayward and haphazard as the early stages of a film. Look at the gulf between the untidy, seemingly almost useless, first draft of Elizabeth Bishop's 'One Art' and the remarkably tight and suggestive final version of her 19–line villanelle. It becomes clear that all the subtleties of nuance and precision of form were achieved during the editing. So much so that it's almost difficult to recognize the link between the original lines and the final poem. (136)

Notes

Introduction

1 Kermode, *Pleasing Myself*, 138.

2 York, 'Whirling Blindfolded in the House of Woman,' 75, 72.

3 De Man, *Allegories of Reading*, 3.

4 Clarke, 'Michael Ondaatje and the Production of Myth,' 1.

5 Solecki, 'An Interview with Michael Ondaatje (1984),' 325.

6 Stevens, *Opus Posthumous*, 164.

7 There are no references to manuscripts or letters because the Ondaatje papers at the National Archives of Canada are not accessible.

8 Scobie, 'The Lies Stay In,' 118. It is worth noting that he goes on to call it 'the greatest single poem in Canadian literature.'

9 Vendler, *The Given and the Made*, xii.

10 Milosz, *Nobel Lecture*, 20.

11 Russell, *Portraits from Memory and Other Essays*, 82.

12 *Globe and Mail*, 18 August 2001, D14.

13 Wachtel, 'Interview with Michael Ondaatje,' 259.

14 Verhoeven, 'Playing Hide and Seek in Language,' 22.

15 Eliot, *The Use of Poetry and the Use of Criticism*, 147–8.

16 Quoted by Mark Strand in *The Weather of Words*, 71.

17 Whalley, *Poetic Process*, 140.

18 Quoted in James Longenbach's *Modern Poetry after Modernism*, 22, 8. Eliot was interviewed by Bishop at Vassar in the spring of 1933, and she published an account of the interview in the *Vassar Miscellany News*, 10 May 1933, 4; Berryman's review, 'À peine ma piste,' appeared in *Partisan Review* 15 (1948): 828.

19 Quoted in Ondaatje, 'Peter,' *How Do I Love Thee*, 149.

20 Ondaatje, 'Mythology in the Poetry of Edwin Muir.' Only Ed Jewinski has noted the importance of the thesis.

21 The quotation from Muir is from *An Autobiography*, 14.

22 Carson, *The Beauty of the Husband*, 33.

23 Also of interest is the comment by Francis Bacon Ondaatje cites: 'I don't want to avoid telling a story but I want very very much to do the thing that Valéry said – to give the sensation without the boredom of its conveyance. And the moment the story enters the boredom comes upon you' (Russell, *Francis Bacon*, 32).

24 The quotation from Muir is from *Latitudes*, 296.

25 Bush, 'Michael Ondaatje: An Interview,' 248.

26 Bowering, 'Ondaatje Learning to Do,' 62–3.

27 No source is given.

28 See Ondaatje, 'Pictures from Vietnam,' *The New Romans*, 131.

29 Ondaatje, 'García Márquez and the Bus to Aracataca,' 19.

30 Gustafson, 'Ondaatje, (Philip) Michael.' For Nichol's influence on Ondaatje, see Jewinski, *Michael Ondaatje: Express Yourself Beautifully*, 70.

31 I was at both events. The concert was at Massey Hall.

32 The words are Robert Lowell's ('Yet why not say what happened?') from 'Epilogue,' *The Dolphin*, 127.

33 Leopardi, *A Leopardi Reader*, 55

34 Shaw, *The Lucid Veil*, 120.

35 Jack Spicer, quoted by Ondaatje in the 'Introduction' to *The Long Poem Anthology*, 3.

36 Ondaatje, 'Mythology in the Poetry of Edwin Muir,' 75.

37 O'Meara, 'The Company of Great Thieves,' 35.

The Dainty Monsters

1 This observation is quoted by Anne Carson in *The Economy of the Unlost*, 6. Sartre makes the point in his *Mallarmé or the Poet of Nothingness*.

2 Chamberlin, 'Let There Be Commerce between Us,' 35.

3 Quoted by William Wootten, 'In the Graveyard of Verse: Review of *The Collected Poems of Vernon Watkins*,' 24.

4 Ondaatje, 'Margaret Atwood's *The Circle Game*,' 23.

5 Atwood, *The Circle Game*, 67.

6 D.H. Lawrence to Edward Garnett, 5 June 1914.

7 Bush, 'Michael Ondaatje: An Interview,' 239.

8 The line 'to mate with our children' may carry a memory of two lines from D.G. Jones: 'And the houses grow like a petrified garden / Of flaking shale

in a sterile sky; / While at Alexandria over the bay / A race is prepared to
unglaze the eye' ('November, Gananoque,' *Frost on the Sun*, 9); 'They wait. /
What will they breed on the daughters of men? / Outside in the un-Christian night, the wind / shifting the metaphor / replies: / Dragon's teeth
across the land' ('Teenagers,' *The Sun Is Axeman*, 18).

9 Jones, *Frost on the Sun*, 25.
10 Muir, *An Autobiography*, 56.
11 Muir, *Collected Poems*, 69.
12 From *Words to a Young Poet*, quoted by James Fenton in *The Strength of Poetry*, 248.
13 Quoted in Bradley and Teitelbaum, *The Art of Betty Goodwin*, 119.
14 Bush, 'Michael Ondaatje: An Interview,' 240.
15 Ford, *It Was the Nightingale*, 90.
16 Whalley, *Poetic Process*, 140.
17 The closing lines of 'The Goodbye' – 'and beyond him the sun / netted in
the hills, throwing back his shape' – may owe something to the red sun
locked or trapped in a net of leaves in Henri Rousseau's *La Jungle*, a painting Ondaatje knows well and describes in 'Henri Rousseau and Friends,'
which refers to 'the beautiful and the forceful locked in suns' (*DM*, 27).
18 The play is discussed in Ondaatje's thesis, 'Mythology in the Poetry of
Edwin Muir,' 25–8.
19 For the historical background, see Hibbert, *The Virgin Queen*, chapters 2
and 3.
20 Harding-Russell, 'A Note on Ondaatje's "Peter,"' 205.
21 Ibid., 207.
22 Ibid., 205.
23 Wilde, *The Picture of Dorian Gray*, 7.
24 Ondaatje, 'Pictures from Vietnam,' *The New Romans*, 131.
25 Interview, *Manna*, 20.
26 Baecque and Toubiana, *Truffaut*, 181.
27 Burke, *Counter-Statement*, 183.
28 See Adorno, 'Commitment,' *Notes to Literature*, 2: 77–94.

Covers

1 Solecki, 'An Interview with Michael Ondaatje (1984),' 330.
2 Auden, *Collected Poems*, 72. I have restored Auden's punctuation.
3 'You know, I wanted to call my new book of poems, *Secular Love*, "a
novel." I structured it like one. For me its structure and plot are novelistic.
Each section deals with a specific time period but the people in them are

interrelated. But, of course, they are drawn in a lyric, perceived by a lyric eye' (Solecki, 'An Interview with Michael Ondaatje [1984],' 324).

4 Adorno, 'Titles: Paraphrases on Lessing,' *Notes to Literature*, 2: 4.

the man with seven toes

1 According to *Colombo's Concise Canadian Quotations*, Borges told Robert Zend that 'Canada is so far away it hardly exists' (31).

2 Bush, 'Michael Ondaatje: An Interview,' 240.

3 Barthes, *S/Z*, 5–6.

4 For other accounts of the story, see Beatty, *Tales of Old Australia*; Wannan, *Legendary Australians*; and White, *A Fringe of Leaves*.

5 Ondaatje, 'O'Hagan's Rough-Edged Chronicle,' 24.

6 Clarke, 'Michael Ondaatje and the Production of Myth,' 1.

7 Ondaatje, 'Introduction,' *The Long Poem Anthology*, 13.

8 Ondaatje quotes from MacInnes in a note at the end of the book. See *the man with seven toes*, 45. All subsequent references will be to the 1969 edition.

9 Bryan Robertson has described this painting as follows: 'This animal-like figure conveys something of the shock and horror of a white, northern European body flung down in the wild bush of a Pacific island, and forced to fend for itself: a body that has not been exposed to the ravages of a strong sun before, straddles horrifically across the land, isolated and lost. Her face is hidden by her hair and this device for anonymity is also employed in all the later paintings of Mrs Fraser' (Clark, MacInnes, and Robertson, *Sidney Nolan*, 74).

10 Atwood, *The Journals of Susanna Moodie*, 7.

11 Francis Bacon's comment about his paintings is relevant here: 'we all need to be aware of the potential disaster which stalks us at every moment of the day' (Russell, *Francis Bacon*, 31). Other points of comparison that could be drawn between Ondaatje and Bacon relate to their interest in the beauty of violence, their mutual attempts to describe motion, and the sense or colour of menace that pervades their work.

12 Solecki, 'An Interview with Michael Ondaatje (1975),' 24.

13 Ondaatje, 'O'Hagan's Rough-Edged Chronicle,' 25–6.

14 Blaser, 'The Practice of Outside,' quoted by Ondaatje in the introduction to *The Long Poem Anthology*, 14.

15 Ondaatje, *Leonard Cohen*, 23.

16 Ondaatje, 'O'Hagan's Rough-Edged Chronicle,' 25.

17 In White's *A Fringe of Leaves* the convict's name is Jack Chance, and his status as a man existing between civilization and wilderness is evident in

the fact that he has almost completely forgotten the English language. White replaces the striped shirt with scars, an image that Ondaatje would probably respond to since, as I mentioned earlier, his own work – 'The Time Around Scars,' *Coming through Slaughter, Anil's Ghost* – reveals a fascination with emotional and physical scars. '[She] realized that she was touching the scars she had first noticed on his first appearing at the blacks' camp, when their apparently motiveless welter distinguished them from the formal incisions in native backs' (290).

18 In his article on *Tay John*, Ondaatje quotes the following sentence from the novel: 'indeed, to tell a story is to leave most of it untold' (30).

19 The paintings *Woman and Billabong*, *Woman in Swamp*, and *Woman in Mangroves*.

20 Lane, 'Drama as History,' 118.

21 White, *A Fringe of Leaves*, 20.

22 'Cramasie' is crimson, more usually spelled 'cramoisy' or 'cramesy.'

23 See Willa Muir, *Living with Ballads*, 224–5. For the earliest treatment of Mrs Fraser's experiences, see the ballad 'Wreck of the "Stirling Castle,"' reprinted in Bill Wannan's *Legendary Australians*, 47–9. As Wannan points out, 'This Copy of "Mournful Verses" was originally published in broadsheet form in 1837, by the printer of broadsides J. Catnach, of Seven Dials, London.' The last two stanzas should give sufficient indication of its quality:

> The chief mate too they did despatch,
> By cutting off his head,
> And plac'd on one of their canoes
> All for a figure head.
> Also, a fine young man they bound,
> And burnt without a dread,
> With a slow fire at his feet at first
> So up unto his head.
>
> When you read the tortures I went thro'
> 'Twill grieve your heart full sore,
> But now thank HEAVEN, I am returned
> Unto my native shore.
> I always shall remember,
> And my prayers will ever be,
> For the safety of both age and sex,
> Who sail on the raging sea.

24 Ondaatje writes in *Leonard Cohen* that in the world of *Let Us Compare*

Mythologies 'the morals are imagistic, as they always are in the context of dreams' (14).

Titles

1 Quoted by Adorno in 'Titles: Paraphrases on Lessing,' *Notes on Literature*, 2: 3. The comment appears originally in Gotthold Ephraim Lessing's *Werke* (Leipzig and Vienna: Bibliographisches Institut, n.d.), 4: 435. For a different approach to titles, see John Hollander's ordering of titles in 'a spectrum along the axis of redundancy,' with 'neutral titles' at one end and titles with 'maximum informativeness' at the other' (Ferry, *The Title to the Poem*, 8).
2 Adorno, *Notes on Literature*, 2: 4.
3 There is also a wink in Hitchcock's direction when Ondaatje walks in front of his camera early in his film *The Clinton Special*.
4 Adorno, *Notes on Literature*, 2: 4.

Rat Jelly

1 Livingston, *The Art of Richard Diebenkorn*, 115.
2 The line disappears in the version printed in *The Cinnamon Peeler*, though it is present in *There's a Trick with a Knife I'm Learning to Do*.
3 Scobie, 'His Legend a Jungle Sleep,' 58.
4 I borrow the phrase from Rochelle Vigurs's 'On Rock and Book and Leaf,' 72.
5 Ondaatje returns to the father-son theme in 'Fabulous shadow' (60), though this link isn't as obvious as it was when the poem was first published in *Quarry* as the last in a sequence of six short lyrics. The first poem, 'Photosynthesis,' names the central figure as 'Icarus.' But it is the fourth poem, 'Daddy,' that establishes a perhaps too obvious link between Crete and Ceylon, Dedalus and Mervyn Ondaatje. In this version of the myth, Icarus is abandoned by a drunk Dedalus. 'Fabulous shadow' names neither the father nor the son. All we have is an anonymous voice describing how his body was 'fished from this Quebec river.' The slightly ambiguous title may refer to the shadow cast from above by a figure from myth, or it may touch closer to home by suggesting that the son either is a 'shadow' of the father or, more probably, lives in his shadow of a 'fabulous' father.
6 Warren, *New and Selected Poems, 1923–1985*, 157. Ransom is quoted in 'Concrete and Abstract,' *Princeton Encyclopaedia of Poetry and Poetics*, ed. Preminger, 149.
7 Stevens, *Opus Posthumous*, 161.

8 The poem first appeared in *IS*, no. 6 (April 1969): 10–11.

9 Sophocles, *Philoctetes*, ll. 228–33.

10 See Borsi and Borsi, *Paolo Uccello*, 256–9.

11 Quoted in Whalley, *Poetic Process*, 141.

12 See Solecki, *Spider Blues*, 246–67.

13 Brooks, *Modern Poetry and the Tradition*, 60.

14 In both poems, as well as in 'I have seen pictures of great stars' (*CWBK*, 41), Ondaatje may be recalling the following passage in Cohen's *The Favourite Game*:

> On one of his walks around the Montreal waterfront he passed a brass foundry, a small firm which manufactured bathroom fixtures ...
>
> Now a huge man wearing an asbestos apron and goggles took over. He guided the crucible over to the moulds. With a lever device he tilted the stone pot and poured the molten brass into the lead-holes of the moulds.
>
> Breavman gasped at the brightness of the liquid metal. It was the colour gold should be. It was as beautiful as flesh ... It was yellow, alive and screaming. It poured out in arch with smoke and white sparks. (104)

15 Solecki, 'An Interview with Michael Ondaatje (1975),' 23.

16 There is, however, an indirect link with Cohen. In *Leonard Cohen* Ondaatje summarizes *The Favourite Game* as follows: 'The book is an autobiography of Breavman told in the third person, like one of those group photographs with a white circle drawn around the central character. Breavman, then, is studying his own portrait while making it, and the stress is on the fact that the portrait is unfinished' (24). I also wonder whether the choice of the 'Shell Vapona Strip' doesn't owe something to the fact that Breavman's girl friend is named Shell?

17 'The Spider as an Artist / Has never been employed – / Though his surpassing Merit / Is freely certified // By every Broom and Bridget / Throughout a Christian Land – / Neglected Son of Genius / I take thee by the Hand – .' For another poem about the spider as artist, see Charles Simic's 'The Spider': 'Teacher of Swedenborg and St. John of the Cross, / First anchorite, mysterious builder – / From the dark corner of my room / His destination / The distant northern star ... [sic] // As he weaves, as he spreads his webs, / He is singing. / I'm certain of it, / He is singing' (*Dismantling the Silence*, 12).

'Letter to Ann Landers,' the earlier 'fly' poem in the collection, is a playful footnote to or elaboration of Cohen's 'You know there was honey in my system' (*Parasites of Heaven*, 20–1).

18 Compare Cohen, *The Favourite Game*: 'There was a pause. He leaped up, ran to the window, smashed his fist through the glass' (216).
19 Stevens, *Collected Poems*, 61.
20 Kong makes a final appearance in a still from the original movie in Ondaatje, *The Conversations: Walter Murch and the Art of Editing Film*, 112.
21 Compare 'He's at the call of Metro-Goldwyn-Mayer' to Cohen's 'Everyone knew my lady from the movies and the art-galleries, / Body by Goldwyn' ('Ballad'). The poem is discussed in Ondaatje, *Leonard Cohen*, 9.
22 Atwood, *The Animals in That Country*, 13; Stevens, *Collected Poems*, 53.
23 Vendler, *The Given and the Made*, 106.
24 Burke, *Counter-Statement*, 124.
25 The image of 'the needle's eye' recurs in 'Buck Lake Store Auction': 'While for her, Mrs Germain, / this is the needle's eye / where maniacs of heaven select' (*TTK*, 79).
26 I wonder whether the implied image of the hot-air balloon – 'Release of sandbags' – wasn't on Ondaatje's mind because of Rousseau's *View of the Bridge of Sèrres* (1908).
27 The image of the crucified figure may also owe something to Edwin Muir's 'The Annunciation,' which is discussed in Ondaatje's thesis: 'Muir also captures the immediacy of the crucifixion by concentrating on the physical aspect of Christ's death and avoiding social comment. By seeing Christ without the cloak of Christian theorizing around him, Muir gives him an even greater timelessness. Christ becomes an archetype akin to Prometheus or Theseus' ('Mythology in the Poetry of Edwin Muir,' 86). Since the thesis also mentions Francis Bacon's work, there's a strong possibility that the image owes something to *Three Studies for Figures at the Base of a Crucifixion* (1944) and *Crucifixion* (1965).
28 McKay, 'Baler Twine,' 27.
29 Kafka, *Complete Stories*, 162.
30 Ibid., 270–3.
31 Stevens, *Collected Poems*, 490.
32 Rilke, *Selected Letters, 1902–1926*, 135–6 (to Clara Rilke, 24 June 1907).

Epigraphs

1 Genette, *Paratexts*, 156.
2 Malory, *Works*, 790.
3 Genette, *Paratexts*, 157.
4 Ibid., 158.
5 Ibid., 160.

There's a Trick with a Knife

1 Stevens, *Opus Posthumous*, 171.
2 The title comes from a Blossom Dearie song: 'There's a Trick with a Knife I'm Learning to Do (Everything I've Got Belongs to You).'
3 Ondaatje probably read 'Ksemaraja' in Merwin and Masson's *Sanskrit Love Poetry.*
4 Quoted by Charles Simic in 'Tragicomic Soup.'
5 Ondaatje, 'O'Hagan's Rough-Edged Chronicle,' 30.
6 Stan Dragland, 'Introduction,' *Poetry and Knowing*, ed. Lilburn, 16.
7 Solecki, 'An Interview with Michael Ondaatje (1984),' 325.
8 For the entire poem, see St. Martin, *Roots and Wings*, 60–1. Ondaatje did not use this translation by Robert Bly.
9 Genette, *Paratexts*, 158.
10 *Descant*, 42 (Fall 1982): 175. I suspect that Ondaatje decided not to reprint 'Wordsworth in the Tropics' because it remains just a catalogue of images that never cohere into a larger aesthetic whole.

In 'Sweet like a Crow' (94) Ondaatje is more playful and comic in trying to deal with otherness and difference. Here he attempts to communicate a sense of someone's voice with a catalogue of often absurd analogies. An epigraph by Paul Bowles asserting 'The Sinhalese are beyond a doubt one of the least musical people in the world' seems to relate the poem to others in which otherness or foreignness is an issue.
11 Stan Dragland, 'Introduction,' *Poetry and Knowing*, ed. Lilburn, 9–10.
12 Describing his uncle's death, Ondaatje writes: 'She told me about his death and the day he died / his eyes clearing out of illness as if seeing / right through the room the hospital and she said / he saw something so clear and good his whole body / for a moment became youthful.' There may be a memory here of Emily Dickinson's letter about the death of her mother that Ondaatje quoted in the Muir thesis: 'Mother was very beautiful when she died ... The illumination that comes but once paused upon her features, and it seemed like hiding a picture to lay her in her grave' (Ondaatje, 'Mythology in the Poetry of Edwin Muir,' 115).

Canon I

1 Solecki, 'Michael Ondaatje,' 341.
2 Gass, *Reading Rilke*, 4.
3 Rochelle Vigurs offers a slightly different and more poetic summary of Ondaatje's body of work: 'If his father's letters were rooms in which he sel-

dom lived, Ondaatje's poems are rooms in which we *can* live, where movement and compression, release and restraint, proportion, scale, and light
co-exist with the sheer physicality of space. Patterns of sound and form that
recur throughout the work confer a sense of order – of "home" perhaps –
similar to the way repetition functions in architecture. As one passes from
collection to collection, poem to poem, there is a sense of travelling from
one space to another all within the same building' ('On Rock and Book and
Leaf,' 88).
4 Solecki, 'An Interview with Michael Ondaatje (1984),' 323.

Secular Love

1 Truffaut, *Le Cinéma selon François Truffaut*, 189.
2 Vendler, *The Given and the Made*, xii.
3 All references will be to the first edition of *Secular Love*. The version
reprinted in *The Cinnamon Peeler* has been revised: some poems have been
dropped, and the order of the last two poems, 'Birch Bark' and 'Escarpment,' has been reversed.
4 Fox, 'Anthropology as It Should Be,' 26.
5 Ondaatje's older brother, Christopher, points out the fictive dimension of
some of the autobiographical scenes in *Running in the Family* in *The Man-
Eater of Punanai*, 38, 50. Michael's swerve from autobiographical realism to
fictional romance when dealing with some aspects of the lives of his father
and his Aunt Lalla hints strongly at his reluctance to write in a confessional
or openly autobiographical mode.
6 Quoted in Olney, *Autobiography*, 41.
7 I quote from memory and am embarrassed to admit that I no longer
remember and cannot find the poem in which these lines occur.
8 Benn, *Primal Vision*, 206.
9 Ondaatje, 'Mythology in the Poetry of Edwin Muir,' 111.
10 Chekhov, 'The Lady with the Little Dog,' *Short Stories*, 240–1.
11 The Lancaster character is another variant of the wounded, scarred, or
limping artist.
12 For the graffiti, written between the sixth and tenth centuries, see Paranavitana, *Sigiri Graffiti*. Ondaatje borrows several images and lines from different poems. The ninth and tenth lines of 'Women like You' come from the
sixty-ninth poem: 'Ladies like you / Make men pour out their hearts / And
you also / have thrilled the body / Making its hair / Stiffen with desire.'
13 See Merwin and Masson, *Sanskrit Love Poetry*.
14 See *At the Crease* in Paul Duval, *Ken Danby*, 149.

Canon II

1 Wachtel, 'Interview with Michael Ondaatje,' 260.
2 Atwood, 'Mathews and Misrepresentation,' in *Second Words*, 142. It's worth noting the following from *Survival*: 'The Canadian concern with doomed and slaughtered animals spreads far beyond the range of the "animal story," however. It is highly visible in poetry, and there's even a recent anthology of "animal poems." Both the title – *The Broken Ark* – and the jacket copy reveal editor Michael Ondaatje's stance, which is firmly in the tradition of Seton and Roberts' (76).

Handwriting

1 Truffaut, '*Citizen Kane*: The Fragile Giant,' *The Films in My Life*, 284.
2 Vigurs, 'On Rock and Book and Leaf,' 76.
3 Ibid., 77–8.
4 J.E. Chamberlin has some prescient comments on Ondaatje's cultural and linguistic in-betweenness in 'Let There Be Commerce between Us': 'Ondaatje is in a curious position as a poet, but a position that is close to that of other contemporary poets writing out of situations that define essentially colonial predicaments, where language or audience or the identity or role of the poet are indeterminate ... Canada offers Ondaatje a geography, but no inheritance; Sri Lanka offers him a family history, but no tradition, no way or passing things on; the English language offers him both an inheritance and a history, but no time and place' (41).
5 See Ramanujan, *The Interior Landscape*, 101.
6 Stevenson, *Collected Poems*, 361. Ondaatje indents the second and fourth lines, and drops the colon at the end of the fourth.
7 Vigurs, 'On Rock and Book and Leaf,' 48.
8 Ondaatje, 'Mythology in the Poetry of Edwin Muir,' 82–3.
9 Donoghue, *The Practice of Reading*, 79.
10 Ingalls, 'General Introduction,' *Sanskrit Poetry*, 13–14. Ingalls's footnote on the shades of meaning within *rasa* is also of interest: 'A particular *rasa* is said to lie in a given literary work as a sweet taste or a bitter taste may lie in a given food or drink. The connoisseur of poetry is also said to have a *rasa* (taste) for the poetry he enjoys, much as a wine taster has a taste for wine. The Sanskrit word for a literary connoisseur is *rasika*' (14).
11 Vigurs, 'On Rock and Book and Leaf,' 81.
12 For the full quotation see ibid., 87.
13 Parsons, 'Letters in Canada: Poetry,' 76.

14 Fu, Lowry, and Yonemura, *From Concept to Context*, 36–7.
15 Reynolds, *An Anthology of Sinhalese Literature up to 1815*, 9. Because of the importance of Buddhism in Sri Lankan life, most native readers would see the allusion to the Buddha in Ondaatje's 'To Anuradhapura,' the Sinhalese city in which a sapling was planted from the Bo tree under which the Buddha attained enlightenment.
16 Eliot, *Complete Poems and Plays 1909–1950*, part IV, ll. 18–33, 136.
17 Stevens, *Collected Poems*, 70.
18 Is 'Western Wind' somewhere behind this line? 'Western wind, when wilt thou blow, / The small rain down can rain? / Christ, if my love were in my arms / And I in my bed again!' Or perhaps this is another example of mnemonic irrelevance?
19 Quoted by Martin Heidegger in 'What Are Poets For?' *Poetry, Language, Thought*, 91.
20 Eliot, 'Little Gidding,' *Complete Poems and Plays 1909–1950*, part V, l. 12.

Last Word

1 Quoted in Solecki, *Prague Blues*, 23.
2 Page references are to *Spider Blues*, ed. Solecki.
3 Page references are to Catherine Bush, 'Michael Ondaatje: An Interview.'
4 Page references are to Eleanor Wachtel, 'Interview with Michael Ondaatje.'

Bibliography

Works by Michael Ondaatje

Poetry

The Cinnamon Peeler: Selected Poems. Toronto: McClelland and Stewart, 1989.
The Collected Works of Billy the Kid. Toronto: Anansi, 1970.
The Dainty Monsters. Toronto: Coach House Press, 1967.
'Elizabeth – Anne.' *Canadian Forum*, Aug. 1968, 111.
'Elizabeth – The House.' *Canadian Forum*, Aug. 1968, 111.
Handwriting. Toronto: McClelland and Stewart, 1998.
the man with seven toes. Toronto: Coach House Press, 1969.
'Peter.' *How Do I Love Thee: Sixty Poets of Canada (and Quebec) Select and Introduce Their Favourite Poems from Their Own Work*. Ed. John Robert Colombo. Edmonton: Hurtig, 1970, 149.
'Pictures from Vietnam.' *The New Romans*. Ed. Al Purdy. Edmonton: Hurtig, 1968. 131.
Rat Jelly. Toronto: Coach House Press, 1973.
Secular Love. Toronto: Coach House Press, 1984.
There's a Trick with a Knife I'm Learning to Do: Poems 1963–1978. Toronto: McClelland and Stewart, 1979.
'Wordsworth in the Tropics.' *Descant* 42 (Fall 1982): 175.

Prose

Anil's Ghost. Toronto: McClelland and Stewart, 2000.
Coming through Slaughter. Toronto: Anansi, 1976.

The Conversations: Walter Murch and the Art of Editing Film. New York: Alfred A. Knopf, 2002.

Elimination Dance. Ilderon, Ont.: Nairn Publishing House, 1978.

The English Patient. Toronto: McClelland and Stewart, 1992.

'García Márquez and the Bus to Aracataca.' *Figures in a Ground.* Ed. Diane Bessai and David Jackel. Saskatoon, Western Producer Prairie Books, 1978, 19–31.

'How Poems Work: "One Art" by Elizabeth Bishop.' *Globe and Mail* 18 August 2001: D14.

In the Skin of a Lion. Toronto: McClelland and Stewart, 1987.

Leonard Cohen. Toronto: McClelland and Stewart, 1970.

The Long Poem Anthology. Ed. Michael Ondaatje. Toronto: Coach House Press, 1979.

'Margaret Atwood's *The Circle Game*: A Review.' *Canadian Forum* April 1967: 22–3.

'Mythology in the Poetry of Edwin Muir: A Study of the Making and the Using of Mythology in Edwin Muir's Poetry.' MA thesis, Queen's University, 1967.

'O'Hagan's Rough-Edged Chronicle.' *Canadian Literature* 61 (Summer 1974): 25–31.

'Pillar of Another World.' *Toronto Life* January 1982: 44–5, 78–9, 82.

Running in the Family. Toronto: McClelland and Stewart, 1982.

Reviews, Critical Essays, and Books on Michael Ondaatje

Barbour, Douglas. 'The Last Time I Wrote "Paris": Ondaatje's First Attempt at a Poetic Sequence in "Troy Town."' *Essays on Canadian Writing* 53 (Summer 1994): 107–24.

– *Michael Ondaatje.* New York: Twain Publishers, 1993.

Bök, Christian. 'Destructive Creation: The Politicization of Violence in the Works of Michael Ondaatje.' *Canadian Literature* 132 (Spring 1992) 109–24.

Bowering, George. 'Ondaatje Learning to Do.' *Spider Blues*, ed. Solecki, 61–9.

Bush, Catherine. 'Michael Ondaatje: An Interview.' *Essays on Canadian Writing*: 53 (Summer 1994): 238–49.

Chamberlin, J.E. 'Let There Be Commerce between Us: The Poetry of Michael Ondaatje,' *Spider Blues*, ed. Solecki, 31–41.

Clarke, George Elliott. 'Michael Ondaatje and the Production of Myth.' *Studies in Canadian Literature* 16 (1991): 1–21.

Gustafson, Ralph. 'Ondaatje, (Philip) Michael.' *Contemporary Poets of the English Language.* Ed. Rosalie Murphy. New York: St Martin's, 1970. 820–2.

Harding-Russell, Gillian. 'A Note on Ondaatje's "Peter."' *Canadian Literature* 112 (Spring 1987): 205–11.

Interview by mail with an anonymous correspondent. *Manna* 1 (1972): 19–22.

Jewinski, Ed. *Michael Ondaatje: Express Yourself Beautifully.* Toronto: ECW, 1994.

Kertzer, John. 'On Death and Dying: *The Collected Works of Billy the Kid.*' *English Studies in Canada* 1 (Spring 1975): 86–96.

Lane, M. Travis. 'Dream as History: A Review of *The Man with Seven Toes.*' *Spider Blues*. Ed. Solecki. 150–5.

Lecker, Robert, and Jack David, eds. *The Annotated Bibliography of Canada's Major Authors.* Vol. 6. Toronto: ECW Press, 1985.

Norris, Ken. 'The Architecture of *Secular Love*: Michael Ondaatje's Journey into the Confessional.' *Essays on Canadian Writing* 53 (Summer 1994): 43–50.

O'Meara, David. 'The Company of Thieves: An Interview with Michael Ondaatje.' *Where the Words Come From: Canadian Poets in Conversation.* Ed. Tim Bowling. Roberts Creek: Nightwood Editions, 2002, 31–43.

Parsons, Marnie. 'Letters in Canada: Poetry.' *University of Toronto Quarterly* 66 (1999): 74–8.

Pearce, Jon, ed. *Twelve Voices: Interviews with Canadian Poets.* Ottawa: Borealis Press, 1980.

Scobie, Stephen. 'His Legend a Jungle Sleep: Michael Ondaatje and Henri Rousseau.' *Spider Blues,* ed. Solecki, 42–60.

– 'The Lies Stay In: A Review of *There's a Trick with a Knife I'm Learning to Do.*' *Spider Blues,* ed. Solecki, 117–20.

Solecki, Sam. 'An Interview with Michael Ondaatje (1975).' *Spider Blues,* ed. Solecki, 13–27.

– 'An Interview with Michael Ondaatje (1984).' *Spider Blues,* ed. Solecki, 321–32.

– 'Michael Ondaatje: A Paper Promiscuous and Out of Forme with Several Inlargements and Untutored Narrative.' *Spider Blues,* ed. Solecki, 333–43.

– ed. *Spider Blues: Essays on Michael Ondaatje.* Montreal: Véhicule Press, 1985.

Spice, Nick. 'Ways of Being a Man: Review of *The English Patient.*' *London Review of Books* 24 Sept. 1992: 3–5.

Verhoeven, W.M. 'Playing Hide and Seek in Language: Michael Ondaatje's Historiography of Self.' *American Review of Canadian Studies* 24 (1994): 21–38.

Vigurs, Rochelle. 'On Rock and Book and Leaf: Reading Michael Ondaatje's *Handwriting.*' *Studies in Canadian Literature* 26 (2001): 71–90.

Wachtel, Eleanor. 'Interview with Michael Ondaatje.' *Essays on Canadian Writing* 53 (Summer 1994): 250–61.

York, Lorraine. 'Whirling Blindfolded in the House of Woman: Gender Politics in the Poetry and Fiction of Michael Ondaatje.' *Essays on Canadian Writing* 53 (Summer 1994): 71–91.

General

Adorno, Theodor W. *Notes to Literature*. Trans. Shierry Weber Nicholsen. 2 vols. New York: Columbia University Press, 1991.

Anderson, Linda. *Autobiography*. London: Routledge, 2001.

Atwood, Margaret. *The Animals in That Country*. Toronto: Oxford University Press, 1973.

– *The Circle Game*. Toronto: House of Anansi, 1966.

– *The Journals of Susanna Moodie*. Toronto: Oxford University Press, 1970.

– *Second Words: Selected Critical Prose*. Toronto: House of Anansi, 1982.

Auden, W.H. *Collected Poems*. New York: Random House, 1976.

Baecque, Antoine de, and Serge Toubiana. *Truffaut*. New York: Alfred A. Knopf, 1999.

Barthes, Roland. *Camera Lucida: Reflections on Photography*. Trans. Richard Howard. New York: Hill and Wang, 1981.

– *S/Z*. Trans. Richard Miller. New York: Hill and Wang, 1975.

Beatty, Bill. *Tales of Old Australia*. Sydney: Ure Smith, 1966.

Benn, Gottfried. *Primal Vision*. New York: New Directions, 1960.

Borsi, Franco, and Stefano Borsi. *Paolo Uccello*. Trans. Elfreda Powell. New York: Harry N. Abrams, 1994.

Bradley, Jessica, and Matthew Teitelbaum, eds. *The Art of Betty Goodwin*. Toronto: Art Gallery of Ontario, 1998.

Brooks, Cleanth. *Modern Poetry and the Tradition*. New York: Oxford University Press, 1965.

Brough, John, trans. *Poems from the Sanskrit*. Harmondsworth: Penguin, 1968.

Burke, Kenneth. *Counter-Statement*. Berkeley: University of California Press, 1968.

Carson, Anne. *The Beauty of the Husband*. New York: Alfred A. Knopf, 2002.

– *The Economy of the Unlost*. Princeton: Princeton University Press, 1999.

Chekhov, Anton. *Short Stories*. Trans. Elisaveta Fen. London: The Folio Society, 1974.

Clark, Kenneth, Colin MacInnes, and Bryan Robertson. *Sidney Nolan*. London: Thames and Hudson, 1961.

Cohen, Leonard. *Beautiful Losers*. Toronto: McClelland and Stewart, 1966.

– *The Favourite Game*. Toronto: McClelland and Stewart, 1963.

– *Parasites of Heaven*. Toronto: McClelland and Stewart, 1966.

Colombo, John Robert, ed. *Colombo's Concise Canadian Quotations*. Edmonton: Hurtig Publishers, 1976.

Costello, Bonnie. *Marianne Moore: Imaginary Possessions*. Cambridge: Harvard University Press, 1981.

de Man, Paul. *Allegories of Reading: Figural Language in Rousseau, Nietzsche, Rilke, and Proust*. New Haven: Yale University Press, 1979.

Dewdney, Christopher. *Demon Pond*. Toronto: McClelland and Stewart, 1994.

Dickinson, Emily. *Selected Letters*. Ed. Thomas H. Johnson. Cambridge: Harvard University Press, 1986.

Donoghue, Denis. *The Practice of Reading*. New Haven: Yale University Press, 1998.

Duval, Paul. *Ken Danby*. Toronto: Clarke, Irwin, 1976.

Eliot, T.S. *The Complete Poems and Plays 1909–1950*. New York: Harcourt, Brace and World, 1962.

– *The Use of Poetry and the Use of Criticism*. London: Faber, 1967.

Fenton, James. *The Strength of Poetry*. New York: Farrar, Straus and Giroux, 2001.

Ferry, Anne. *The Title to the Poem*. Stanford: Stanford University Press, 1996.

Ford, Ford Madox. *It Was the Nightingale*. New York: Ecco Press, 1984 [1933].

Fox, Robin. 'Anthropology as It Should Be.' *London Review of Books* 9 Aug. 2001: 25–6.

Fu, Shen, Glenn D. Lowry, and Ann Yonemura. *From Concept to Context: Approaches to Asian and Islamic Calligraphy*. Washington: Smithsonian Institution, 1986.

Gass, William H. *Reading Rilke: Reflections on the Problems of Translation*. New York: Alfred A. Knopf, 2000.

Genette, Gérard. *Paratexts: Thresholds of Interpretation*. Cambridge: Cambridge University Press, 1997.

Heidegger, Martin. *Poetry, Language, Thought*. New York: Harper Colophon, 1975.

Hibbert, Christopher. *The Virgin Queen: The Personal History of Elizabeth I*. New York: Viking, 1990.

Ingalls, Daniel H.H., trans. *Sanskrit Poetry from Vidyakara's 'Treasury'*. Cambridge: Harvard University Press, 1968.

Jones, D.G. *Frost on the Sun*. Toronto: Contact Press, 1957.

– *The Sun Is Axeman*. Toronto: University of Toronto Press, 1961.

Kafka, Franz. *The Complete Stories*. Ed. Nahum N. Glazer. New York: Schocken Books, 1971.

Kermode, Frank. *Pleasing Myself*. London: Penguin, 2001.

Leopardi, Giacomo. *A Leopardi Reader*. Ed. and trans. Ottavio M. Casale. Urbana: University of Illinois Press, 1981.

Lilburn, Tim, ed. *Poetry and Knowing: Speculative Essays & Interviews*. Kingston: Quarry Press, 1995.

Livinston, Jane, ed. *The Art of Richard Diebenkorn*. New York: Whitney Museum of American Art, 1997.

Longenbach, James. *Modern Poetry after Modernism*. New York: Oxford University Press, 1997.

Lowell, Robert. *The Dolphin*. New York: Farrar, Straus and Giroux, 1973.

Lynn, Elwyn. *Sidney Nolan: Myth and Imagery*. London: Macmillan, 1967.

Malory, Sir Thomas. *The Works of Sir Thomas Malory*. Ed. Eugène Vinaver. London: Oxford University Press, 1962.

McKay, Don. 'Baler Twine: thoughts on ravens, home, and nature poetry.' *Poetry and Knowing*, ed. Tim Lilburn, 17–28.

Merwin, W.S. (with J. Moussaieff Masson). *Sanskrit Love Poetry*. New York: Columbia University Press, 1977.

Milosz, Czeslaw. *Abecadlo Milosza*. Kraków: Wydawnictwo Literackie, 1997.

– *The Collected Poems: 1931–1987*. New York: The Ecco Press, 1988.

– *Nobel Lecture*. New York: Farrar Straus Giroux, 1980.

Muir, Edwin. *An Autobiography*. London: Hogarth Press, 1954.

– *Collected Poems*. London: Faber and Faber, 1960.

Muir, Willa. *Living with Ballads*. London: Hogarth Press, 1965.

Olney, James, ed. *Autobiography: Essays Theoretical and Practical*. Princeton: Princeton University Press, 1980.

Ondaatje, Christopher. *The Man-Eater of Punanai*. Toronto: HarperPerennial, 1992.

Paranavitana, S., ed. and trans. *Sigiri Graffiti*. 2 vols. London: Oxford University Press, 1956.

Pound, Ezra. *Collected Early Poems of Ezra Pound*. New York: New Directions, 1976.

Preminger, Alex, ed. *Princeton Encyclopedia of Poetry and Poetics*. Princeton: Princeton University Press, 1974.

Ramanujan, A.K., trans. *The Interior Landscape: Love Poems from a Classical Tamil Anthology*. Bloomington: Indiana University Press, 1967.

Reynolds, C.H.B., ed. *An Anthology of Sinhalese Literature up to 1815*. London: George Allen and Unwin, 1970.

Rilke, Rainer Maria. *Selected Letters 1902–1926*. Trans. R.F.C. Hull. London: Quartet, 1988.

– *The Selected Poetry of Rainer Maria Rilke*. Trans. Stephen Mitchell. New York: Random House, 1982.

Russell, Bertrand. *Portraits from Memory and Other Essays*. London: George Allen and Unwin, 1956.

Russell, John. *Francis Bacon*. London: Thames and Hudson. 1971.

Sacks, Sheldon, ed. *On Metaphor*. Chicago: University of Chicago Press, 1979.

St. Martin, Hardie, ed. *Roots and Wings: Poetry from Spain 1900–1975*. New York: Harper and Row, 1976.

Sartre, Jean-Paul. *Mallarmé or the Poet of Nothingness*. Trans. E. Sturm. University Park: Pennsylvania State University Press, 1991.

Shattuck, Roger. *The Banquet Years: The Origins of the Avant Garde in France, 1885–World War 1*. New York: Vintage, 1968 (1955).

Shaw, W. David. *The Lucid Veil: Poetic Truth in the Victorian Age*. London: Athlone Press, 1987.

Simic, Charles. *Dismantling the Silence*. London: Jonathan Cape, 1971.

– 'Tragicomic Soup.' *New York Review of Books* 30 Nov. 2000: 11.

– 'Working for the Dictionary.' *New York Review of Books* 19 Oct. 2000: 11–13.

Solecki, Sam. *Prague Blues: The Fiction of Josef Skvorecky*. Toronto: ECW, 1990.

Sophocles. *Philoctetes*. Trans. David Grene. *The Complete Greek Tragedies*, vol. IV. New York: Random House, 1957.

Stevens, Wallace. *Collected Poems of Wallace Stevens*. London: Faber and Faber, 1955.

– *Opus Posthumous: Poems, Plays and Prose*. Ed. Samuel French Morse. New York: Alfred Knopf, 1957.

Stevenson, Robert Louis. *Collected Poems*. Ed. Janet Adam Smith. London: Rupert Hart-Davis, 1971.

Strand, Mark. *The Weather of Words: Poetic Invention*. New York: Alfred A. Knopf, 2000.

Truffaut, François. *Le cinéma selon François Truffaut*. Ed. Anne Gilain. Paris: Flammarion, 1988.

– *The Films in My Life*. Trans. Leonard Mayhew. New York: Simon and Schuster, 1978.

Vendler, Helen. *The Given and the Made*. London: Faber and Faber, 1985.

– *Seamus Heaney*. London: Harper / Collins, 1998.

Wannan, Bill. *Legendary Australians*. Adelaide: Rigby, 1974.

Warren, Robert Penn. *New and Selected Poems 1923–1985*. New York: Random House, 1985.

Whalley, George. *Poetic Process*. London: Routledge and Kegan Paul, 1953.

White, Patrick. *A Fringe of Leaves*. New York: Viking, 1977.

Wickramasinghe, M. *Landmarks of Sinhalese Literature*. Colombo: M.D. Gunasena, 1948.

Wilde, Oscar. *The Picture of Dorian Grey*. Harmondsworth: Penguin, 1998.

Williams, Hugo. 'Freelance.' *Times Literary Supplement* 25 Feb. 2000: 16.

Wootten, William. 'In the Graveyard of Verse: Review of *The Collected Poems of Vernon Watkins*.' *London Review of Books* 9 Aug. 2001: 23–4.

Index